Understanding Abusive Families

Understanding Abusive Families

—~~— An Ecological Approach to Theory and Practice

James Garbarino
John Eckenrode

*With the staff of
the Family Life Development Center
at Cornell University*

Frank Barry
Kerry Bolger
Patrick Collins
Martha Holden
Brian Leidy
Michael Nunno
Jane Levine Powers
Marney Thomas

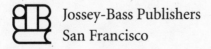

Jossey-Bass Publishers
San Francisco

Substantial discounts on bulk quantities of Jossey-Bass books are available to corporations, professional associations, and other organizations. For details and discount information, contact the special sales department at Jossey-Bass Inc., Publishers (415) 433–1740; Fax (800) 605–2665.

For sales outside the United States, please contact your local Simon & Schuster International Office.

Jossey-Bass Web address: http://www.josseybass.com

 Manufactured in the United States of America on Lyons Falls Turin Book. This paper is acid-free and 100 percent totally chlorine-free.

Library of Congress Cataloging-in-Publication Data

Garbarino, James.
    Understanding abusive families: an ecological approach to theory and practice/James Garbarino. John Eckenrode: with the staff of the Family Life Development Center at Cornell University, Frank Barry . . . [et al.].—1st ed.
        p.   cm.
    This new version is a mostly new book written by mostly new authors.
    Originally published: Lexington: Lexington Books, ©1980.
    Includes bibliographical references and index.
    ISBN 0-7879-1005-8 (alk. paper)
    1. Child abuse—United States.   2. Abusive parents—United States.
I. Eckenrode, John.   II. Barry, Frank D.   III. New York State
College of Human Ecology.   Family Life Development Center.
IV. Title.
HV6626.52.G38   1997
362.82′92′0973—dc21   97-20812
    CIP

FIRST EDITION
HB Printing   10 9 8 7 6 5 4 3 2 1

⎯⎯ Contents

—ᴧᴧ— Preface

The original version of *Understanding Abusive Families* was published in 1980. Much has happened in the field of child abuse and neglect since that time. Thousands of professional papers have been written, presented, and published. Hundreds of thousands of workshops have been presented at conferences. Millions of children have experienced child maltreatment, and many of them have been handled by the child protection system. Many of the pioneers in the field have left the scene through retirement or death: Vincent DeFrancis, Ray Helfer, Jolly K., Henry Kempe, Norman Polansky, Donna Stone, and Roland Summit, to name but a few. New organizations have sprung up; others have come and gone. Professionals formed the American Professional Society on the Abuse of Children. The National Committee for the Prevention of Child Abuse matured into the National Committee to Prevent Child Abuse. The federal government's leadership role in dealing with child maltreatment has waxed and waned. This new version of *Understanding Abusive Families* reflects all these historical developments while retaining its original vision.

The original preface of *Understanding Abusive Families* began as follows: "This book presents an ecological and developmental perspective on the maltreatment of children and adolescents. As a perspective book, it seeks to develop and present a particular view of maltreatment, one that we believe will shed light on prevention, protection, and rehabilitation. Our goal is to tell the story of abusive families in a way that will humanize and normalize them. We seek to make them and the things that go on inside them more comprehensible."

In this second edition we affirm that goal. We have brought together staff of the Family Life Development Center at Cornell University as collaborators. The Family Life Development Center began in the mid 1970s as part of New York State's commitment to do something about child abuse and neglect. Over the years the center has become an important locus for training, demonstration projects, and research. The center staff members contributing to the second edition of *Understanding Abusive Families* have roots that run deep and strong into the history of the field and can trace their intellectual lineage to the "pioneer" generation—those leaders who invented modern child protection in the 1960s and early 1970s. A look at their biographies confirms this.

How does this book differ from the 1980 version? In places we have sought to maintain the flavor of the original version, especially where we felt the material was still timely. On the other hand, the book has been updated in two important ways. First, the selection and organization of topics and chapters reflects our best current understanding of the field. Of the 1980 edition's fourteen chapters, only two—the first and last chapters—retain their basic structure and place. Second, we have sought to include up-to-date references and examples while retaining the classic sources (for example, the early works of Henry Kempe, Ray Helfer, and Brandt Steele.)

This, then, is a mostly new book written by mostly new authors. Part One begins with Chapter One, which still offers an introduction to child maltreatment and includes both definitions of the basic concepts and ecological and developmental perspectives. Chapter Two presents a history of child maltreatment as an issue in policy and practice and grounds the presentation with the most up-to-date data on patterns of incidence and prevalence. Chapter Three deals with the community context of child maltreatment and the issue of social support. Part One concludes with Chapter Four, which focuses on understanding why and how some family relationships become abusive.

Part Two opens with Chapter Five, in which we look at psychological maltreatment. The focus on special issues continues in Chapter Six, where we look at sexual abuse, and in Chapter Seven, where we look at abuse in institutional families—"child maltreatment in loco parentis." In Part Three—Chapters Eight and Nine—we examine the special issues involved in adolescent maltreatment. We conclude in Chapter Ten with a perspective on "family life development and child protection." This reflects our basic commitment to understanding, preventing, and treating child maltreatment in the context of broader efforts to support healthy families, communities, and children.

—∿∿—

As staff and faculty of the Family Life Development Center, we acknowledge the supportive role played by our collective institutional home—Cornell University's College of Human Ecology. We dedicate this book to John Doris, founding director of the Family Life Development Center, who retired in 1993 as professor emeritus of Human Development and Family Studies. We thank Dean Francille Firebaugh for supporting and encouraging this project. We thank our colleagues at the Center who supported this effort technically—especially Suzanne Aceti, who coordinated the references and manuscript. We also thank and acknowledge our many colleagues at the center and around the world whose work has enriched our thinking and increased our knowledge. And we thank our families, who sustain us.

Ithaca, New York   JAMES GARBARINO
July 1997   JOHN ECKENRODE

For John Doris
Founding Director of the Family Life Development Center
Mentor and Friend

Understanding Abusive Families

PART ONE

An Introduction to Basic Concepts

CHAPTER ONE

The Meaning
of Maltreatment

James Garbarino
John Eckenrode

———∿∿———

The social problem we call the maltreatment of children and youth has myriad faces:

• Dick Brown is a caseworker for the Child Welfare Department in a medium-sized city. At any one time he is responsible for investigating and managing more than thirty cases of child abuse and neglect. This includes deciding just how dangerous a family situation is and what the prospects are for improvement. On a given day he may have to judge whether a six-month-old is in danger of being murdered, a teenage mother is able to care for her two children currently in foster care, or a father known to have sexually molested his ten-year-old stepdaughter has progressed enough in counseling to return home without threatening the girl again. In the course of his work, Dick may be harassed by an irate father, bullied by a defense attorney, and worn to a frazzle by various competing demands. Like his coworkers, Dick faces a burnout problem and may not last more than a year in his current position.

• Joan Havens is a twenty-three-year-old mother of three children, ages five, three, and one. Her life is a bleak procession of work as a waitress and children that she faces alone. She no longer lives with the children's father. She has few friends, none of whom are doing much better than she is in coping with day-to-day life. Her money goes for rent, cigarettes, beer, and whatever food she buys for her family. Each of her children shows signs of neglect. Often unattended, they have the dull eyes of children whose emotional and physical diet is inadequate. They do not see a doctor regularly and have little contact with anyone outside the family.

Joan often feels like giving up, and she sometimes does. On one such occasion, a neighbor called the police when the three children were left alone overnight with no food in the house. Much of the time Joan is lonely and apathetic; sometimes she is very angry. This is nothing new. Her life has been this way as long as she can remember.

• Melinda Sue Jones is a fifteen-year-old runaway. She left home two weeks ago when things got so bad that she could not take it anymore. Her mother remarried four years ago, and Melinda Sue does not get along with her stepfather. To make sure Melinda Sue did not get into trouble, he was very strict with her at first. That was bad enough. Then last year things changed, and suddenly he was really nice to her. He began to act funny, telling her to sit on his lap and "accidentally" walking into the bathroom when she was taking a bath. A few months ago, while her mother was out shopping, he came into her room and had sex with her. She told him she did not want to, but he threatened to kill her if she refused or if she told anyone about it. So she did what he told her. It happened three more times before Melinda Sue ran away. She now is out on the street and living with a guy she met hitchhiking.

• Bob Thompson is sixteen. When he was a kid his father spanked him, and Bob behaved pretty well. When Bob got to be a teenager he started hanging out with a bunch of guys from school who had a reputation for being wild. His father forbade him to go around with "those punks" (as he called them), but Bob said he would do what he pleased. His father beat him with a belt and his fists to teach Bob a lesson about "mouthing off." No more was said about Bob's friends until a couple of weeks later, when Bob was picked up by the police for breaking into the school one night with his friends and hitting the janitor who caught them. The assault charge means Bob is facing a one-year sentence in the state's training school.

How can we help Dick provide adequate service to his case load and handle the deluge of new reports, each requiring thorough investigation and each indicating a situation that may present an immediate threat of death or permanent injury to a child? How can we help Joan get her life into better shape and provide more responsible care for her children? How can we reach Melinda Sue before she falls victim to further tragedies on the street? How can we stop the chain of events in Bob's life in which escalating violence is going to land him in jail for assault?

Where can we find the resources to deal with the problem of abuse and neglect? Until the 1970s, there was little public awareness of the plight of abused and neglected young children. This has been largely rectified through the efforts of crusading pediatricians, social workers, judges, psychologists, journalists, researchers, politicians, and private citizens. By the early 1980s nine in ten Americans identified child abuse as one of the top problems facing our country (Magnuson, 1983). In the 1990s, we find public awareness at an all-time high, but we sense that the battle, if not yet lost, is not being won either. A federally funded study shows a 98 percent increase in the national incidence rate of child maltreatment between 1986 and 1993. In 1990, the U.S. Advisory Board on Child Abuse and Neglect declared the country's response to this social problem as a national emergency (U.S. Advisory Board on Child Abuse and Neglect, 1990).

More than two decades of professional research and public discussion and debate has significantly helped us understand abusive families and what it takes to help them care for their children or, failing that, to protect children from harm. Our goal in this book is to look anew at the maltreatment of children and youth and to clarify the issues of prevention and treatment. To do this, we must view maltreatment both developmentally (from infancy to adolescence) and ecologically (from the perspectives of individual, family, cultural, and institutional systems). We hope these perspectives will help professionals deal with abuse and neglect in a useful and scientifically sound way.

To begin, we must examine the meaning of *maltreatment* while retaining our developmental and ecological perspectives. We use the general term *maltreatment* to include the more common terms *abuse* and *neglect*. There is so much social significance attached to these terms that we feel we must use them; but for the purposes of our discussion, fine distinctions are not necessary (Walters, 1975). We begin with several sources that treat abuse as the central concept and issue; later we will insert neglect into the discussion and eventually come around to maltreatment (Fontana, 1968).

PROBLEMS WITH THE DEFINITION OF ABUSE

Defining abuse is difficult, but this difficulty should not stop us from examining the problem. There are many things in life that we cannot define precisely but must deal with nonetheless. Lack of a precise definition of time does not prevent us from using our watches. Our inability to produce a conclusive definition of love does not stop us from loving. Neither time nor love has been defined satisfactorily, yet each exists and supports a body of scientific evidence. So it is with abuse (Bourne & Newberger, 1979). As one of the best analyses of child abuse concluded, "A variety of definitions of child abuse have been offered and none is free of ambiguities" (Parke & Collmer, 1975).

The basic problem in defining abuse is that the meaning of most actions is determined by the environment in which they occur, which consists of (1) the intention of the actor, (2) the act's effect upon the recipient, (3) an observer's value judgment about the act, and (4) the source of the standard for that judgment. These four elements—intentionality, effect, evaluation, and standards—are the fundamental issues in defining abuse. Initially, *abuse* may be defined as any behavior by a parent that results in injury to a child. The proof of abuse, according to this definition, is found in the effect of parental behavior upon the child. But does a child who is beaten but escapes injury negate the abusiveness of the beating? Resilient children who thrive despite deprived childhoods would be exempt from being classified as abused, no matter how they were treated. Conversely, children who were injured accidentally through innocent parental actions would be classified as abused nonetheless. Recent definitions of child maltreatment also classify children who have been endangered but not yet harmed as being maltreated (Sedlak & Broadhurst, 1996).

This brings us to the issue of intention. Two pioneers in the treatment of child abuse include intention in their definition. They defined abuse as "*nonaccidental* physical injury that results from acts or omissions on the part of parents or guardians" (Kempe & Helfer, 1975). While this definition has problems—it still relies upon injury but only considers physical injury—it represents an advance by stating that the parent need only intend to perform the act and does not seem to require that the parent intend to perform the act. Thus one can be abusive because one is ignorant about the possible effects of one's behavior.

One might argue that force itself is abusive, even without specific physical injury. The researcher-theoretician David Gil (1970) suggests that the use of any physical force to punish a child is abusive. Sociologist Murray Straus agrees, and his book *Beating the Devil Out of Them* (1994) marshals an impressive array of research to document this position. In this view, abuse is intentional, nonaccidental use of force aimed at a child. This definition regards spanking as abuse, in which case the term *abusive* might apply to most parents. In other words, a parent need not intend to injure a child in order to abuse him or her. It leads naturally to saying that any use of force against a child is abusive. Many researchers reject this definition on the grounds that it is too broad (and also perhaps because they cannot envision a practical nonviolent style of childrearing) (Parke & Collmer, 1975). Yet many scholars believe that cultural support for the use of force against children is at the heart of the child-abuse problem (Garbarino, 1977; Straus, Gelles, & Steinmetz, 1980).

The next issue is the judgment made by an observer. Some investigators rely on community standards as the criteria of child abuse (Parke & Collmer, 1975). They define abuse as "non-accidental physical injury as a result of acts (or omissions) on the part of parents or guardians *that violate the community's standards concerning the treatment of children*" [emphasis added]. According to this view, those within the community can best interpret its norms and identify acts that violate those norms. Empirical evidence exists to support the view that though such standards do vary, there is a surprising degree of consensus across ethnic groups in the United States (Giovannoni & Becerra, 1979).

From an anthropological perspective, other scientists see abuse as a culturally determined label that is applied to behavior and injuries (Walters & Parke, 1964). For example, facial scarification as part of a tribal rite of passage is not the same as facial scars sustained from a violent argument. Specific events and behavior derive their meaning from the context in which they occur. This anthropological point is well taken. Although the environment determines the impact of such actions, there are limits to the power of culture to make things right. Some cultures support practices harmful to children. Infanticide in ancient Sparta is but one (albeit extreme) example. Our own culture contains elements (such as racism and sexism) that harm children.

The point is that some cultural differences are just that, differences in style, while others represent actions that are intrinsically harmful to the children involved. We constantly face the problem of knowing how to distinguish legitimate differences in style from practices based on cultural errors; that is, antichild values. One anthropologist recalls being questioned by native Hawaiian mothers about the "abusive" American practice of forcing infants to sleep in cribs and rooms apart from their parents (Korbin, personal communication, 1978). Is this emotional abuse or cultural difference?

In our definition of child abuse, there needs to be some authority beyond the opinions held by parents. At worst, those opinions may be modeled after abusive parental behavior or be based on incorrect assumptions about children. Therefore, our definition includes a second standard—our best scientific understanding of parent-child relations—in addition to the already established criterion of beliefs about child rearing based on custom. The evaluation that leads to the judgment of parental behavior as abusive must be made by both science and culture.

Scientists know, for example, that rejection can be injurious to the psyche of a developing child (Rohner, 1975). Some researchers are convinced that the evidence demonstrates a connection between the use of physical punishment and impaired psychological development and social competence. However, this culture so strongly supports physical punishment that only the most devoted child advocates say that spanking in and of itself is abusive, and the empirical evidence is debatable. Reasonable people of good will can and do differ.

Abuse is a conclusion drawn about family life, and we think it must be based on a mixture of community standards and professional knowledge. The Hawaiian mothers' concern cited earlier is a good example. As much as we may hate the ambiguity it implies, the process of defining abuse is, in practice, one of negotiation between culture and science, folk wisdom and professional expertise. It is not easy, but it is the way things work. Cultural differences are only that, unless there is evidence to the contrary.

ELEMENTS OF A DEFINITION OF ABUSE

Up to this point we have used the term *child* in our discussion. This is because much of the research has looked at abuse of young children without considering adolescents. We have used this material because it is most of what we have. However, one of our goals in this book is to work out the implications and applications of any definition of abuse for adolescents. Briefly mentioned here, these implications and applications are expanded in Chapters Eight and Nine.

Our interest in adolescence takes us beyond the established child-abuse literature. We define *maltreatment* as acts of omission or commission by a parent or guardian that are judged by a mixture of community values and professional expertise to be inappropriate and damaging. This definition covers the four issues mentioned earlier: intention, effect, evaluation, and standards. *Inappropriate* describes parental action; *damaging* covers the effect upon the development of the victim. Both are defined by a value judgment based upon community standards and professional expertise. Inappropriate parental behavior may produce physical, emotional, or psychosocial damage.

We cannot always accurately predict what effects abuse will have, because victims most often suffer multiple damage, and individual susceptibility to harm differs. Also, while each type of maltreatment is distinct in principle, in practice there is so much overlapping that we rarely see only one type of abuse, at least when we observe a troubled family over a long period of time. This overlapping and coincidence is one reason we are inclined to link abuse and neglect under the broader term *maltreatment*.

Acts of commission (the typical distinguishing mark of abuse) often accompany acts of omission (the primary characteristic of neglect). In practice, neglect and abuse often are found in the same family, with some estimates indicating they occur together 50 percent of the time (Garbarino & Crouter, 1978a; Garbarino & Carson, 1979a). A recent study in Florida reports that over half of the physically abused children in a sample of families referred to Child Protective Services were also exposed to psychological maltreatment (Crittenden, Claussen, & Sugarman, 1994). Abuse and neglect may occur in sequence as well, as when neglect by one parent exposes the victim to abuse by the other. (This often seems to happen in cases of sexual abuse.) Whether we use the terms *abuse, neglect,* or *maltreatment,* the central issue remains one of protecting the child or teenager from damage and exploitation and of setting and enforcing high standards of care for children and youth.

The whole point of defining abuse is to articulate both what parents and guardians must do and what they may not do. When we speak of guardians we include the state (certainly no paragon of virtue in these matters, as we shall see). The concept of inappropriateness is very important, particularly in adolescent abuse. It reflects the idea that parenting behaviors must be evaluated in the context of the developmental stage of the child. Behaviors that might be appropriate in the rearing of young children (such as a high level of coercion) lose their meaning and appropriateness for teenagers.

A fairly common problem parents face is difficulty in changing the habits formed while rearing young children when those children become adolescents. Teenagers are far more capable of abstract thought than children and can independently evaluate both their own motives and those of others. This capability demands that parents reason and consult with their adolescent children when making family decisions and setting rules. This may be hard to do at a time when adolescents are first asserting their independence, and it produces disturbance even among otherwise smoothly functioning families (Hill, 1980; Steinberg, 1977).

Most parents eventually recognize the need for some adjustment to the new situation of having adolescent children. Some do not and are at special risk for abusing their teenagers. We must direct our attention to those patterns of behavior that impose a high level of risk on their victims; that is, treatment that would cause most normal children and teenagers to suffer some social or psychological harm. The consequences of abuse and neglect are incompletely documented, and the resilience of the human being rules out any simple cause-effect relationship between maltreatment and impaired development. We must go beyond damage and focus on risk and endangerment.

Many of us are drawn to the fever analogy in explaining the meaning of child abuse and neglect. Typically we speak of abuse and neglect as indicators of underlying problems with the family, just as a fever indicates infection in the body. We think the analogy is a good one and can be pursued still further. Most fevers are not, in themselves, intrinsically dangerous. They are generally indicators, posing no direct threat to the organism. Very high fevers, on the other hand (particularly among very young children), are themselves dangerous. We liken this to child abuse and neglect.

Most of the *physical* damage done by abusive and neglectful parents, while socially distressing and morally unconscionable, is not itself a threat to the long-term health of the child (Martin, 1976). Only the most extreme instances of physical abuse and neglect are life-threatening or produce substantial impairment. These injuries mainly affect very young children and are not too common. Information from the Third National Incidence Study shows that, of the estimated 2.8 million children maltreated in the United States in 1993, a relatively small number (1,600) suffered fatalities and about 560,000 suffered serious injury or impairment (Sedlak & Broadhurst, 1996). As we shall see at a later point, there is growing interest in finding ways to focus special attention on the most severe cases, for example, by requiring specialized services for "catastrophic" maltreatment (Haugaard & Garbarino, 1997).

Figures such as these give rise to the hardheaded assessment that child abuse and neglect are not major medical problems. Three decades ago, Gil (1970) made this point when, after reviewing the data available, he concluded that the scope of the problem of child abuse that results in serious injury is minor, at least in comparison with other more widespread problems that undermine the developmental opportunities of millions of children in U.S. society, such as poverty, racial discrimination, malnutrition, and inadequate provisions for medical care and education.

While the massive increase in reported cases since Gil's study was undertaken in the late 1960s would certainly enlarge the scope of the problem, the figures presented in the Third National Incidence Study data still indicate that serious physical harm is only a relatively small part of the child maltreatment problem (Sedlak & Broadhurst, 1996). Does this mean that child maltreatment is a minor problem? Clearly, this is untrue. Most professionals and members of the general public almost instinctively recognize that the problem of maltreatment goes well beyond serious physical harm to children. Consider, for example, the problem of sexual abuse. While physical assault does accompany sexual abuse in numerous cases, the absence of such assault does little to diminish the seriousness of sexual abuse (Summit & Kryso, 1978). Why?

The coercive climate in which most sexual abuse takes place produces an emotional threat to the child. Although our formal statements about child maltreatment focus their attention on physical consequences, most of us recognize that the heart of the matter lies not in the physical but in the emotional and psychological domains. This recognition permits us to distinguish between the culturally approved and common use of force against children, what we might provocatively term "normal domestic violence," and abuse, while at the same time recognizing that "normal domestic violence" may be one of the principal underlying causes of abuse (Gelles, 1978). We are concerned with physical damage, of course. No one with any moral sensibility can dismiss a battered or bruised child.

What is more important, however, is developmental damage. Garmezy (1977) argues that the effects of child abuse (defined primarily as physical assault) are neither so simple nor so absolute as many public pronouncements would have us believe. Many victims of child abuse survive it and do not repeat the pattern with their own children. The real issue, therefore, is not any specific action but rather the overall pattern of parent-child relations and the probable impact of that pattern on the child's social, intellectual, and moral competence. By *competence* we are referring to the child's ability to adequately use resources for the accomplishment of tasks relevant to particular developmental stages.

TYPES OF MALTREATMENT

Thus the issues facing our efforts to formulate a practical definition of abuse will shift as the developmental agenda of the victim shifts. Physical force may raise different issues for young children than it does for teenagers; emotional abuse may take one form in childhood and another in adolescence. By focusing on inappropriateness and developmental damage, our definition draws the study of abuse and neglect back into the mainstream of issues in human development. This will benefit both mainstream child-development research and the study of maltreatment. Having defined maltreatment, we will now describe its various forms.

Physical Abuse

When we got there this baby was crying and we could see his leg was twisted kind of funny to one side. He had bruises on his face. He looked pretty bad.

You can't say my dad didn't like me, but you can't say that he did, either. When he hit me he used anything from a belt to a beer bottle. And a beer bottle slightly smarts. You could go through a window very easy around him if he is mad. . . . I've gone through a window or two.

Physical abuse involves the inappropriate and developmentally damaging use of force. The actual injury is not as important as the way it comes about. Youngsters who are injured in athletic pursuits typically bear none of the emotional scars that victims of abuse carry. A boy may be proud of the scar above his eye from a boxing match if he sees it as representing athletic prowess. But if the scar came as a result of a beating from his drunken father over a curfew violation, the boy probably would feel differently about it.

Even here, however, there is variation. Some children and youth are proud of their ability to receive and withstand physical assault. We believe this represents a warped value system and refuse to validate violence in this form. Physical wounds, unless extremely severe, heal relatively quickly. Emotional injury lasts longer. The use of physical force against children seems to reflect a mixture of positive belief in force as a tool for shaping behavior, lack of effective alternatives to force, and emotional tension in the parent: "A good swat on the rear lets him know I mean business"; "What else am I going to do when he runs into the street or breaks something?"; "I was so mad I could spit, but I felt better once I let him have it!"

Straus, Gelles, and Steinmetz (1980) explored the significance of violence in the family and concluded that violence is deeply rooted in basic aspects of the way our families work, particularly their focus on power assertion and authoritarian values. We explore further the central role of the culture-of-violence hypothesis in Chapter Two.

If the use of force against children is of dubious value, the use of force against adolescents is an outright disaster. More so than any other type of abuse, the use of physical force against adolescents illustrates parents' failure to adapt to adolescence. As children grow up, some parents who use spanking for discipline increase the level of force they use. Patterson (1982) has discussed this in terms of "fight cycles," where inept discipline strategies can escalate into physical confrontations when parents are faced with a resisting adolescent. The adolescent growth spurt significantly increases the child's size, and parents who continue to rely on corporal punishment may feel they have no choice but to increase the amount of force they use. We think that the sheer amount of force necessary to subdue a teenager makes the practice abusive. Corporal punishment is a poor disciplinary tactic in childhood, but it is worse in adolescence (Coopersmith, 1967; Homans, 1975; Jeffrey, 1976; Bandura, 1977; Gilmartin, 1978).

This view is reflected in the finding from a national survey that the overall use of force by most parents against their children decreases with the onset of adolescence (Gelles, 1978). Common sense dictates a shift away from physical discipline toward more mature, psychologically oriented discipline. Because of their size, adolescents (particularly males) who are physically abused usually sustain only minor injuries. The amount of force used to produce a concussion in an infant will probably cause only a black eye for a teenager. The adolescent body is better equipped to handle the shock. This understandably contributes to the fact that adolescents often are pushed aside by Child Protective Service agencies in favor of younger children when excessive case loads force such a choice. The teenager's tolerance for physical abuse may mask an equal or even greater susceptibility to emotional abuse, however.

Emotional Abuse

When my mom would look at me and say, "You're worthless—I wish you were never born," I wanted to disappear.

I just wanted my mom to tell me that she loved me. And she couldn't even do that, you know. Like, I fought with her so much. I just remember getting into fights with her. Just screaming at her, "Why can't you tell me you love me? Why can't you just tell me that?" She never hugged me or nothing.

Psychological maltreatment in the form of emotional abuse is extremely difficult to define theoretically and practically, but it is at the heart of the maltreatment of children and youth. Chapter Five deals with this issue in some detail, so we will only outline the matter here. For infants, emotional abuse typically involves parental refusal to be responsive. It may mean punishing normal behavior such as smiling and vocalization. It may mean rejecting the child and stunting the normal parent-infant attachment. For older children, it involves a pattern of behavior that punishes the child for normal social behavior and self-esteem. It means actively preventing the child from becoming socially and psychologically competent. There are many inappropriate parental behaviors that can damage teenagers emotionally. One is overcontrol. Our interviews with young victims provided good illustrations.

My dad started grounding me for finding dirty spots on the dishes. The last time he grounded me like that, it went on for six months, and it got so bad that I had to start asking for everything: if I could get up, if I could go to the bathroom, if I could sit down and eat with him, if I could get ready to go to bed, if I could take a bath. You know, everything you take for granted. And his answer to me always was, "Do you deserve it, do you think you deserve it?" Well, of course, I deserved to eat. I have to eat to live, you know. And it just got really bad.

It is inappropriate to force teenagers repeatedly to do things that will disgrace them before their peers or to expect them to respect socially and psychologically suffocating restrictions. A parental need to control an adolescent's every action can make life unbearable for teenagers who are naturally programmed to become more rather than less independent. Overcontrol can retard development by robbing youth of opportunities for making decisions and learning from normal mistakes. When an overcontrolling parent is faced with a resistant teenager, the parent may be assaultive or rejecting—and parental rejection is an extremely damaging form of emotional abuse.

> I think that I was always rejected. I think that often my parents would set me up. They would be very good to me until I was feeling [a] warm feelings type of thing, and then they would totally reject me. I never remembered doing anything good enough for them.
>
> I was twelve years old, and I was pregnant, and I was being very much rejected by my family, and my mother would not allow anyone to know that I was pregnant, and so I was very alone. I was dropped out of school, and when people came to visit I was put in my room and stayed there, sometimes for up to a day and a half. But the last time I cried was when I was in the hospital. I was taken there by my mother, and they had decided to do a cesarean section on me because she didn't want anybody to know or to have anybody around to take me to the hospital. I had really nobody to talk to, and I wanted to see the baby, and they wouldn't let me, and so my mother had decided that my baby should be baptized before he was taken to where he was being adopted. And so after they had baptized the baby, she came strolling in my room and said, "I got to hold the baby, and we baptized it, and they gave it a name." And she had left then because I couldn't go home until the next day. Then I did cry that night, and it was the last time I cried, when I was thirteen.

Parental rejection is harmful. Its damaging effects are so well documented that it can justifiably be called psychologically malignant (Rohner, 1975). Beyond the gross cases just described, a pattern of smaller assaults, such as constant criticism, disdain for personal idiosyncrasies, and contempt for dress styles can have a seriously corrosive effect. Rejection unquestionably meets our two criteria for abuse: it is inappropriate, and it is damaging. It can produce low self-esteem and compromise the achievement of important developmental goals. Children who are not loved and cherished by their parents tend to conclude that they must be unlovable. Parental rejection can take even more extreme forms.

I ran because I didn't think they cared about me. The night before, my mom told me that they never liked me. She says, "Go live with your friend." And then she goes, "I don't give a damn about you. Just get the hell out of here. I never want to see your face in this house again."

Some parents reject their children so completely that they physically throw them out of the house, without making adequate provisions for their care. In twentieth-century America it is inappropriate to expect a teenager to be able to support or provide shelter for himself or herself without any assistance. Denial of a home endangers adolescents physically, emotionally, and sexually. Many of these teenagers are called runaways, but they are really "throwaways."

Sexual Abuse

He told me to sit on his lap on the bed while we watched TV after my bath. Mom was out at the store and he was taking care of me like he always does. Then he told me to take off my pajamas and touch him there. I said I didn't want to, but he made me, and then he touched me all over. I felt real bad afterwards, and kinda scared.

Children are off limits to adults sexually, and sexual abuse is therefore inappropriate behavior in its most extreme form. Sexual abuse—particularly at the hands of a relative or responsible adult—forces an inappropriate choice upon the child or youth, between obedience and integrity. It can cause many types of damage, the most predictable being sexual dysfunction and internalizing problems such as fear, anxiety, and depression (Kendall-Tackett, Williams, & Finkelhor, 1993). These are discussed in Chapter Six, where we take a special look at sexual abuse.

Neglect

I called the protective service people because those children never have enough to eat. They're left alone in that apartment, sometimes four nights a week. The older one is only nine, and that's too young to be in charge of the baby like that. Then when I read in the paper about

those children on the North Side who were killed in that fire 'cause
they were all alone, I decided I had to do something.

For children, neglect is probably a greater social threat than active
abuse. More than half the reported incidents of maltreatment investigated by Child Protective Service agencies involve neglect (National
Center on Child Abuse and Neglect, 1995). A classic study by Downing (1978) looked at thirty children who had died after having been
protective service cases but whose death certificates listed natural
causes. Downing found that half of these deaths were directly attrib-
utable to parental neglect, such as failure to give prescribed medica-
tion. Among infants, neglect can mean all kinds of damage and
exposure to needless risk because the infant is so totally dependent on
the parents for basic care.

For older children, neglect can mean physical and psychological
impoverishment when the basic necessities of life are denied. In both
cases, we must look beyond the parents to the community that permits neglect. Since adolescents are much more capable of handling
their own daily living and personal hygiene needs than children, physical neglect per se is much less an issue once adolescence is reached.
For teenagers, neglect usually means parental failure to sustain contact or to provide realistic supervision. Failure to care about the whereabouts of a twelve-year-old at midnight is neglectful, as is an indefinite
refusal to talk (even to a noncommunicative teenager).

Neglect is distinct from abusive forms of maltreatment because it
is not identified with inappropriate physical contact between a child
and a caretaker and on the surface may appear more passive than
active. But many neglected children and adolescents seem to be
harmed just as severely as victims of more active sorts of abuse. Indifference, forgotten promises, and withdrawal are all inappropriate
parental behaviors, damaging to children and teenagers who may feel
they are not worth their parents' concern and care. Neglect of this sort
may lead its victims to very self-destructive behavior.

―∿―

These examples provide a picture of the forms maltreatment may take.
We have not tried to present an exhaustive list of abusive behaviors,
nor have we tried to categorize their causes and effects; neither task is
really feasible, nor is it necessary at this point. Our concern is the well-
being of children. From our perspective, the big issue is whether or

not families are working well on behalf of children. When they are, the natural human capacity for adaptation and growth reassures us that the process will result in a complete human being. When families are not working, children will suffer, as will their parents in their own way.

Much abuse happens simultaneously (for example, sexual and emotional) or in sequence (emotional abuse followed by physically throwing the teenager out of the house; rejection followed by the child's rebellion, which leads to a beating).

> They beat me. It hurts me real bad inside. It hurts right now. They yell at me about my hair and say I'd never amount to a hill of beans or something. Then they start to hit me with a belt or something, anything that was handy.

> My dad would get so pissed off if I didn't get dinner fixed on time. He would just throw me against the wall and say, "You deserve this, you lazy slut." I never could go to games or go out with boys or anything. I could never make the house nice enough for him, so he'd always say I had more stuff to do. Finally, I just ran away.

One final issue around definition worth mentioning is the concept of catastrophic maltreatment. Catastrophically maltreated children are those who have been the victims of attempted murder, torture, mutilation, violent rape, enforced prostitution, and denial of the necessities required for minimal development. These children are at high risk for dying or otherwise developing serious physical and psychological disabilities as a result of this maltreatment. When parents perpetrate catastrophic maltreatment, the extreme nature of the parental violation justifies a presumption that parental rights will be terminated (in contrast to the current presumption of family reunification after initial protective separation). What is more, resident siblings of children subject to catastrophic maltreatment (such as siblings of a child murdered by a parent) are themselves to be considered at extreme risk for the development of the same problems as the immediate victims themselves and would be removed from the parent's care on the same basis.

Maltreatment is a many-faceted phenomenon. To understand its pieces and the whole we need an ecological perspective on human behavior and development.

AN ECOLOGICAL PERSPECTIVE

Nature and nurture can work in harmony or in opposition. The level of risk and damage experienced by a specific individual depends upon the interplay of these two forces. In extreme cases, facts of nature can all but overwhelm environmental differences. Likewise, environmental conditions can be so extreme (either positive or negative) as to override all but the most powerful and extreme conditions of biology. This is human nature; our nature is to be what conditions encourage.

Understanding the interaction between nature and nurture in producing social and personal risk is difficult—so difficult, in fact, that most researchers do not even try to handle both parts of the equation at once. Rather, they tend to let one side vary while they hold the other constant—as in studying genetically identical twins reared apart to learn about the role of nature and nurture in intelligence, or in seeing how different newborns respond to a constant stimulus such as a smiling face.

Researchers may also vary one factor systematically while letting the other vary randomly—as in presenting school-age children with three different teaching styles and seeing the overall effect of each. It is rare that a researcher is able really to look at the interplay of nature and nurture in development. Where risk is concerned, this is extremely unfortunate. Policymakers need reliable information demonstrating the costs and likely benefits of alternative strategies for dealing with child maltreatment. These "cost/benefit" studies must include the impact of these alternatives on both the individual child and family as well as on the whole community. In computing these costs and benefits, we need to understand where history fits into individual and cultural development. In a sense, our interest in development is really an interest in biography.

We must discover how the lives of individuals, families, and societies are interdependent. Events taking place at the level of nations (the big picture) can reverberate into the day-to-day life of the individual and the family (the little picture). One example is when global shifts in labor markets result in unemployment that affects domestic relationships and deprives a child of a nurturing relationship with her or his parents. Conversely, millions of individual decisions can add up to major social changes, as when millions of women decide to delay childbearing so that they can pursue careers. Understanding the interplay of biography and history is at the heart of understanding human development.

One important aid in applying this concept practically is an emerging ecological perspective on human development. In using the word *ecological* here, we mean to convey an interest in the way the organism and its immediate environment (the ecological niche) affect and respond to each other. This process of mutual adaptation and accommodation means that influences and behaviors are always shifting, sometimes subtly, sometimes drastically. It means that in cases of maltreatment the intimate relationships between children and parents cannot be understood without understanding how environmental conditions affect the interaction between child and parent.

The framework proposed by Urie Bronfenbrenner (1979) is the most useful approach to the ecology of human development. Like most frameworks, it relies on some special terms, which we now will define. As stated previously, the ecology of human development is the scientific study of how the individual develops interactively with the social environment, defined as a network of interrelated systems. The newborn shapes the feeding behavior of its mother but is largely confined to a crib or a lap and has limited means of communicating its needs and wants. The ten-year-old, on the other hand, influences many adults and other children located in many different settings and has many ways of communicating. The adolescent's world is still larger and more diverse, as is his or her ability to influence it. The child and the environment negotiate their relationship over time through a process of reciprocity. One cannot predict the future of either reliably without knowing something about the other. Does economic deprivation harm development? It depends on how old one is when it hits, what sex one is, what the future brings in the way of vocational opportunity, what the quality of family life was in the past, what one's economic expectations and assumptions are, and whether one looks at the short term or the long run.

In short, it all depends. In asking and answering questions about developmental risk we can and always should look at the next level of larger and smaller worlds to find the questions to ask and answer. If we see husbands and wives in conflict over lost income, we must look outward, to the economy that put one spouse out of work and now may welcome the other into the labor force. We must also look to the culture that defines a person's personal worth in monetary terms and that blames the victims of economic dislocation for their own losses.

In addition, we must look inward, to the parent-child relationships that are affected by the changing roles and status of the parents. Then we must look "across," to see how the myriad systems involved (family, workplace, and economy) adjust to new conditions over time. Bronfenbrenner offers a terminology to express these concerns in a systematic way that permits scientific study and promises to increase our understanding.

Microsystems

Most immediate to the developing individual is the *microsystem,* the actual setting in which the child experiences and creates reality. At first, for most children, the microsystem is quite small: it is the home, involving interaction with only one person at a time (dyadic interaction) in simple activities such as feeding, bathing, and cuddling. As the child develops, complexity normally increases: the child does more, with more people, in more places. In Bronfenbrenner's view, the expanding capacity to do more is the very essence of development.

Play figures prominently in the development process from the early months of life and eventually is joined by work. Playing, working, and loving (what Freud called the essence of normal human existence) are the principal classes of activities that characterize the child's microsystem. One characteristic of maltreatment is that it undermines the child's capacity for complexity and thus impoverishes development.

However, the extent to which playing, working, and loving take place and their level of complexity are variable. Thus one source of sociocultural harm or risk is a narrowly restricted range and level of activities, which creates impoverished experience and, consequently, a stunted microsystem where reciprocity is limited; that is, where genuine interaction is lacking and where either party seeks to avoid or to be impervious to the other. One of the most important aspects of the microsystem as a force in development is the existence of relationships that go beyond simple dyads. A child's development is enhanced by observing and learning from other dyads (such as the mother and father), where the presence of a third party can highlight differences in the child's own dyadic experience.

So long as increased numbers in a child's microsystem mean more enduring reciprocal relationships, larger and more complex microsystems as a function of the child's age mean enhanced development (Summit & Kryso, 1978). A child's social riches are measured by enduring, reciprocal, multifaceted relationships that emphasize playing, working, and loving. This is a crucial point for understanding abusive families. First, however, we should examine the next level of systems.

Mesosystems

Mesosystems are the relationships between contexts in which the developing person experiences reality. The richness of mesosystems for the child is measured by the size (quantity) and depth (quality) of connections. Bronfenbrenner uses the example of the child who goes to school on the first day unaccompanied. This means there is only a single link between the home and school microsystem; namely, the child's participation in both. Were this weak linkage to persist, it would place the child at risk, particularly if there is disagreement between home and school in terms of values, experiences, objects, and behavioral style.

Homes that do not value schooling, do not have books or educated people, do not involve reading and other basic academic skills, and do not use the formal language used for instructional purposes jeopardize the child's academic development. Where all these links are strong, the odds favor the development of academic competence. Where the similarity of the two settings is bolstered by actual participation of people other than the child in both settings, academic success is still more likely.

Thus it is important that the parents visit the school and even that the teachers visit the home. The central principle here is that the stronger and more diverse the links between settings, the more powerful the resulting mesosystem will be. Such mesosystems are important in providing feedback to the parent and protection from maltreatment to the child. There can be much more to child care than the microsystem of the family. A rich range of mesosystems is both a product and a cause of development. A poor set of mesosystems both reflects and produces impaired development, particularly when home and school are involved.

Exosystems

What governs the quality of the child's mesosystems? Events in systems where the child does not participate but where things happen that have a direct bearing on parents and other adults who interact with the child. Bronfenbrenner calls these settings *exosystems*—situations that influence a child's development but that the developing child does not engage in directly. They include the workplaces of the parents (where most children are not participants) and those centers of power, such as school boards and planning commissions, that make decisions affecting the child's day-to-day life. In exosystem terms, risk comes about in two ways.

The first is when the parents or other significant adults are affected in a way that impoverishes their behavior in the child's microsystem. For example, Melvin Kohn (1977) found that when parents work in settings that demand conformity rather than self-direction, they reflect this orientation in their child rearing, which stifles important aspects of the child's development. Other examples include elements of the parents' working experience that result in an impoverishment of family life, such as long or inflexible hours, traveling, or stress.

The second way risk flows from the exosystem is when decisions made in those settings adversely affect the child or treat the child unfairly. For example, when the school board suspends extracurricular programs in the child's school, or the planning commission runs a highway through the child's neighborhood, these events jeopardize the child's development. Thus exosystem risk comes when the child lacks effective advocates in decision-making bodies. Psychologist George Albee (1979) identifies powerlessness as the primary factor leading to impaired development and psychopathology.

Powerlessness certainly plays a large role in determining the fate of groups of children and may even be important when considering individual cases, such as whether parents have the pull to get their child a second chance when he or she gets into trouble. Risk at the exosystem level is largely a political matter.

Macrosystems

Mesosystems and exosystems are set within the broad ideological and institutional patterns of a particular culture or subculture. These are *macrosystems.*

Macrosystems are the blueprints for the ecology of human development. These blueprints reflect a people's shared assumptions about how things are done. To identify a macrosystem is to do more than simply name a group: Israeli, Arab, Swiss, Latino, African American, Anglo, Indian. It goes beyond simple group identification to focus on the values, beliefs, collective experiences, interests, and ideas that make up culture, for example, Judeo-Christian tradition, the Protestant ethic, communism, or fascism. We need variables rather than simply labels. We must compare these groups systematically on some common scales of measurement, such as collective versus individual orientation or schooled versus unschooled.

But macrosystems are more than even these broad descriptive factors. *Macrosystem* refers to the general organization of the world as it is and as it might be. The existence of historical change demonstrates that the *might be* is quite real. The *might be* occurs through evolution (many individual decisions guided by a common perception of reality) and through revolution introduced by a small cadre of decision makers. The suburbanization of the United States in the post–World War II era happened because of an intricate set of individual decisions, technological developments, and corporate initiatives. Together, they reshaped the experience of millions of children in families and schools (Straus, Gelles, & Steinmetz, 1980). The breakup and war in the former Soviet Union in the 1990s altered the institutional and ideological landscape for the millions of families who no longer lived in one communist system but rather in many national systems. We can assume these changes have reverberated through schools and homes in all those rapidly differentiated social systems.

What is risk when it comes to macrosystems? It is an ideology or cultural alignment that threatens to impoverish children's microsystems and mesosystems and set exosystems against them. It is a national economic policy that tolerates or even encourages economic dislocations and poverty for families with young children. It is institutionalized support for high levels of geographic mobility that disrupt neighborhood and school connections. It is a pattern nonsupportive of parents that tolerates or even condones intense conflicts between the roles of worker and parent. It is a pattern of racist or sexist values that demean some parents and thus raise the level of stress for their children. In general, it is any social pattern or societal event that impoverishes the ability and willingness of adults to care for children and children to learn from adults.

Macrosystem risk is the world set against children. This takes place in microsystems. As noted before, the microsystem is the immediate setting in which the child develops. Microsystems evolve and develop much as the child does—influenced by forces from within and from without. The setting "school" is very different in June than it is in September for the same children (who are themselves, of course, not the same). The setting "family" as experienced by the firstborn child is different from that experienced by subsequent children. We must remember that the microsystem has a life of its own; it develops, too.

It is also important to remember that Bronfenbrenner's definition speaks of the microsystem as a pattern experienced by the developing person. The cognitive maps we carry around in our heads are the reality we live by and act upon. One might consider who said it better: Shakespeare in *Hamlet* ("for there is nothing good or bad/but thinking makes it so") or sociologist W. I. Thomas ("If men define situations as real, they are real in their consequences") (Thomas & Thomas, 1928, p. 572; Coopersmith, 1967; Homans, 1975; Jeffrey, 1976; Bandura, 1977; Gilmartin, 1978). The individual child constructs the microsystems much as he or she is shaped by them. The child's microsystem becomes a source of developmental risk when it is socially impoverished. He or she suffers when there are too few participants, too little reciprocal interaction, and/or psychologically destructive patterns of interaction. A microsystem should be a gateway to the world. Bronfenbrenner recognizes this when he offers the following proposition about microsystems and individual development: "The developmental status of the individual is reflected in the substantive variety and structural complexity of the activities which he initiates and maintains in the absence of instigation or direction by others" (Bronfenbrenner, 1979, p. 55). The product of a healthy microsystem is a child whose capacity for understanding and dealing successfully with ever-wider spheres of reality increases. Such a child learns to have self-respect and self-confidence, to be socially and intellectually competent. Child maltreatment affects these developmental areas directly.

CHAPTER TWO

The Scope and History of Child Abuse and Neglect

Frank Barry
Patrick Collins

H ow widespread is the problem of child abuse and neglect? This controversial question has been at the heart of the child welfare debate for over one hundred years, yet a definitive answer remains elusive. One of the greatest hindrances to resolving this issue, and to advancing the child maltreatment field in general, has been a lack of consensus regarding definitions of maltreatment. Legal definitions of child maltreatment vary by state, making it difficult to compare data from different states. Scientific definitions have also varied widely, making it difficult to compare results across studies.

OFFICIAL SOURCES OF DATA ON CHILD ABUSE AND NEGLECT

In response to the growing concern about child maltreatment and the lack of consensus on the scope of the problem, the federal government began dedicating significant resources to measuring the incidence of child abuse and neglect in the early 1980s. The federal government currently provides three official sources of data on maltreated children and youth. The National Child Abuse and Neglect Data System (NCANDS) provides data on children who were reported to state Child Protective Services (CPS) offices. The National Incidence Studies of Child Abuse and Neglect (NIS-1, NIS-2, and NIS-3) provide data on children whose maltreatment was known to a range of community professionals in addition to CPS. The FBI's Uniform Crime Report (FBI-UCR) provides information about child fatalities. While all of these data sources are considered official, each has particular strengths and limitations. Each source will be discussed in terms of what it can and cannot tell us about the scope of child abuse and neglect in the United States. It is important to note that the availability of official statistics concerning child maltreatment has done little to quell the debate concerning the scope of the child maltreatment problem.

Child Protective Services Data

The National Child Abuse and Neglect Data System (NCANDS) is a voluntary national data collection and analysis system that was developed through a federal-state partnership. Since the passage of the Child Abuse Prevention and Treatment Act in 1974, all states have been required to maintain records of reported and suspected maltreatment. Although this federal legislation requires that states identify and respond to maltreatment, it does not require states to report these data to the federal government. The goal of NCANDS is to compile data from the states at the national level through voluntary agreements. NCANDS has been collecting data from the states since 1990.

Prior to this time the American Humane Association (AHA) and the National Committee to Prevent Child Abuse (NCPCA) conducted annual surveys of the states and compiled similar summary level data. NCPCA continues to conduct an annual fifty-state survey, and the results of this survey are highly consistent with those from NCANDS. Figure 2.1 presents both the rate of reports of maltreatment for the years 1976 to 1995 and the rate of substantiated cases for the years 1990 to 1995 using data from AHA, NCPCA, and NCANDS. (*Substantiated cases,* also known as *founded cases,* are those that have been investigated by CPS and deemed legitimate cases of maltreatment.)

Estimates derived from CPS sources reveal a substantial and steady increase in the rate of reported cases over the nineteen-year period for which data are available. The rates of substantiated cases, while available only for the years 1990 to 1995, show only a very moderate increase. These data indicate that the rate of substantiation is decreasing as CPS

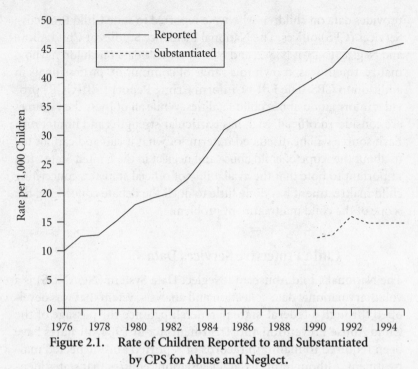

Figure 2.1.   Rate of Children Reported to and Substantiated by CPS for Abuse and Neglect.

Sources: American Humane Association, 1988; National Committee to Prevent Child Abuse, 1996.

handles more and more reports. One common explanation for this trend is that professionals and the general public have become more sensitive to child maltreatment and are therefore reporting less severe cases which are, in turn, less likely to be substantiated. Another explanation for the falling substantiation rate is that resources devoted to investigations have not increased at the rate at which the public have reported cases of maltreatment, leading to less thorough investigations.

The major limitation of child maltreatment estimates from NCANDS, AHA, and NCPCA is that they represent only the subset of cases known to Child Protective Services (CPS). Although there is a wide range of opinion as to what proportion of all cases are known to CPS, it is generally agreed that a large number of cases are never reported to CPS. The national incidence studies, which are discussed in detail later in this chapter, give us some insight into this issue, because these studies provide estimates of the number of maltreated children known to several types of community professionals, including cases that were not reported to CPS.

Another problem with state level reports and using CPS data to determine the pervasiveness of child maltreatment is that the types of cases that are investigated by CPS are biased. One form of bias relates to the type of maltreatment (such as abuse versus neglect) involved in the case. Because abuse is often easier to detect than neglect, and therefore more likely to be reported, CPS data are biased toward abuse. For example, in 1993, CPS investigated 40 percent of abuse cases but only 18 percent of neglect cases identified through the more comprehensive NIS-3. These biases are also observed within abuse and neglect categories. For example, physical abuse is far more likely to be investigated than emotional abuse, and physical neglect is more likely to be investigated than emotional or educational neglect.

Another commonly cited bias of reporting data is known as a surveillance bias. According to this hypothesis, families with few economic resources are more visible to the social services system and are therefore more likely to be subjects of maltreatment reports. In contrast, families with ample social and economic resources may be able to seek help from private sources (such as therapists) and are therefore less visible to the social services system and less likely to interact with it.

The National Incidence Study of Child Abuse and Neglect

The National Incidence Study of Child Abuse and Neglect (NIS) is a congressionally mandated, periodic study conducted by the National Center on Child Abuse and Neglect. Three waves of the study have been completed, and data are available for the years 1980, 1986, and 1993. The national incidence study gives a more comprehensive measure of the incidence of child maltreatment than NCANDS or other sources of CPS data because it surveys community professionals in hospitals, law enforcement agencies, schools, and day-care centers in addition to CPS agencies. Thus the national incidence study contains data on children who were not reported to CPS or who were screened out by CPS without investigation. Another major advantage of the NIS is that it employs a standard set of definitions across all cases, regardless of the state in which a case originated.

An important difference between the three waves of the NIS is that two sets of standardized definitions of abuse and neglect were employed in the NIS-2 and NIS-3, whereas the NIS-1 used only one set of definitions. The original definitions employed in the NIS-1 used a harm standard, under which children were considered maltreated only if they had already experienced harm from abuse and neglect. Definitions based on an endangerment standard were added to the NIS-2 and NIS-3 in response to criticism that the harm standard was too conservative. The endangerment standard counts children who experienced abuse or neglect that put them at imminent risk of harm. It is important to note that these categories are not mutually exclusive. That is, children whose maltreatment met the harm standard are generally included in both groups. Figure 2.2 presents the NIS-3 estimates of the rates of abused or neglected children in the United States for the years 1980, 1986, and 1993 according to each definitional standard.

These data show substantial and statistically significant increases in rates of maltreatment since the first wave of the study was conducted in 1980. The rate of increase is most dramatic during the seven-year interval between the NIS-2 in 1986 and the NIS-3 in 1993. During this period, the rate of maltreatment under the endangerment

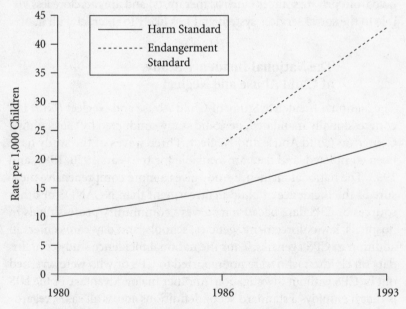

**Figure 2.2.   Rate of Child Maltreatment Under Harm and
Endangerment Standards.**

Source: Sedlak, A. J., & Broadhurst, D. D. (1996). *The third national incidence study
of child abuse and neglect (NIS-3): Final report.* Washington, DC: U.S. Department
of Health and Human Services, National Center on Child Abuse and Neglect.
Reprinted by permission.

standard nearly doubled to a rate of 42 per 1,000 for a total of 2,815,600 children nationwide (Sedlak & Broadhurst, 1996). The rate of maltreatment under the harm standard increased by 67 percent for the same interval.

Data from the National Incidence Study reveal that the majority of maltreatment goes unreported and that the proportion of unreported cases is increasing. For example, the NIS-3 study found that only 28 percent of all maltreatment cases were investigated by CPS in 1993. The remaining 72 percent were either not reported or were screened out by CPS without investigation. This figure represents a significant drop from the 44 percent of cases that were investigated in 1986 and the 33 percent that were investigated in 1980. Figure 2.3 graphs the overall incidence of maltreatment for each of the three national incidence studies, showing the percentage of children in each study whose maltreatment was investigated by CPS.

Many critics have argued that such large proportions of maltreated children were not reported to CPS because they had milder forms of maltreatment. They attribute the increase in the number of child maltreatment reports over time to increased sensitivity and awareness

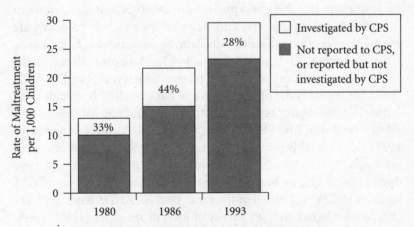

**Figure 2.3.   Proportion of Maltreated Children
Investigated by CPS by Year.**

Source: Sedlak, A. J., & Broadhurst, D. D. (1996). *The third national incidence study of child abuse and neglect (NIS-3): Final report.* Washington, DC: U.S. Department of Health and Human Services, National Center on Child Abuse and Neglect. Reprinted by permission.

rather than actual increases in maltreatment. This viewpoint is further supported by the greater increase in cases meeting the endangerment standard than the harm standard and the decrease in the CPS substantiation rate noted earlier. However, it is unlikely that increased sensitivity accounts for the entire increase in incidence. The NIS-3 revealed a fourfold increase over NIS-2 in the rate of children who were seriously injured or endangered by maltreatment, and only 26 percent of these seriously injured children were reported to CPS. It is very unlikely that such a large number of serious injuries could have gone undetected by the community professionals who responded to NIS-2, so increased sensitivity alone cannot explain this change. In all likelihood, both factors are at work—heightened sensitivity and real increases in maltreatment.

FBI Uniform Crime Report (FBI-UCR)

Fatal child maltreatment affects a very small number of children compared to other forms of maltreatment, but it is very difficult to know exactly how many child deaths are due to maltreatment. Estimates of the incidence of child maltreatment fatalities vary widely, but there is a growing consensus that fatal child maltreatment is seriously under-identified and underreported because of poor medical diagnoses, incomplete police and child protection investigations, inaccurate or incomplete crime reports, and flaws in how causes of death are recorded on death certificates (McClain, Sacks, Froehlke, & Ewigman, 1993; Ewigman, Kivlahan, & Land, 1993). Data on maltreatment-related child fatalities comes from numerous sources. The FBI-UCR homicide report is the official source of data on child homicides, but it does not distinguish between maltreatment and non–maltreatment-related fatalities. The FBI-UCR reported 2,521 child homicides for 1994 (U.S. Federal Bureau of Investigation, 1995). The National Committee to Prevent Child Abuse identified 1,278 child deaths in 1995 due to maltreatment, based on their annual fifty-state survey of CPS agencies (NCPCA, 1996). For the same year, NCANDS reported 1,111 child deaths based on their survey of forty-three states (U.S. Department of Health and Human Services, 1996).

Recent research in this area indicates that a large percentage of maltreatment fatalities are systematically misidentified. Ewigman, Kivlahan, and Land (1993) found significant underreporting of maltreatment as a cause of death in vital statistics, FBI-UCR homicide data, and the Missouri CPS records of 384 children under age five. Other record review studies in New York and Cook County Illinois have found similar results. McClain, Sacks, Froehlke, and Ewigman (1993) created three models for estimating the actual number of child maltreatment fatalities using death certificates, and found death rates were stable over the ten-year period from 1979 to 1988. Findings of the NCPCA fifty-state survey found that the incidence of fatal maltreatment increased from 1.30 per 100,000 in 1985 to 1.81 per 100,000 in 1995, a total increase of 39 percent (NCPCA, 1996). In comparison, the overall murder rate in the United States is 10 per 100,000.

These study findings have led to the widespread establishment of child death review teams. These teams, made up of medical, legal, and child protective experts, determine the circumstances of a child's death and recommend appropriate follow-up. The first such team was established in Los Angeles County in 1978. Since then teams have been established at the local or state level in forty-five states. In 1992 alone, eight states passed statutes mandating child death review teams. The teams have been successful in creating a better understanding of child maltreatment fatalities, increasing the rate of identification and prosecution of perpetrators, and promoting systemwide changes that may ultimately prevent fatalities. While more work is clearly needed in this area, child death review teams appear to be a useful approach.

HISTORY OF SOCIETAL RESPONSE TO CHILD MALTREATMENT

For a deeper understanding of the dynamics affecting child maltreatment, it is useful to review the evolution of the public response to this problem. Child maltreatment is not a new phenomenon, but society's view of it has changed dramatically over time. Biblical advice regarding discipline recommends beating one's child with a rod to drive foolishness from him and to "deliver his soul from Hell" (Proverbs, 23:13–14, King James Version). While such methods were apparently accepted then, they would be generally considered outright abuse in this country today. Charles Dickens described harsh discipline in mid nineteenth-century England (Dickens, 1839), as did Mark Twain in the United States after the Civil War (Twain, 1885). But times were already changing—unlike those whose sayings were recorded in the Bible, Dickens and Twain did not advocate or condone abuse; on the contrary, those who used brutal discipline were the villains in their novels.

This raises a crucial question: to what extent are the effects of child maltreatment culturally determined, and to what extent do they occur regardless of cultural context? If society genuinely believes beatings benefit a child, to what extent will the effects be negative? Some answers may emerge as the reader proceeds, but it is worth noting here that Jane Goodall's fascinating accounts of mothering among chimpanzees clearly document the negative effects of neglect on the growth and development of their young (Goodall, 1990). Some effects transcend not only culture and time but the human species itself.

For our purposes in understanding history, the crucial question is not when or how child maltreatment started, or even what its effects were, but rather when and why it became a public issue. At what point did society decide it was wrong? In the United States, public concern with child abuse is generally considered to have begun in 1874, with the highly publicized case of Mary Ellen Wilson, an illegitimate child whose mother abandoned her after her father died in the Civil War. Left in the care of her deceased father's lawful wife and the wife's second husband—neither of whom had any direct relationship to her—the child was found severely beaten and neglected. Mary Ellen's predicament was discovered by Etta Wheeler, a church social worker, following a tip from a concerned neighbor. There was no agency to look after children's rights then, but Wheeler went to the American Society for the Prevention of Cruelty to Animals, which convinced a judge to remove Mary Ellen and imprison her stepmother (Nelson, 1984; Lazoritz, 1990).

Many children had suffered similar plights before, especially those born out of wedlock. Mary Ellen's case most likely attracted attention not because of its uniqueness but because of its timing. The industrialization of the latter half of the nineteenth century brought technological changes that stimulated the growth of a new, educated leisure class whose members became influential in literature, education, politics, and the arts (Grotberg, 1976; Nelson, 1984). Education grew in importance as industrialization required more sophisticated technology. There was an active women's movement that advocated not only women's suffrage but also kinder, more gentle forms of child discipline than the beatings that were still commonly used as punishment (Gordon, 1988). The "natural rights" ideology became popular during the Radical Reconstruction period after the Civil War and was applied to both children and adults. Changes in religious beliefs that began with the Reformation started to affect childrearing as the harsh doctrine of "original sin" began to yield to a more benign concept of childhood innocence. In the eighteenth century, Jean-Jacques Rousseau and John Locke had argued that children were born with innate goodness and were shaped by their environment and those around them—not by a devil within. These views gained acceptance in the United States in the nineteenth century, especially as more people were educated after the Civil War (Grotberg, 1976; Garbarino, 1982; Nelson, 1984).

During the Middle Ages, about half of all children had died by the time they were five; in the 1800s, major advances in public health reduced infant mortality drastically, so that during the Industrial Revolution the figure fell to roughly 10 percent. Before then, children were not viewed as a good investment, due to their short life expectancy (Garbarino, 1982, 1995; Grotberg, 1976; Jordan, 1987). Pediatrics emerged as a specialty after the Civil War, and this period saw the beginnings of neighborhood social work in the 1880s and the first recreational organizations for children a decade earlier (Grotberg, 1976).

All these forces converged to produce an enlightened view of childhood as a protected time for education and development, different from adulthood and free of the pressures, obligations and dangers adults face (Grotberg, 1976; Nelson, 1984; Garbarino, 1995). Before then, children were not understood to be separate from adults, and there was less awareness of the significance of age. In fact, early paintings show children as miniature adults, with adult features; childlike features did not even appear in art before the thirteenth century (Aries, 1962; Garbarino, 1982). Through the eighteenth century, children were often expected to work almost as soon as they were physically able, and there was little understanding of the importance of play in a child's development (Garbarino, 1982, Grotberg, 1976, Gordon, 1988).

Organizing to Protect Children

Considering both the changes after the Civil War and the prior conditions and beliefs, it is easy to see why child abuse began to be challenged—and why few institutions were available to remedy it. The Mary Ellen case generated intense newspaper coverage and resulted in the establishment of the first Society for the Prevention of Cruelty to Children (SPCC) in New York City, as an extension of the Society for the Prevention of Cruelty to Animals (SPCA) (Nelson, 1984). By 1880, more than thirty similar organizations had been formed throughout the country (Gordon, 1988).

The New York SPCC adopted a law-and-order approach; the organization obtained police officer status for its staff and the power to prosecute parents. Its aim was to identify abusive families, punish the parents, and "rescue" the children, who were often placed in orphanages or other large institutions (Nelson, 1984). The Massachusetts Society for the Prevention of Cruelty to Children, which formed later, adopted a similar approach at first. After studying early case records in Boston, Gordon (1988) concluded that the SPCC's major concern was controlling lower-class immigrant families who were widely perceived as inferior by the upper-class men and women who ran the organization. The many desperately poor Catholic immigrants who had arrived from Ireland were seen as a threat by well-established Anglo-Saxon Protestants who had controlled Boston unchallenged for two hundred years. In fact, by 1850, 35 percent of Boston's population was foreign born. Consequently, it is not surprising that the SPCC became not only a means of protecting children but also a method of social control. It is likely that some freewheeling child protection "agents" may have committed abuses of power themselves; certainly most poor immigrant families had little protection against them.

This changed in 1907, when the Massachusetts SPCC employed Carl Carstens of the New York Charity Organization Society as its head. Carstens introduced the concept of casework to child protection. Rather than freewheeling male law enforcers, Carstens employed and trained middle-class women as caseworkers—to investigate families' situations and attempt to resolve major problems. Casework was evolving in settlement houses and other branches of social work as a scientific extension of the volunteerism initiated by reformers from wealthy families of the previous generation. It was viewed as scientific and more effective than punishment and removal, and it would eventually form the basis for modern social work theory (Gordon, 1988).

The Massachusetts SPCC was the first major child-protection agency to adopt the social work model, and others soon followed. But some child-protection agencies rejected this approach, and a split resulted between the "restrictionists" and the "liberals" (Gordon, 1988). The New York SPCC continued to emphasize law enforcement, rescue, and punishment of offending parents, while Massachusetts led toward a problem-solving casework approach. While the "progressive"

Massachusetts model eventually gained much wider acceptance than the New York approach, the tension between these philosophies has permeated child protection work ever since and continues even today.

The professionalization of social work led to a focus on reforming and changing individual families as opposed to rescuing children and punishing abusers. According to Gordon, this resulted in a shift in focus away from abusive and often alcoholic men toward women who, for whatever reason, were not providing proper care of their children. Social workers often tried to teach such mothers about child rearing and housekeeping and to push them to live up to middle-class standards—but this was difficult to do without a middle-class income (Gordon, 1988; Nelson, 1984).

The intense concern over child abuse in 1874 did not last. While the *New York Times* published fifty-two articles on "cruelty to children" from 1874 to 1877, this category (which appeared for the first time in 1874) was dropped from the newspaper's index altogether by 1877 (Nelson, 1984). Nearly a century would pass before child abuse would become a major public issue again.

THE CHILDREN'S BUREAU— A GOVERNMENT RESPONSE

Nevertheless, overall concern about children led to the creation of the federal Children's Bureau in 1912, as a result of the First White House Conference on Dependent Children, hosted by President Theodore Roosevelt in 1909. The bureau was given a mission to conduct research on "all matters pertaining to the welfare of children and child life among all classes" (Nelson, 1984, p. 35). To avoid opposition that could have led to an early demise, the new bureau did not take on the most controversial matters of the time such as child labor—where new views of children's rights clashed with powerful economic interests. Instead it took up "politically safe, yet socially important issues," many of which had a public health focus (Nelson, 1984, p. 36).

The 1935 Social Security Act moved the Children's Bureau beyond research by giving it responsibility for administering Title V, which included child welfare services. It was significant that this major response by the federal government to child welfare issues emphasized social workers rather than peace officers, further institutionalizing the shift away from the law enforcement approach. By the 1930s, child abuse had effectively disappeared as a major public issue, and concerns about maltreatment were largely left to professional social workers (Nelson, 1984).

A NEW PROFESSION GETS INVOLVED

But in the prosperous period after the Second World War, seeds were planted for a major rekindling of public interest and concern that would far outstrip everything that occurred in the reform period at the end of the previous century. The first critical developments took place among professionals and largely escaped public notice. New X-ray technology now permitted radiologists to discriminate between old healed fractures and new ones, which allowed them to identify consecutive injuries from previously hidden physical evidence (Grotberg, 1976).

In 1946 John Caffey, a radiologist, reported on the mysterious occurrence of repeated long-bone fractures and subdural hematomas in infants whose parents reported no injury serious enough to cause them (Caffey, 1946). In 1953, Roy Astley of Birmingham Children's Hospital in England, studied six babies exhibiting this phenomenon and hypothesized that they were victims of extremely fragile bone structure (Astley, 1953). In the same year, Frederic Silverman, a Cincinnati radiologist, examined three similar cases and proposed that the attending physicians had not obtained adequate histories (Silverman, 1953). Then, in 1955, P. V. Woolley and W. A. Evans, of the Michigan Children's Hospital and Wayne State University College of Medicine, respectively, extensively examined twelve cases of infants with unexplained fractures, hematomas, and other injuries. They found no evidence to support Astley's fragile bone concept and concluded that the conditions they saw were most likely caused by "undesirable vectors of force." They observed that all occurred in households with a "high incidence of neurotic or psychotic (adult) behavior" and that there were no new injuries to babies who were removed from their home (Woolley & Evans, 1955, p. 543). In 1957 Caffey reexamined his 1946 data and concluded that the trauma might have been willfully caused by the infants' parents (Nelson, 1984).

These and a few similar articles constituted the first tentative steps toward involvement of a potent new force in the child maltreatment arena—the medical profession. Although it would be at least another decade before physicians would fully accept the possibility that parents might be deliberately injuring their children, the involvement of medical professionals would have a profound impact on the field and the public's response (Nelson, 1984).

The social work profession also took important steps during this time. In 1954 Vincent De Francis, director of the New York SPCC, became director of the American Humane Association (AHA), the national umbrella for SPCAs and SPCCs. Under his direction the AHA began a national survey of services for neglected, abused, and exploited children. In 1955 he reported his results to the Children's Bureau, and his findings were published the following year (Nelson, 1984).

De Francis also persuaded national child welfare agencies to meet annually. Dissension surfaced at the first meeting over his emphasis on imposed services for the child as opposed to voluntary services to the parent—a sort of a replay of the punishment-versus-rehabilitation issue. Both his report and the annual meetings increased the visibility of child maltreatment in professional circles. The report emphasized neglect—"the endangerment of children's health, morals, welfare or emotional development," rather than physical abuse, as neglect reflected what caseworkers saw in most of their cases (Nelson, 1984).

In 1960 the Children's Bureau received a new and permanent unrestricted research allocation of $1 million. According to Nelson, the availability of this windfall funding, just as professionals were becoming more aware of child maltreatment, provided the necessary groundwork for the reemergence of child abuse as a public issue. As preliminary research findings attracted attention among professionals, the Children's Bureau programmed some of its new money to learn more about this issue. The resulting research generated new findings that periodically spilled over into the popular media, bringing the issue once again into public view.

The Role of the Media

The first article to attract major public attention was prepared by C. Henry Kempe, a Denver pediatrician, and his colleagues and published in the *Journal of the American Medical Association* in 1962. Titled "The Battered Child Syndrome," it was based on 302 emergency room cases of "serious physical abuse" to small children. In their first sentence, Dr. Kempe and colleagues boldly asserted what most prior writers had only hinted—that these injuries were inflicted by the parents (Kempe, Silverman, Steele, Droegemueller, & Silver, 1962). The journal editorialized (with little supporting data) that this phenomenon might cause more child deaths than better-known diseases such as leukemia and muscular dystrophy. This quickly caught the attention of the mass media, and articles on child abuse soon appeared in *Newsweek, Time, Life,* and the *Saturday Evening Post* (Nelson, 1984).

The fact that Kempe's article had attracted public attention while De Francis's earlier report had not may have been due to Kempe and colleagues' emphasis on physical abuse—a far more sensational subject than neglect, as De Francis had defined it. Also, medicine enjoyed high public status in view of its recent success in eliminating smallpox, polio and several other childhood diseases that had worried virtually every parent of the era. And Dr. Kempe brought more than a routine knowledge of pediatrics; he was a believer in public health principles and had played a significant role in the campaign to eradicate smallpox in India. He knew well the importance of the media in health campaigns.

The 1962 article by Kempe and colleagues kicked off a stream of publicity that continues to this day. The *Readers Guide to Periodical Literature* listed 124 articles on child maltreatment between 1960 and 1980, and over 1,700 articles were published in professional journals between 1950 and 1980, almost all of them after 1962 (Nelson, 1984). Other physicians took up the cause, writing books and articles and offering training—among the best known were Ray Helfer in Michigan, Vincent Fontana in New York, and Eli Newberger in Boston.

Legislative and Private Sector Responses

The Children's Bureau responded to the public attention by developing model legislation for the states that would require physicians to report suspected cases of child maltreatment. Professional organizations such as the American Humane Association and the American Academy of Pediatrics offered legislative alternatives. There was disagreement over whether the reporting should be mandatory or voluntary, where the reports should go, and who should be required to report. In another replay of the punishment-versus-rehabilitation debate, the Children's Bureau proposed reporting to the police "because they are always there," while the AHA recommended reporting to child welfare agencies, as they were more likely to bring services rather than punishment. Different versions of reporting legislation passed in all fifty states between 1963 and 1967—an incredibly rapid rate of diffusion for a new law (Nelson, 1984).

In the early 1970s two private efforts began that would shape the public's response. Parents Anonymous, a self-help movement for parents who feared they might abuse their children, formed when Leonard Lieber, a psychiatric social worker in California, put two of his clients together thinking they might help each other, after everything else had failed. Help each other they did, and one of the women, who became known as Jolly K., went on with Lieber to form self-help groups that spread across the country. To some extent this group formed in reaction to overprofessionalization—from a frustration with professional responses that did not work and professionals who did not personally understand the problem (Gordon, 1988). Then in 1972, Donna Stone, the daughter of a wealthy industrialist, founded what is now the National Committee to Prevent Child Abuse. This organization began by mobilizing private sector support to address the problem, and it has since become a major player in implementing preventive models throughout the country.

The strong response at the state level and the professional and private sector responses just described prepared the ground for federal legislation. In 1971 Senator Walter Mondale (D., Minn.) succeeded in getting legislation through Congress to establish a major day care program, only to have it vetoed by President Nixon on the grounds that supporting "communal" child care would be improper for the federal government. As head of the new Subcommittee on Children and Youth, Mondale wanted a victory that would benefit children and could get by a hostile president. He took up the child abuse issue in part because it had almost no opposition—who would be against fighting child abuse? Jolly K. of Parents Anonymous was a star witness, and her eloquence in describing the pain of abusive parents made a deep impression on legislators and the media (Nelson, 1984).

There was debate about whether the bill should focus only on physical abuse or should also include neglect. Some influential physicians, including Dr. Kempe, favored limiting it to physical abuse, but AHA's Vincent De Francis argued successfully that "we must solve the whole problem" by including the many children who are neglected or sexually or emotionally abused (Nelson, 1984).

New Federal Leadership

Mondale's bill, the Child Abuse Prevention and Treatment Act, was signed by President Nixon in January 1974—just one hundred years after the Mary Ellen case first brought the issue to public attention.

The bill created a new government entity, the National Center on Child Abuse and Neglect, which would disburse federal funds for research and demonstration projects on child abuse and funds that would go directly to states that met the requirements of the legislation. For example, states were required to have reporting laws in place with confidentiality statutes to protect the identity of those who reported child abuse; they were also to have in place a system to investigate the reports. Guardians ad litem were required to represent children in court—on the assumption that the child's interests might be different from those of her or his parents or the child protection agency.

The new legislation advanced the concept of protective custody—forcible removal (rescue) of the child from the family by law enforcement or protective workers—in order to protect the child. This concept was not new, but its explicit inclusion in child protection legislation pushed the field back toward the "rescue" end of the continuum. It became easier (and perhaps a little safer) for the protective worker to remove a child when in doubt (Nelson, 1984).

The new National Center provided a level of leadership that had not existed before. Douglas Besharov, the center's first director, pushed the states hard to develop effective reporting in accordance with the law. He believed that child maltreatment was too big a problem to be left to one field, such as medicine or social work, and actively promoted interdisciplinary cooperation and the involvement of other fields, including education, mental health, and private efforts. The center produced manuals on child maltreatment for virtually every profession in every relevant field. It funded child abuse and neglect resource centers and other efforts around the country to disseminate information locally and to mobilize and assist state and local efforts.

As these various initiatives began to work, new awareness developed in the media and in police departments, schools, and hospitals. The reporting legislation of the 1960s had required mainly doctors to report, but a second round of legislation initiatives in response to the new federal legislation caused states to designate others who worked with children as mandated reporters. These included nurses, day care workers, teachers, counselors, and in some cases even the general public.

The increase in mandated reporters and in public awareness dramatically increased the number of reports. Dr. Kempe had studied only 302 cases of battered children in emergency rooms in 1962—a serious but definitely manageable problem. After the 1974 federal legislation and new laws at the state level, reported cases skyrocketed. In 1974, sixty thousand cases were reported, but that number rose to 1.1 million in 1980 and over 3 million by 1995 (U.S. Advisory Board on Child Abuse and Neglect, 1995; National Committee to Prevent Child Abuse, 1996). In Florida the number of reported cases went from 17 in 1970 to 19,120 in 1971, after initiation of a well-publicized hot line (Nelson, 1984).

According to Nelson, one reason state governments acted to pass reporting legislation was the belief that it would not cost taxpayers money. Reporting was viewed as a simple action that could be followed up at the appropriate level. Only one state—Illinois—initially appropriated funds to receive and follow up on the reports. Others apparently assumed that reported cases could be absorbed by existing staff (Nelson, 1984).

But while there had been money to increase funds for the Children's Bureau in the early 1960s, escalation of the Vietnam War created a severe drain on funding in the 1970s, and attempts by President Reagan to cut domestic spending in the 1980s squeezed funds even further. As time passed and the numbers of reports increased, local child protective units became more and more overwhelmed. Staff had been added at first, but in the 1980s expansion stopped or slowed in many places, even though the number of reports continued to grow.

Broadening the Definitions

Part of the increase in reports resulted from a broadening of definitions. The article by Dr. Kempe and colleagues mentioned earlier had focused on the most serious type of physical abuse, which was of greatest concern to physicians—hence the term *battered child*. But social work professionals, who had been addressing the issue of child maltreatment for many years, argued successfully for also addressing neglect. Then during the 1980s the federal legislation was expanded to address abuse in out-of-home situations such as child care institutions, day care centers, and schools. Child pornography was also added to the legislation, and finally the definition of maltreatment was expanded to include failure of doctors to provide medical treatment for seriously disabled infants.

This expansion represented a shift in philosophy. Initially, child protection intervention was justified because the parents who were supposed to be protecting the child were in fact causing the child harm. Since they obviously could not protect their children from themselves, the government stepped in as protector of last resort. Services were often provided because it was difficult to punish the parent without also punishing the child, who was already a victim. But these principles became less clear as the definition expanded. When the source of harm was outside the home, the parents could presumably provide some protection—at least to the point of removing their children from a harmful situation or calling in law enforcement (except in the case of a child care institution, where parents typically had little say about placement or opportunity to protect the child once it got there). And services to the perpetrator were hardly relevant. But in each case the child protection role expanded in reaction to a perceived threat to children—even though some threats (such as medical neglect to disabled infants) represented very small numbers.

Perceived susceptibility to maltreatment became an important issue. Was child maltreatment a threat, like many childhood diseases, that could develop in any community or neighborhood, regardless of economic and social class? Or was it a problem primarily confined to the poor? Political support has traditionally been strongest for issues that affect—or benefit—everyone. Dr. Kempe and others who sold the initial child abuse legislation to the federal government knew this, and Senator Mondale knew it too. During the hearings there was an emphasis on the classless nature of child abuse—that it could happen in the best of families. Senator Mondale believed this view was essential to ensure the passage of his bill (Nelson, 1984).

Dr. Kempe had argued that physical child abuse cuts across class and social lines—a radical switch from the elite view of the 1870s, which held that it could only occur in "inferior" lower-class families. Even Woolley and Evans had found abuse only in dysfunctional families (Woolley & Evans, 1955). But in 1972 it was clear that neglect was heavily concentrated among the poor—who had the fewest resources to provide for their children and therefore were least likely to provide adequately. In most states, a majority of the reports in fact concerned neglect rather than physical abuse, and this was true even in the early days of the SPCCs. In fact it did not take the SPCCs long to discover that the occasional instances of physical abuse had much more power to generate financial and other support for their work than descriptions of the neglect that occupied most of their time (Gordon, 1988). Since those early days it has become clear that, while all forms of maltreatment occur at all income levels, reports of all types are far more common among low-income people than those at higher income levels (Sedlak & Broadhurst, 1996).

A related question was causation. Did child maltreatment result from internal psychological or emotional problems of the parents— or simply from a lack of information on childrearing? Could it be cured? Or does it result from deeper factors in communities and society that would be difficult to change and would generate substantial opposition if change were attempted? The early reformers had blamed maltreatment on cultural inferiority, immorality, and alcoholism (Gordon, 1988). During the Mondale hearings child abuse was presented as a serious but relatively small-scale individually based problem, for which remedies could be found. Dr. Kempe represented the medical model, which viewed pathology in terms of specific disease agents that could be eliminated once they were identified. As indicated earlier, this approach had successfully eliminated several serious childhood diseases.

Environmental Factors

Dr. Ray Helfer, a Michigan pediatrician, developed a popular causal theory that he called the World of Abnormal Rearing (WAR). Helfer believed child abuse resulted from serious deficiencies in the parent's own upbringing, which made bonding difficult, and this caused the problem to pass from generation to generation, unless intervention took place to break the cycle. But as more research took place it became clear that causes were more varied and complex. Some causal factors were undoubtedly psychologically or emotionally based and lay within the individual. But environmental factors were also found to be important, as when Garbarino and others discovered much higher rates of child abuse in weaker neighborhoods than stronger ones, even when income levels were similar (Coulton, Korbin, Su, & Chow, 1995; Garbarino & Kostelny, 1992; Garbarino & Sherman, 1980; Garbarino & Crouter, 1978a; Deccio, Horner, & Wilson, 1994). In 1988 Lizbeth Schorr published her popular work *Within Our Reach,* which explained how environmental and economic factors interact with personal factors, often producing devastating results for poor children with deficits in poor communities—even though children with similar deficits develop very successfully in families with higher incomes in stronger communities (Schorr, 1988). This led to a realization that families "on the edge" might perform adequately in a healthy community with lots of supports but fail to do so in a dysfunctional community, with child maltreatment an unfortunate result.

Unfortunately, conditions in both inner cities and some rural areas worsened considerably during the 1970s and 1980s, as a result of factory closures and the disappearance of jobs. Throughout the Second World War and much of the 1950s, urban blacks had been confined largely to inner-city neighborhoods as a result of discrimination and restrictive housing policies. When the Civil Rights movement lessened these barriers, many blacks with ability left inner-city neighborhoods, just as generations of white immigrants had done before. In addition, cities used highway construction and urban renewal literally to destroy many urban neighborhoods. This deprived the inner-city neighborhoods not only of physical infrastructure, such as housing and stores, but also of the organizational leadership and stable role models they had enjoyed in the past (Halpern, 1995). These two trends produced a concentration of poverty in some neighborhoods, and substance abuse, teen pregnancy, violence, and child maltreatment all increased as a result (Coulton, Korbin, Su, & Chow, 1995; Wilson, 1987). Some community environments became bad enough to be described as an "ecological conspiracy against children" (Garbarino & Kostelny, 1992, p. 463). In some rural areas economic changes resulted in the loss of community institutions such as businesses, schools, stores, churches, and other organizations that brought people together. This increased both the isolation of poor families and the community's ability to support them (Fitchen, 1981).

Between 1986 and 1993 the incidence of child maltreatment nearly doubled, increasing from 22.6 to 41.9 per thousand children (U.S. Department of Health and Human Services, 1996). Some of the increase was related to the emergence of crack cocaine in low-income neighborhoods. Studies in Washington and Los Angeles in 1989 found substance abuse to be involved in 80 to 90 percent of the child maltreatment cases reviewed (U.S. Advisory Board on Child Abuse and Neglect, 1990). Unlike many earlier drugs, which were used mainly by men, crack cocaine has been popular also among women, with devastating effects on childrearing. This put a severe strain on services, especially since few professionals had experience with the new drug, and substance abuse treatment was very limited and primarily addressed to men.

Sexual Abuse

Another factor causing increased reporting in the 1980s was an increased awareness of sexual abuse. The sexual exploitation of children had been raised as an issue by feminists and other activists in the post–Civil War period in both the United States and Great Britain. In Britain they succeeded in raising the age of consent from ten to thirteen in 1875 and to sixteen in 1885. Incest was outlawed there in 1908. In Vienna Sigmund Freud heard many stories of sexual abuse from his clients, and in 1896 he published a groundbreaking paper that related many of their emotional problems to childhood sexual abuse (Olafson, Corwin, & Summit, 1993).

But the interest in sexual abuse generated a powerful backlash that led to suppression of talk about it. In fact, Freud actually recanted his 1896 paper thirty years later, confessing that he had been naive and asserting that the stories he had heard had been childhood sexual fantasies. A 1932 paper by Sandor Ferenczi identifying sexual abuse as an important pathogenic factor, even in respectable families, was not translated into English for seventeen years. An initial translation was destroyed by E. Jones with Freud's consent; Freud said Ferenczi was making the same mistake he himself had made thirty years before. But it later turned out that Jones himself was the subject of accusations of indecent behavior toward three young girls and sexual irregularities toward his patients. Although it is not clear that any of these accusations were ever proven, they ultimately caused him to resign his position. It appeared that the backlash may have come partly because influential people were adversely affected—and partly because the extent of the problem may simply have been too great for people to accept (Olafson, Corwin, & Summit, 1993).

A major backlash milepost was the formation of Victims of Child Abuse Laws (VOCAL) in 1984 by a group of parents in Minnesota who claimed to have been falsely accused of child abuse and that they and their families had suffered as a consequence. The group included two parents who had been acquitted of sexual abuse in an unsuccessful prosecution concerning allegations of a sexual abuse ring in Jordan, Minnesota. (Charges were later dropped against twenty-one others accused.) VOCAL spread rapidly and soon had over 100 chapters in more than 40 states. False sexual abuse allegations have been a major concern of the group (Hechler, 1988).

Some have questioned the motives behind this movement, and it seems probable that some of the members of VOCAL have, in fact, sexually abused children and have taken advantage of the organization as a shield (Hechler, 1988). But it is equally clear that many members have been falsely accused and that they and their children have suffered as a result. Although VOCAL may be considered extremist or irresponsible by some, many of its concerns are widely shared—particularly those involving incompetent investigations and the unnecessary removal of children from their families (Hechler, 1988).

Hechler (1988) and Wexler (1995) have both drawn analogies between sexual abuse allegations and the seventeenth century Salem witchhunts. Sexual abuse, like witchcraft, invokes horror and fear, which can lead to a form of public hysteria. Defending oneself against such an allegation is difficult, and the removal of children can be done without proof of guilt, despite the fact that it may cause serious psychological damage to the child.

As with physical abuse, several key sexual abuse studies were undertaken in the 1950s. The main conclusion drawn from them was that sexual abuse, including incest, was far more widespread than most people imagined—affecting as many as 25 percent of female respondents. In 1955 Weinberg estimated that there were a million incest victims in the United States. But some researchers claimed that the victims themselves were responsible for seducing their abuser and expressed more concern for accused abusers than the victims (Olafson, Corwin, & Summit, 1993).

Nevertheless, revelations continued. In 1979 Finkelhor found that 19 percent of female college students had been sexually abused as children, and in that year funding for a focus on sexual abuse was added to the Child Abuse Prevention and Treatment Act (CAPTA). Russell found that 38 percent of a random sample of San Francisco women had suffered sexual abuse as children. By this time, these and other studies had caught the attention of the media (Olafson, Corwin, & Summit, 1993). Several public personalities, including Florida Senator Paula Hawkins and television personality Oprah Winfrey, confessed publicly to having been sexually abused as children. Reports of sexual abuse grew dramatically. But according to Olafson, Corwin, & Summit (1993) the backlash continues in various forms, as "sexuality and sexual regulation impinge centrally on powerful social interests and privileges" (p. 19).

Sexual abuse is a far more complex problem than other forms of maltreatment, and, initially at least, many of the perpetrators seemed less curable. There is rarely any physical evidence, so the child's testimony becomes more important than in other forms of abuse where more evidence is available (Doris, Mazur, & Thomas, 1995). While most parents who have raised children can at least understand how mild physical abuse might occur, sexual abusers do not generate much tolerance or sympathy among a large section of the public. Prosecution has been emphasized over rehabilitation, and sexual abuse cases are often more likely to be referred to court than other types. In fact, the first serious treatment option, Parents United, began in 1971 among men already imprisoned for sexual abuse. Some experts believe the rise in sexual abuse cases has helped to push the whole child protective system toward a more legalistic approach, making prevention and rehabilitation more difficult for other forms of abuse (Douglas Besharov, personal communication, December 1996).

CHILD ABUSE AND POLITICS

Over time, the federal focus on child maltreatment weakened. Although President Nixon had supported the establishment of the National Center on Child Abuse and Neglect (NCCAN) in 1974, it languished under his successors. To cut federal spending, the Reagan administration initiated a "reduction in force" among federal employees that caused many of the most innovative and energetic NCCAN staff to leave. Travel and publication funds for those who remained were drastically reduced or eliminated altogether, which greatly reduced the center's visibility and effectiveness. In 1984, the regional resource centers were defunded, and thus the center's reach was reduced even further (U.S. Advisory Board on Child Abuse and Neglect, 1991).

Under pressure from advocacy groups, such as the National Committee to Prevent Child Abuse, the American Humane Association, the Child Welfare League, and the American Public Welfare Association, some key congressmen became concerned about lack of attention in the executive branch. As a result of leadership by Senator Christopher Dodd (D., Conn.) and Representative Major Owens, D., N.Y.), the 1988 CAPTA amendments established an advisory board on child abuse. The intent was partly to pressure the administration and partly to provide key Congressional committees and the national center with advice on child abuse policy.

The new advisory board was far more outspoken than many expected. Its first report, in 1990, declared that child maltreatment had become a "national emergency." The board found that the system for responding to child abuse and neglect was failing: "It is not a question of acute failure of a single element. . . . [T]here is chronic and critical multiple organ failure. . . . Indeed the system itself can at times be abusive to children" (U.S. Advisory Board on Child Abuse and Neglect, 1990, p. 2). This referred to the overwhelming caseloads, high caseworker turnover, crushing loads on court calendars, and extreme difficulties within the overwhelmed foster care system—as well as the diminishing availability of preventive and treatment services. The board offered thirty-one recommendations for immediate action and promised a more detailed strategy for action in the future.

Investigation or Prevention?

Some of the board members felt that the child protective system had strayed from its intended mission of helping families and children and had become too closely aligned with the court system. Child protective workers, instead of coming to help, were there to conduct an investigation, which in many cases would do little to help the children directly. Since all states required investigations but few mandated treatment or prevention, more and more emphasis was focused on the investigation as the gap between needs and resources widened. "As a result it has become far easier to pick up the telephone to report one's neighbor for child abuse than it is for that neighbor to pick up the telephone to request and receive help before the abuse happens" (U.S. Advisory Board on Child Abuse and Neglect, 1990, p. 80).

With increasing publicity of extreme cases by the media, the stakes in caseworker decisions grew higher. A child's death might now result in a lawsuit against the caseworker and/or dismissal of the county social services commissioner. On the other hand, placing a child in foster care unnecessarily could be costly for local government and damaging to the child. As a new risk assessment technology swept the country, training for caseworkers began to focus more on assessment of risk in families. The intent was to establish a much-needed uniform and comprehensive standard for deciding when to remove a child, based on assessment of various types of risk. But risk assessment came also to be used as a means of protecting caseworkers and their agencies from lawsuits, ironically blurring the initial focus on protecting the child.

As reports increased and money for services grew scarcer, services were prioritized, and risk assessment became a basis for triage. Reported families with serious problems were often given preference over others who had not been reported. The system became more oriented toward crisis response than prevention or treatment. This meant that families often did not get help until they had gotten into such serious difficulty that they were reported—or threatened with removal of their child. Only then would services be available. Presumably, if help had been provided earlier, much of the expense and trauma resulting from the report and investigation could have been avoided, and the chance for success would have been higher (U.S. Advisory Board on Child Abuse and Neglect, 1995). But how to get off this crisis treadmill?

Richard Wexler (1990) went further than the U.S. Advisory Board by blaming these problems on a "child saver" mentality, whose proponents carry the rescuer approach much too far. His book *Wounded Innocents* offers appalling examples of a system gone awry by unnecessarily damaging both children and innocent parents while diverting attention from those who really need it. He blames all this on system and worker overload and incompetence, as well as on society's unwillingness to pay the cost of assigning skilled workers to protect children in difficulty. The result, Wexler says, is a carryover from the last century, in which poverty is confused with neglect, and the system is used to control or punish the poor. Many cases of so-called neglect involve impoverished families who are struggling against overwhelming odds. What they need is help in paying for food or rent. What they get is a humiliating investigation and, sometimes, the placement of their children in foster care, with perhaps some counseling thrown in. Usually the foster care costs far more than the help these families need. Wexler advocates narrowing the grounds for coercive intervention into families and eliminating the bias in federal funding streams that favor foster care over help for families. He strongly supports Family Preservation, which channels intensive help and support to families threatened with the removal of children to foster care (Wexler, 1990).

In its second report (1991) the U.S. Advisory Board on Child Abuse and Neglect advocated universal voluntary neonatal home visitor programs as one of its two top recommendations to prevent child abuse.

Regular visits to at-risk parents by trained staff before and after the birth of an infant had demonstrated positive results in Elmira, New York, and in the state of Hawaii (U.S. Advisory Board on Child Abuse and Neglect, 1991). Although ignored by the federal government at first, this recommendation was quickly promoted by the National Committee to Prevent Child Abuse, which was awarded a $1 million grant from the Ronald McDonald House to establish home visiting programs throughout the country under the name Healthy Families America.

In 1992 a Government Accounting Office report concluded that child abuse prevention incentives to the states would pay for themselves by reducing the use of foster care (U.S. Government Accounting Office, 1992). The report recommended home visiting services. On the strength of this the federal government authorized funding for home visiting programs, although money ($2.5 million) did not actually start to flow until two years later (National Child Abuse Coalition, 1994).

Strengthening the Environment

In 1993 the U.S. Advisory Board produced its recommendations for a national strategy, promised in its first report three years earlier. The board advocated a strong focus on strengthening neighborhoods and a reshaping of funding for services to make it at least as easy to provide voluntary preventive services as it is now to provide foster care. It made a strong case for more treatment, noting that the emphasis on investigation was consuming too great a share of available resources at the expense of the people who are reported (U.S. Advisory Board on Child Abuse and Neglect, 1995).

The board's new recommendations sparked professional discussions, and many advocates and grantseekers drew on its recommendations for their work, but this report did not attract the same media attention as the 1990 declaration of a "national emergency." However, the board's work may have helped to move the government toward the prevention end of the spectrum. The 1994 budget, drawn up in 1993, included a new $930 million, five-year Family Preservation and Support Services program, for which $60 million was appropriated initially, with increasing amounts in later years. Family Preservation, developed with support from the Edna McConnel Clark Foundation, would provide intensive services to families in crisis to avoid placing children in foster care; family supports are "community based services to promote the well being of children and families, designed to increase the strength and stability of families" (Social Security Act, Title IV-B, Part 2, Section 431, 1993 Amendments). This was a significant new funding opportunity that allowed communities to develop new treatment and preventive programs (National Child Abuse Coalition, 1993a).

The 1994 budget also added $1 billion to the Title XX social services block grants to states for social services in empowerment zones and enterprise zones. The new funds were to "prevent and remedy the neglect and abuse of children" through alcohol and drug prevention and treatment programs. (National Child Abuse Coalition, 1993b) The 1995 budget, developed in 1994, increased child abuse prevention funds by about $5 million, and the amount for Family Preservation and Support more than doubled, to $150 million.

The 1994 election radically changed the nature of Congress, however, and Republicans gained control of both houses for the first time in many years. The new Republican leaders believed they had a mandate to cut government spending on social programs and did so. Community-based family resource funds were cut by 26 percent for 1996, the NCCAN was reduced in scope, and specific funding for the advisory board was eliminated altogether in the 1997 budget. But the Family Preservation and Support funds were not cut, as the law had been written to provide them as an entitlement, subject only to an overall funding cap.

CONCLUSION

During the last thirty years the issue of child maltreatment has moved from being perceived as a relatively small and little-known phenomenon to a problem overwhelming in its incidence and serious in its effects. For most of this century there has been tension between the punitive and the rehabilitative response, and that tension continues today. Despite some encouraging increases in funding for prevention, the U.S. system still places its primary emphasis on a legalistic response after the crisis has occurred.

Policy is affected by the public perception of the problem as opposed to its reality. From the beginning, legislation and action have frequently resulted from dramatic but relatively rare cases of severe abuse rather than the cases of neglect that are far more common. The dramatic cases have been effective in generating concern and support, both legislatively and financially, but the public and legislative response to such cases may have produced a more punitive system than is consistent with day-to-day reality.

Causal theories of child maltreatment have varied according to politics, social evolution, and prevailing beliefs. In politically conservative times, the emphasis has been on psychological or individual causes and solutions, while social reform movements have tended to emphasize social causes such as poverty, unemployment, isolation, and environmental factors. (Gordon, 1988; Levine & Levine, 1970). Psychological causes place the onus for change on the individuals affected, while social causes put the onus for change on society itself—including those who are trying to help (Lofquist, 1983). Psychological solutions are much less sweeping and expensive than those dealing with social causes that affect many people. Unfortunately, they may also be less effective. In the absence of conclusive studies, however, policy choices tend to be made on the basis of beliefs and ideology rather than hard data.

Where are we now? It is easy to identify such swings of opinion in retrospect, but more difficult to do so as they occur—especially since not all indicators are pointing in the same direction. In the 1980s and 1990s worsening conditions in some neighborhoods have begun to focus more attention on the effect of neighborhood environments on families, childrearing and child outcomes. Despite Mondale's recognition that the child maltreatment issue would lose support if it were perceived to require major changes in societal conditions, there are now many articles in the popular press about conditions in low-income neighborhoods and their effects. There seems to be growing recognition that various problems people exhibit that were once thought to be psychologically based may have been affected or even caused by neighborhood or environmental conditions. This means that changing such conditions could reduce many other problems besides child maltreatment.

But the 1994 elections installed the most conservative Congress to take office for many years, and the 1996 elections have produced little change. As of this writing it is too early to say which trends—conservative or reformist—will predominate as we move toward the end of the twentieth century. In its last report, at the request of Congress, the U.S. Advisory Board on Child Abuse and Neglect focused on fatal child abuse. It recommended more fatality review boards and argued that some families cannot provide a safe home for their children—and children must be removed (rescued). It also reaffirmed its earlier emphasis on building more preventive services and strengthening neighborhood environments (rehabilitation) (U.S. Advisory Board on Child Abuse and Neglect, 1994). Clearly both approaches have merit—our challenge is to understand more clearly when each is appropriate.

CHAPTER THREE

The Community Context
of Child Abuse and Neglect

James Garbarino
Frank Barry

Human ecology is a way of thinking about human beings that flows from the proposition that behavior and development arise out of a mutual adaptation of person and environment occurring within an ecological niche, defined in large part by politics and economics (Hawley, 1950). Starting from this perspective, an individual's environment, particularly a child's environment, can be understood as a series of settings, each nested within the next broader level, from the microenvironment of the family to the macroenvironment of the society (Bronfenbrenner, 1979; Garbarino & Associates, 1992). One of the implications of this approach to child development is the recognition that as children grow and mature socially and biologically, the size of their environment increases. They experience directly more and more social systems; more is immediately relevant to them.

Concepts such as rejection and acceptance do not exist apart from social contexts. Rather, they operate in concrete settings. The great value of the ecological perspective derives in part from its ability to help us explore systematically this aspect of human development. The nature of the phenomenon makes for an approach in which we move back and forth between process and context. Subsequent chapters will examine various processes in families that produce child maltreatment; now we look at the neighborhood context of abuse and neglect in general.

Think of the geography of human development. People in general and families in particular do not really live in countries or states. They live in communities and in neighborhoods (using that term at this point only in a descriptive sense). The neighborhood is a primary context for the family with a young child. In developing our ecological perspective on child maltreatment and neighborhoods we have been drawn to work from diverse sources. A patchwork quilt of evidence results, a set of findings that roots parent-child relations in context.

In an essay titled "Space: An Ecological Variable in Social Work Practice," Germain (1978) concluded, "Where the environment is supportive, creative adaptation and growth occur. Where the environment is nonprotective or depriving, stress is created and growth and adaptive functioning may be impeded" (p. 522). One research strategy that leads us from a general concern with the social environment to the quality of the neighborhood and community comes from efforts to construct social indicators, or measures that indicate good and bad trends. For decades social scientists have been seeking such social indicators to understand the context of child development and family well-being (Kogan, Smith, & Jenkins, 1977). Recently, Mirringhoff (1996) has offered the Social Quality Index as one way to capture what is happening in the social evolution of the society.

In this chapter, we focus on child maltreatment as a social indicator and seek to link it to other forces and factors at work in the society. Economic deprivation and inequality are the principal deleterious influences. Problems of family violence increase as we go lower on the social class ladder in our society. What is more, economic inequality rather than absolute level of material deprivation, is most strongly predictive of group differences in the rate of violence, because we find that rates of severe violence (such as homicide) are highest in social environments in which the gap between rich and poor is greatest. This puts poverty in a somewhat different light, because it highlights the role of social impoverishment. Social impoverishment means denuding the child's life of supportive relationships and protective behaviors, and it reflects the shame that comes from feeling rejected as a second-class human being (Gilligan, 1996). It stands in contrast to social enrichment and affirmation, in which the child is enmeshed in an elaborate web of caring that can compensate for individual failings.

Jane Howard describes this social enrichment when she says of her strong family, "But we are numerous enough and connected enough not to let anyone's worst prevail for long. For any given poison, our pooled resources can come up with an antidote" (Howard, 1978).

The goal of our analysis is to identify situations in which the conditions of life conspire to compound rather than counteract the deficiencies and vulnerabilities of parents. In this respect our approach moves beyond the individualistic orientation that dominates social theory and policy and focuses jointly on social support and social control (Garbarino, 1977; Slater, 1970). We are most interested in the circumstances of life as families experience them. Our principal interest is with those circumstances that can be subsumed under the term *neighborhood*.

THE MEANING OF NEIGHBORHOOD

Neighborhood is typically the ecological niche in which families operate, and neighborhoods are one of the principal places where one finds the conditions of life that can conspire either to compound or to counteract the deficiencies and vulnerabilities of parents. Defining a neighborhood is the first problem we face in working out the practical implications of this idea for understanding and dealing with child maltreatment. There is no neat and airtight solution to the problem of defining neighborhood. Both geographical and social concerns must be reflected in whatever definition is used. We think Kromkowski (1976) does a good job of highlighting the essential features of a neighborhood, however. In so doing, he presents the criteria with which to evaluate the quality of the neighborhood as a social environment, and this is the central concern of our work in this area. Kromkowski notes, "The organic life of a neighborhood, created by the persons who live in a particular geographic area, is always a fragile reality. A neighborhood's character is determined by a host of factors, but most significantly by the kinds of relationships that neighbors have with each other. A neighborhood is not a sovereign power—it can rarely write its own agenda. Although neighborhoods differ in a host of ways, a healthy neighborhood has pride in the neighborhood, care of homes, security for children, and respect for each other" (p. 228).

These themes are reflected in Warren's research (1980) and in other studies of how neighborhoods work for or against families (Tietjen, 1980; Wandersman, Florin, Friedmann, & Meir, 1987). A neighborhood can be rich economically but poor socially and vice versa. The consequences of a poor (or weak) neighborhood differ for rich and poor families, however. Low income and economic inequality increase vulnerability (Gil, 1970; Tolan & Guerra, 1993). Here then is our thesis: economic factors affect the adequacy of personal resources and, therefore, the compensatory importance of social resources for successful parenthood. Poor people generally have fewer personal resources, and thus their need for social resources is greater if they are to succeed as parents. Rich people generally have more personal resources and therefore are less dependent upon social resources. For this reason, the importance of neighborhood is different for people with different levels of economic resources.

Rich people can afford a weak neighborhood better than poor people, who must rely much more heavily on the social resources of their ecological niche for support, encouragement, and feedback. As always in human behavior, the important outcomes (in this case, adequate child care) are the product of interacting factors (in this case, the personal and social resources of the parent). In this sense, an ecological perspective sheds light on child maltreatment. It directs our attention to personally impoverished families clustered in socially impoverished places: high-risk families and high-risk neighborhoods. We have a lot of information about high-risk individuals and families, even if we do not really know much that is definitive. We have much less information about high-risk environments.

In our work we have sought to discover the meaning of "high risk" when it is applied to the immediate social environment of the family, particularly in the neighborhood (Garbarino & Sherman, 1980; Garbarino & Kostelny, 1992). What we have learned has strengthened our belief that an ecological approach to child maltreatment can complement anthropological and psychological perspectives, thereby enhancing our understanding of etiology and improving the delivery of services. We use four working assumptions to guide our efforts.

1. *Economic forces are significant but not exclusive determinants of neighborhood character.* Within given economic levels there can be considerable variation in the quality of life for families. Thus poverty is as much a social concept as it is an economic one.

2. *Residential segregation based on socioeconomic factors presents a serious threat to family well-being because it produces concentrations of high-need, low-resource families.* The resulting neighborhoods lack people who are free from drain (that is, who have surplus personal and social resources) and can thus afford (materially and psychically)

to offer help to others. Just as diversity in the gene pool is a hedge against biological disaster, so social diversity is a bulwark against psychological disaster.

3.   *The process by which socially impoverished neighborhood character affects child maltreatment is threefold:* (1) the high level of neediness inhibits sharing; (2) the lack of positive models reinforces inappropriate and inadequate behavior; and (3) the lack of intimate and confident interaction inhibits nurturance and feedback. All three contribute to a vicious cycle of social impoverishment in which the (socially) rich get richer while the (socially) poor get poorer. Outside intervention is typically necessary to reverse the trend in socially impoverished areas.

4.   *Values and attitudes of a family that place it at risk for maltreatment are accentuated by the stresses of social impoverishment.* Stress is a challenge. It tends to exaggerate characteristics. Thus people who are prone to violence, apathy, depression, or inadequate child care will become worse when faced with socially harsh circumstances.

AN ECOLOGICAL PERSPECTIVE IN ACTION

What does an ecological approach to child maltreatment look like in practice? We think it begins with a *geographic* orientation to cases. This means plotting cases on a map in much the same way public health officials plot a variety of health-related phenomena. We like to recall one particular example of such mapping because it reveals how the process can stimulate creative scientific thinking. The example comes from a classic discussion of scientific method by Bronfenbrenner and Mahoney (1975): Dr. Louis DiCarlo, serving as director of a speech clinic in Syracuse, New York, was surprised by the unexpectedly high proportion of cases of cleft palate coming from certain sparsely populated counties in upstate New York. He was so struck by the phenomenon that he reported it to the district office of the U.S. Public Health Service, directed by Dr. John Gentry. Gentry responded by doing what public health physicians have done for decades: he started putting up pins on a map, in this instance a map of New York State, one pin for each case, not only of cleft palate but of all reported congenital malformations (deformities present at birth). When all the pins were in place, they made a pattern that Gentry found familiar. Where had he seen it before? After some effort, he remembered. It was in a geology course, on a map of igneous rock formations in New York State. Igneous rocks are those that were originally extracted from within the earth's surface. They are found in mountainous areas and glacial deposits. What is more, some of these rocks emit natural radiation, and, as Gentry knew, radiation had been suspected as a possible source of cleft palate and other deformities present at birth.

Odd though it may seem, this story has much to tell us about identifying neighborhoods that are at risk for child maltreatment, for just as cases of cleft palate can be mapped and their underlying geological causes exposed, so cases of child abuse and neglect can be understood by exposing the ecological conditions associated with them. Because counties typically are the unit for providing service in child protective-service work (Helfer & Schmidt, 1976), and because report data are most likely to be systematic when analyzed using counties as units (Garbarino & Crouter, 1978a), counties are usually the appropriate context for studying the human ecology of child maltreatment.

Counties typically contain subunits that correspond more or less to neighborhoods, as defined earlier. For example, in one Midwestern county where we worked, there were some twenty neighborhood areas (Garbarino & Sherman, 1980), while in a major metropolitan country there were ninety-three such areas (Garbarino & Kostelny, 1992). These areas have historical significance, are used for public-planning purposes, and conform more or less to people's ideas about neighborhood identity. These areas include two to six census tracts, and therefore socioeconomic and demographic data are available from published U.S. census sources. The U.S. Census Bureau has made a commitment to organize and report census data on the basis of neighborhoods as defined by local authorities if those authorities will work with the Census Bureau in defining the neighborhood units.

Mapping can identify clusters of reported child-maltreatment cases. It should be remembered that child maltreatment is being used as a social indicator here, an indicator of the quality of life for families. Its relation to other social indicators (such as measures of economic adequacy, family composition, population dynamics, and "social problem" measures such as births to unmarried teenagers and juvenile crime rates) is a matter of interest on both theoretical and practical grounds. As such, it lends itself to research from a variety of perspectives, employing a range of methods from the simplest to the most complex. In our work we limited ourselves to relatively simple (and thus gross) indicators readily available from existing census data. Naturally, where the researcher possesses the necessary expertise and resources, more methodologically sophisticated variables can be employed and analyses undertaken.

The possibilities range from a simple comparison of child-maltreatment rates with the proportion of an area's population having low incomes to complex multivariate analyses (Garbarino & Kostelny, 1992). Various treatments of income adequacy are possible, as are alternative computations of the child-maltreatment rate, for example, for different age groups and by type of mistreatment. The levels of sophistication and resources combine with the scientific and service obligations of the investigator to shape the questions asked. Computing a child-maltreatment rate in cases per hundred families requires up-to-date population figures. These data permit us to compute the relationship between socioeconomic and demographic characteristics on the one hand and rates of child maltreatment on the other. We thus obtain a correlation between economic resources and the treatment of children, the first step toward our goal of understanding the human ecology of child maltreatment.

The next step is to explore and validate the concept of social impoverishment as a characteristic of high-risk family environments and as a factor in evaluating support and prevention programs aimed at child maltreatment. The starting point was identifying the environmental correlates of child maltreatment and community violence (Garbarino, 1976; Garbarino & Crouter, 1978a). This provided an empirical basis for "screening" neighborhoods to identify high- and low-risk areas.

The foundation for this approach is the link between low income and child maltreatment and other forms of violence (Garbarino, 1987; Pelton, 1978; Pelton, 1981; Pelton, 1994). Poverty is associated with a significantly elevated risk of child maltreatment and other forms of violence. In their study of low-income neighborhoods in Coulton, Korbin, Su, & Chow (1995) concluded that child abuse is embedded within a set of forces in the community that also produces deviant behavior, such as violent crime, drug trafficking, juvenile delinquency. From this flows a twofold conception of "risk" as it applies to neighborhoods and families (Garbarino & Crouter, 1978a). The first refers to areas with a high absolute rate of violence (based on cases per unit of population). In this sense, concentrations of socioeconomically distressed families are most likely to be at high risk for violence—most notably child maltreatment. For example, in one city (Omaha, Nebraska), socioeconomic status accounted for about

40 percent of the variation across neighborhoods in reported rates of child maltreatment.

The magnitude of this correlation may reflect a social policy effect. It seems reasonable to hypothesize that in a society in which low income is not correlated with access to basic human services (such as maternal and infant health care), the correlation would be smaller. In a society totally devoid of policies to ameliorate the impact of family-level differences in social class it might be even larger. The hypothesis merits empirical exploration but is consistent with the observation that socioeconomic status is a more potent predictor of child development in the United States than in some European societies (Bronfenbrenner, 1979). This is evidenced by lower infant mortality rates in some poor European countries—such as Ireland and Spain—than in the United States as a whole, and much lower than in poor communities in this country (Miller, 1987). Thus we see that social support is a concept operating at the macrosocial level, not just at the neighborhood level (Thompson, 1994).

The actual rate of violence against children is the first measure of risk; however, it is a second meaning of high risk that is of greatest relevance. High risk can also be taken to mean that an area has a higher rate of child maltreatment than would be predicted, knowing its socioeconomic character. Thus two areas with similar socioeconomic profiles may have very different rates of child maltreatment. In this sense, one is "high risk" while the other is "low risk," although both may have higher rates of child maltreatment than other areas. Figure 3.1 illustrates this.

In Figure 3.1, areas A and B have high actual observed rates of child maltreatment (36 per 1,000 and 34 per 1,000, respectively). Areas C and D have lower observed rates (16 per 1,000 and 14 per 1,000, respectively). However, areas A and C have higher observed rates than would be predicted (10 per 1,000 predicted for A; 7 per 1,000 for C), while areas B and D have lower observed rates than predicted (55 per 1,000 for B; 54 per 1,000 for D). In this sense, A and C are both high risk, while B and D are both low risk. Areas E and F evidence a close approximation between observed and predicted rates. This classification system can provide the basis for identifying contrasting social environments. Unfortunately, this sort of community risk analysis is lacking in virtually all programmatic efforts aimed at preventing child maltreatment (indeed in all areas in which social support programs might be aimed at improved family functioning).

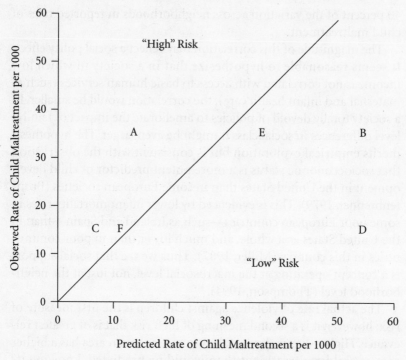

Figure 3.1.   Two Meanings of Risk in Assessing Community Areas.

THE HUMAN SIGNIFICANCE OF "COMMUNITY RISK"

What do low- and high-risk social environments look like? Answering this question is important if we are to understand the essential elements and likely outcome of social support programs seeking to prevent child maltreatment. Addressing this question involves examining pairs of real neighborhoods with similar predicted rates but different observed rates of child maltreatment (in other words, one neighborhood is high risk and the other is low risk). This permits a test of the hypothesis that two such neighborhoods present contrasting environments for childrearing and thus may impose contrasting imperatives on prevention and intervention efforts.

A study of contrasting neighborhoods in Omaha, Nebraska, selected to illustrate this phenomenon, provided support for this hypothesis: relative to the low-risk area, and even though it was socioeconomically equivalent, the high-risk neighborhood was found to represent a socially impoverished human ecology (Garbarino & Sherman, 1980). It was less socially integrated, had less positive neighboring, and represented more stressful day-to-day interactions for families.

Thus, a comprehensive strategy for obtaining information about the neighborhood-level characteristics associated with maltreatment is necessary before a neighborhood initiative can be undertaken. According to Zuravin and Taylor (1987), this involves three techniques. First, a comparative mapping allows a quick visual test of how the distribution of a particular problem correlates with the distribution of maltreatment. Second, a multiple-regression analysis determines how neighborhood characteristics predicted on the basis of theory or comparative mapping account for variation in child maltreatment rates in different neighborhoods. The analysis provides an equation for predicting the at-risk status of a neighborhood based on the characteristics identified by theory or mapping and identifies neighborhoods whose actual degree of risk for maltreatment differs sharply from the degree of risk predicted by the regression analysis. Third, random surveys of neighborhood residents provide neighborhood-specific information about correlates and possible determinants of the three types of child maltreatment (Zuravin & Taylor, 1987).

Other studies have reaffirmed the general outline of this analysis while refining the meaning of social impoverishment—away from a simple concept of social support and toward a more complex phenomenon of social integration (particularly as reflected in employment and neighboring patterns—see, for example, Deccio, Horner, and Wilson's 1994 study in Spokane, Washington; Chamberland, Bouchard, & Bevadry's 1986 study of Montreal neighborhoods; Sattin and Miller's 1971 study of two neighborhoods in a Texas city; and Garbarino and Kostelny's 1992 study of Chicago neighborhoods).

Deccio, Horner, and Wilson (1994) replicated Garbarino and Sherman's study of neighborhoods that were economically similar but had different rates of child maltreatment. In two economically similar neighborhoods in Spokane, the "high-risk" neighborhood had reported rates of child maltreatment more than two times the "low-risk" neighborhood. Although differences in perceived social support were not found, differences in social integration were. For instance, the unemployment rate in the high-risk neighborhood was three times greater than that of the low-risk neighborhood. While the average family income was a few hundred dollars higher in the high-risk neighborhood, so was the percentage of families living below the poverty level—26 percent versus 17 percent.

Differences were also found in stability of residence, possession of a telephone, and vacancy rates. A greater percentage of families in the low-risk neighborhood had lived in their current home for more than five years—52 percent, versus 35 percent in the high-risk neighborhood. Moreover, there were three times as many families in the high-risk neighborhood who lacked telephones compared to the low-risk neighborhood. (Absence of a telephone is both a cause and effect of social isolation as we define it here.) Finally, the high-risk neighborhood had more than twice as many vacant housing units as the low-risk neighborhood—16 percent versus 7 percent.

Thus, social integration, which connoted membership, participation, and belonging, was found to be an important factor in explaining differences in reported rates of maltreatment. More of the low-risk neighborhoods' residents were employed, had incomes above the poverty level, had a history of stable residence, and were connected to friends, neighbors, and relatives by a telephone.

THE INNER-CITY EXAMPLE

Perhaps the most comprehensive analysis to date concerns Chicago neighborhoods (Garbarino & Kostelny, 1992) and illustrates acutely the challenges to mounting a plausible social support–oriented prevention program in the face of the extremely high levels of socioeconomic deprivation, community violence, and negative social momentum that characterize many inner-city neighborhoods, where child maltreatment is a disproportionately severe problem.

Much of the variation among community rates of child maltreatment (using a composite measure that includes all forms but is largely composed of physical abuse and neglect) is linked to variations in nine socioeconomic and demographic characteristics (with the multiple correlation being .89, thus accounting for 79 percent of the variation). We also conducted this analysis for 113 census tracts contained within our four target community areas. These results show a multiple correlation being $r = .52$, and the proportion of variance accounted for is 27 percent.

The higher proportion of variance in the results from the analysis of community areas reflects the larger units of analysis used in community areas and the apparently idiosyncratic nature of the four target areas as social environments. Since community areas encompass a greater number of individuals than the census tract analysis, the estimates of the predictors (such as poverty, unemployment, female-headed households, and so on) and measures of the rate of child maltreatment are more numerically stable (and thus reliable in a statistical sense). They are thus more likely to produce a higher correlation. This statistical artifact is also present in other studies (Garbarino & Crouter, 1978b).

In addition, the variation or range of socioeconomic, demographic, and child maltreatment measures is much greater when contrasting all 77 community areas than when comparing the 113 census tracts within the four target areas—all of which have major difficulties. For example, within the two predominantly African American areas, the census tract with the lowest poverty rate still has 27 percent living in poverty—in contrast to the full range of 77 community areas, in which 33 have poverty rates of less than 10 percent, and 7 have more than 40 percent.

We can look at child maltreatment rates in four areas—"Lower," "West," "North," and "Grand"—for the years 1980, 1983, 1985, and 1986. In "Lower" and "West," child maltreatment rates have been consistently below the city average during these four years. From 1985 to 1986, rates reached a plateau in the "Lower" area, while they decreased in the "West." In contrast, in "North" and "Grand," rates of child maltreatment have been consistently above the city average.

Additionally, while there had been a steady increase of child abuse and neglect in these two communities from 1980 to 1985, there had been a decrease of maltreatment in "Grand" in 1986 (from 24.5 in 1985 to 21.6 in 1986), while rates in "North" continued to climb (from 16.9 in 1985 to 18.5 in 1986).

Analysis of maltreatment rates by census tracts within each community area reveals that wide variations also exist at this level. In "North," for example, while indicated rates of child maltreatment increased at the community level, analysis at the census tract level revealed that rates had actually reached a plateau or decreased in 54 percent of the tracts. Thus, the escalation in rates was due to a large increase in the remaining 46 percent of the tracts (some of which had rates as high as 34.5, compared to a city average of 10.6).

Additionally, multiple-regression analyses were conducted for each of the four years. While thirteen out of "North's" twenty-four census tracts fell within the predicted range for maltreatment for at least two out of the four years (Types E and F in Figure 3.1), the remaining eleven tracts had rates that fell outside the predicted range; six tracts had rates that were consistently lower (Type D in Figure 3.1), while five tracts had rates that were consistently higher than predicted based upon their socioeconomic and demographic profile (Type A in Figure 3.1).

This is the statistical picture of the context in which prevention programs must operate. To make this context speak more clearly to those who seek to employ social support programs to prevent child maltreatment in these contexts, we can examine information provided by professionals supporting families in these neighborhoods.

THE VIEW FROM THE TRENCHES

Interviews with community leaders based in human service agencies shed some light on "community climate": in "North" as a community with a higher than predicted abuse rate and "West" as a community with a lower than predicted abuse rate (using a sixteen-item questionnaire based upon prior research)(Garbarino & Sherman, 1980).

In the high-abuse community, do social service agencies mirror the high social deterioration characteristic of the families and the community? And, conversely, do we observe a strong, informal support network among the social service agencies in the low-abuse community? The answer from these interviews appears to be yes. This is evident in a question-by-question analysis of the interviews. People are more negative about "North," how it looks physically and socially. They see the quality of life as being lower and recognize the problem of child maltreatment as being bigger. They see little neighboring and fewer human service agencies than in "West."

The results of this small study suggest that there is a clear difference in the climate of these two communities. The strength of this difference is perhaps best illustrated as follows. Jobs were mentioned as being of primary importance in both communities, but they were talked about very differently. In "North," three respondents reported that it was important to remember that "North" had only an 18 percent employment rate; in contrast, five of the "West" respondents described "West" as a community of the working poor.

The consequences of these differences in employment are profound. Indeed, recall that Deccio, Horner, and Wilson (1994) reported that it was precisely such a measure of employment that differentiated the low- from the high-risk neighborhoods in their study. Employment, even at low wages, is a social indicator of prosocial orientation and of functionality—apart from the income implications of being employed.

The general tone of the "North" visits was somewhat depressed; people had a hard time thinking of anything positive to say about the situation. The physical spaces of the programs themselves seemed dark and depressed, and to a casual visitor the criminal activity was easily spotted. In "West," people were eager to talk about their community. While they listed serious problems, most of them felt that their communities were poor but decent places to live. "Poor but not hopeless" was the way one respondent described it. While "West" subjects also reported drug and crime problems, those activities were not apparent to the casual visitor.

In "North," the subjects knew less about what other community services and agencies were available and demonstrated little evidence of a network or support system, either formal or informal. One exception to this seemed to be the Family Focus program. Everyone knew about Family Focus, and the staff at Family Focus knew people in other programs by name. In "West," there were more services available, agencies knew more about what was available, and there were very strong formal and informal social support networks. The subjects in "West" also reported strong political leadership from the local state senator. The "North" subjects did not report positive feelings about their political leaders.

In "North," the leaders interviewed described a situation in which their agencies mirrored the isolation and depression of their community. In "West," the agencies mirrored the strong informal support network that exists between families in their community. Workers in the agencies seemed hopeful because many of their families were hopeful. At least in terms of this study, it seems fair to say that the social service agencies in a community mirror the problems facing the community.

The interviews with professionals complement our statistical analyses and provide further indication of the serious difficulties facing "North" as a social system. The extremity of the negative features of the environment—poverty, violence, poor housing—seem to be matched by negative community climate—lack of community identity and fragmented formal support system networks.

The final piece of evidence available to us in our analysis concerns child deaths due to maltreatment. Such child deaths are a particularly telling indicator of the bottom line in a community. There were nineteen child-maltreatment deaths reported for the four community areas we studied from 1984 to 1987. Eight of these deaths occurred in "North," a rate of 1 death for each 2,541 children. For "West," the rate was 1 death for each 5,571 children. The fact that deaths due to child maltreatment were twice as likely in "North" seems consistent with the overall findings of our statistical analyses and interviews. In "North" there is truly an ecological conspiracy against children (Garbarino, 1995). As such it directs our attention to the need to approach the concept of social support to prevent child maltreatment, with our eyes open.

Such an open-eyed approach involves refusing to accept superficial, quick, conventional efforts. Anyone with an appreciation for the depth and pervasiveness of the social impoverishment in neighborhoods such as "North" understands that social support must be part of a sweeping reform of the neighborhood and its relations with the larger community. In our previous work we have used this same approach of identifying areas for special attention. For example, in Omaha, Nebraska, we identified a pair of areas that offered intriguing comparisons based upon the statistical analysis that indicates one area has a much higher rate than would be predicted based upon its socioeconomic and demographic character (high risk), while the other area is low risk in the sense that it has a lower actual rate than would be predicted.

These statistical results were reinforced by discovering how people perceive high-risk versus low-risk neighborhoods through interviews with matched samples of parents in a high-risk versus a low-risk area. The high-risk neighborhood is seen as an unsupportive environment for family life both by observers (parish priests, visiting nurses, educators, and police officers) and by participants (parents living in the area). We found that in well-matched samples of parents randomly selected from the two neighborhoods, those in the high-risk area had more stresses, less support, less adequate child care, and a less positive view of family and neighborhood life. Here are some of the things our community informants said about the two areas:

LOW RISK: "That's one of the most sedate areas." (police officer); "That's a good quick area." (postman)

HIGH RISK: "That's a little less tranquil. The bars are just pits. The crowd is hoodlums, Hell's Angels, and cowboys." (police officer); "There's a lot of 'night activity' there." (visiting nurse)

LOW RISK: "I see it as a stable neighborhood. People have roots in the neighborhood. It's not a very mobile place." (visiting nurse)

HIGH RISK: "The parents cling to this school as a sign of hope. The neighborhood is facing a lot of change and deterioration. They probably felt threatened by the construction of the interstate through the neighborhood. Just this year we've had several new cases of loiterers, and some families report burglaries where they have never happened before. The parish bought up a building opposite the school that had been recently turned into a rough place." (principal of a parochial school)

LOW RISK: "We have very few cases there, only six families with children." (visiting nurse)

HIGH RISK: "That's an area that needs plenty of scrutiny as far as quality of life." (director of a neighborhood community center); "There's stealing from each other." (visiting nurse); "That's one of our heaviest case loads, both as number of families and as problems within each family. Alcoholism is quite a big problem. There are mental health problems, a very high death rate, a high birthrate to unmarried mothers, poor nutrition. . . . Medical knowledge is only of emergency care. . . . Many of the girls are early school dropouts." (visiting nurse)

LOW RISK: "These women often rely on the help available to them through their families. One client of mine lives next door to her mother-in-law, whom she turns to for help." (visiting nurse)

HIGH RISK: "The family unit is not real strong here." (parochial school principal); "The women sometimes form a buddy system, but there is not a lot of interlinking between them. . . . They don't know very many people. They don't associate very much. They don't have a lot of family supports. They may be on bad terms with the family. This area is sometimes a hideout for them. . . . There are a lot of teenage girls with their babies who want to get away from their families downtown." (visiting nurse)

Another measure of interest is the level of stress based on the Holmes-Rahe Scale, a checklist of events requiring social readjustment. While subject to a number of limitations, the scale does provide a gross indication of the uproar and stress in a family's life. What is more, other investigators found an association between this score and child abuse. Parents interviewed in the low-risk area neighborhood were two and a half times more likely to be in the no-crisis range than are parents in the high-risk neighborhood. While 74 percent of the families in the low-risk area were in the "no crisis" range on the scale, only 37 percent of the high-risk neighborhood's families were in the no crisis range. (For more information on this, see Garbarino & Sherman, 1980.)

NEXT STEPS

The conditions described by the informers are, of course, the stuff of which child maltreatment is made: high-risk families in high-risk environments. It has been noted repeatedly by students of child abuse that abuse-prone parents seem adept at finding mates who also are prone to abuse. There is certainly truth in this assertion, at least in terms of identifying clusters of domestic violence across generations and within kinship groups (Straus & Gelles, 1987). The explicit or implicit collusion of spouses in child maltreatment is a significant aspect of the problem, as is the more general principle that violence attracts violence. For our purposes, the likes-attract-likes hypothesis can also be applied to neighborhoods. Socially impoverished families tend to be clustered together. This geographic clustering influences not only the incidence of mental health problems (Lewis, Shanok, Pincus, & Glaser, 1979) but also successful coping with those problems (Smith, 1976). We find this in our neighborhood analyses, which go beyond earlier efforts of this sort that involved case studies (Sattin & Miller, 1971).

Using a statistical technique called nearest-neighbor analysis, Lewis, Shanok, Pincus, & Glaser (1979) provided an illustration of the general hypothesis noted earlier that neighborhood is a more important force for low-income than high-income families, thus adding to the evidence gathered by Stack and others (Stack, 1974). This finding is of special interest for training, because professionals tend to come from middle-class settings, where neighborhood may be less important than it is for their lower-class clients. Given that child maltreatment is a more serious issue for low-income populations, the ecological approach can make its greatest contribution in understanding and helping these families. Indeed, fragmentary evidence from our own pilot studies suggests that high-risk families may be more influenced by neighborhood social climate than low-risk families.

Our results reveal stronger correlations between neighborhood characteristics and relevant behavior (use of social services, for example) among high-risk families. (These results are based on a self-selected group of high-risk parents who may be presumed to be more oriented toward community participation than their peers, due to the fact that they did agree to participate in the study.) Thus just as some high-risk individuals marry low-risk individuals (and are in effect saved from their backgrounds), so some high-risk families find themselves in low-risk settings that can help them overcome their special vulnerabilities. There is no substitute for a socially competent friend when it comes to childrearing. It is worth recalling Jane Howard's conclusion about healthy families and social networks: "For any given poison, our pooled resources can come up with an antidote" (1978, p. 60).

Residential segregation of personally impoverished people tends to produce social impoverishment, unless there are countervailing forces at work. We need to recognize countervailing forces where they exist naturally (and then not tinker with them) and to learn how to generate and sustain them where they do not already exist. This theme is echoed in a report of the National Neighborhood Commission. Community organizing is inseparable from child protection in this sense (see Garbarino, Stocking, & Associates, 1980).

CHANGING AND PRESERVING NEIGHBORHOODS

Moving people is rarely an option on a large scale basis. It is not necessary that we move people so much as that we alter the nature and structure of the high-risk neighborhood as a social entity. Technologies for doing this exist (Fawcett, Bernstein, Czyzewski, & Greene, 1988), which involve teaching community organization and helping skills. We think the goal of these efforts is to achieve a neighborhood where each family is participating in informal support systems, where the level of need matches the level of resources, where there is good morale, where there are effective links between formal and informal helping services, and where children are enmeshed in a web of caring and protective relationships. This ideal is simply that—a description of what we should be seeking in our efforts at social policy and practice. But as an ideal, it can make an important contribution to our understanding of child maltreatment, for, as what Bronfenbrenner calls

Dearborn's Dictum reminds us, "If you want to understand something, try to change it" (Bronfenbrenner, 1979).

We can expand our understanding of child maltreatment by including a better appreciation of how a family's ecological niche accounts for some of the variation in parental behavior. Without denying the importance of psychological factors, we can profit from incorporating the role of economic and social impoverishment into our calculations. This will help us see that we have several fronts on which to combat the problem of child maltreatment and that child maltreatment is woven into the fabric of our society.

In its 1993 report, the U.S. Advisory Board on Child Abuse and Neglect noted that "Environmentalists have developed legal procedures and standards to preserve individual species of fish and wildlife . . . [and that] . . . the children who live in dangerous neighborhoods are surely no less important to the survival of our civilization than the snail darter fish or spotted owl. . . . Neighborhoods in which children are at high risk should receive special attention, just as the discovery of a high level of pollution brings special attention to a body of water" (p. 18).

At a minimum, public policies should not worsen the condition of vulnerable neighborhoods. As an example, Wallace (1989, 1990) documented catastrophic deterioration in neighborhood quality as a result of the closure of fire stations in New York City's South Bronx in the early 1970s. Fewer fire stations allowed more fires to burn out entire buildings instead of being stopped in the apartments in which they originated. This led to an increasing number of burned-out shells, and mass emigration resulted—some neighborhoods lost nearly two-thirds of their inhabitants between 1970 and 1980. An invisible but tragic side effect was the destruction of many neighborhood social networks. Wallace linked this loss with dramatic increases in crime, substance abuse, and intentional violent deaths (homicide and suicide). These results, which Wallace attributed to a conscious policy of "planned shrinkage" in poor neighborhoods, clearly increased the level of neighborhood risks that are generally associated with child abuse. It also caused deterioration of nearby wealthier neighborhoods, as 1.3 million white residents fled to the suburbs (taking their tax base with them), presumably to avoid living next to poor black and Hispanic refugees from the burned-out areas. Other destructive public policies included the urban renewal and urban highway construction of the 1950s and 1960s, which again were used to destroy urban minority communities and displace their residents (Halpern, 1995). Again business and social networks were destroyed, greatly weakening the community for those who remained.

LIFE AT THE MARGINS

Biologists and environmentalists have developed the concept of a "marginal environment," or "life at the margins." This can perhaps best be observed along the edge of a well-tended cornfield, where some corn plants grow outside the main rows in which cornstalks are carefully fertilized and cultivated. The corn plants outside the cultivated area are generally stunted, and if they bear any corn at all, the ears are often deformed and lacking in kernels.

This "life at the margins" concept applies to human beings, too. Rosenbaum, Fishman, Brett, and Meaden (1993) followed two groups of low-income families who moved out of a violent housing project in Chicago with the help of Section 8 housing certificates. Some moved to other locations in the same inner-city neighborhood, while others moved to housing in suburbs outside the city. The selection was relatively random, as it depended on the availability of housing when the application was made rather than the family's choice of where to move. Rosenbaum and colleagues found that the children who moved to the suburbs were roughly twice as likely to go on to college and to get jobs as those who moved elsewhere in the inner-city neighborhood. In other words, neighborhood quality has a potent effect on child-development outcomes—regardless of factors within the family.

Wilson (1987) paid particular attention to the availability of jobs. He found that much of the decline in inner city neighborhoods in the 1970s and 80s resulted from the disappearance of factories and employment opportunities in inner cities. This, coupled with relaxation of suburban housing discrimination in the 1950s and 1960s, led to a massive exodus of educated families with good jobs and incomes, who had served as role models, leaders, monitors of behavior and advocates of the community. Their departure had catastrophic effects.

Gladwell (1996) found that the incidence of crime may bear a relationship to community characteristics, somewhat resembling the "tipping point" phenomenon observed in epidemiology, in which small changes in one variable may lead to big changes in another variable at one point (the tipping point) but may have little effect below and above that point. His article was based in part on the work of Crane (1991), who found a strong relationship between the proportion of "high-status occupation" (managerial and professional) workers living in the neighborhood and the incidence of teen pregnancy and high school dropouts. Crane found that both dropouts and out-of-wedlock teen births increase moderately as the proportion of high-status workers drops—but that the rate of increase climbs sharply and abruptly when the proportion of high-status workers drops below 5 percent. The impact of changes at the tipping point is 300 times greater than the impact of changes above the tipping point (Crane, 1991, p. 1238).

Putnam (1993) paid special attention to the concept of *social capital*—friendships, networks, associations, trust, and norms that easily and naturally meet basic needs for acceptance, safety, purpose, association, and information and are essential for economic activity and community. Putnam challenged the notion that social capital depends on economic health—that trust, networks, and community norms are products of a strong economy: "(Italian) communities don't have choral societies because they are wealthy; they are wealthy because they have choral societies—or more precisely, the traditions of engagement, trust and reciprocity that choral societies symbolize" (p. 106). These traditions, he says, seem to be necessary preconditions for the kind of business relationship that is perquisite to economic development.

Whether economics or social capital comes first, both are critical determinants of neighborhood quality, and therefore both affect a neighborhood's incidence of child maltreatment. While some parents might abuse their children regardless of the setting, there is a large number whose parenting will be heavily influenced by the neighborhood in which they live. A hostile, violent neighborhood will bring out their worst characteristics, while a friendly, supportive environment will encourage them to function at their best, suffering fewer and milder crises than otherwise.

All of this suggests that reducing child maltreatment requires us to devote significant efforts to strengthening community as well as helping individuals. Farmers assume that if they take care of the soil, the individual corn plants will produce healthy ears of corn. This analogy appears relevant to our human species also: if we carefully tend our neighborhoods, we substantially increase the likelihood that our families will raise their children effectively and successfully. Lofquist

(1983) has prepared a useful matrix that separates human services according to whether they focus on prevention or remediation and whether they are targeted to affect individuals or communities. He notes that most of our resources go into programs that attempt individual remediation, while very few go to prevention at the community level. Woodson (1996) illustrates the effects of this by noting that there are many programs for drug addicts, unwed teen parents, and high school dropouts, but "if, against the same odds, you have stayed in school, resisted drugs and abstained from irresponsible sexual activity, there is virtually nothing for you."

Preventive work at the community level means building social capital and strengthening economic development in poor neighborhoods. Both are essential if we are to reduce the number of individuals who need special help (remediation) after getting into trouble. Prevention, according to Lofquist, is generic; if we properly care for our communities we will prevent not only child abuse but many other social problems also. Healthy communities not only provide the cultivation families need to properly nurture their children but also provide an environment that goes beyond the parents' efforts and helps to nurture, monitor, and inspire those children directly.

PRIVACY VERSUS COMMUNITY

What stands in the way of an ecological approach to child protection? One impediment is the issue of privacy in the United States. To most Americans, the value of privacy is unquestioned, and any invasion of privacy is a kind of cultural treason. This orientation is reflected in our laws, in speeches made by politicians, in policies of both government and private agencies, and in opinions of citizens in public polls. Although privacy may be valuable, it does not come without costs to the individual and to the community; some are paid by children in the form of abuse and neglect. Looked at this way, social isolation is the price we pay for privacy in the United States.

We have established the role of isolation from potent prosocial support systems in child maltreatment. While public attention is drawn to only the most lurid and dramatic cases of child maltreatment, we are surrounded daily with the more mundane incidents. An infant is dropped repeatedly. A toddler is whipped. A kindergartner is punched. A teenager is assaulted regularly by a parent for minor misbehavior. These events rarely reach the general public, but they are at the core of the problem. As Henry Kempe (1973) repeatedly has pointed out, our society tends to kiss newborns good-bye at the hospital door and not have any systematic and official contact with them until they enter school. As a parent moving to a new community, one author of the current chapter (Garbarino) recalls, "I brought a three-year-old car and my three year old daughter into my new community and the community made it very clear that it cared about . . . *cars!* I was told to register my car, insure my car, have my car inspected, but no one asked about my child. As far as the community was concerned, she was invisible."

By permitting this we encourage the conditions that spawn child maltreatment; we allow it by valuing privacy above the essential support-system functions of feedback and nurturance. Parenthood is a social contract, not an individual act. Families need information from the outside world in order to do well by their children. Information consists of both regular feedback on parent-child relations and general knowledge of appropriate norms, expectations, and techniques concerning childrearing. Adequate information depends upon three factors: (1) regular observation and discussion of parent-child relations; (2) informal folk wisdom based on extensive, historically validated firsthand experience; and (3) formal, professional expertise, particularly in the areas of solving behavior problems. The need for information is related directly to the situational demands of the parent-child relationship. As these demands increase, so does the need for information. Formal institutions can become effective sources of information if they are linked actively to the family's social network, either directly through the parent or indirectly through the parent's relationship with some other person. Privacy can be hazardous to social health and development because it undermines the processes of information flow to and from the family.

The Price of Privacy

In analyzing the social experience of U.S. youth, Edward Wynne (1975) reported on the value they place on being alone, being autonomous, and being removed from observation, monitoring, and evaluation. Wynne makes a useful distinction between personal and impersonal observation. Youngsters seem to be receiving less and less personal observation (that is, behavior being evaluated in the context of enduring relationships with adults) and more impersonal observations characterized by disinterested bureaucratic contacts of short duration and narrow focus. Bronfenbrenner (1975) reinforced this interpretation in his analysis of the roots of alienation, and we can see it as an important dimension of social toxicity.

Impersonal observation has supplanted personal observation. Moreover, this pattern seems to apply to both adults and children. Families have become less and less dominated by kinship and neighborhood relationships and more and more dominated by individual privacy coupled with reliance on mass media and personal services. The social history of the United States reveals an ambivalence concerning individualism and collectivism, freedom and authority, privacy and social integration. This dynamic has been identified by a variety of authors. Webb (1952) called it "the parabola of individualism." Philip Slater (1970) more recently termed it "the pursuit of loneliness," and David Riesman (1950) labeled it "the lonely crowd." The phenomenon is noted in Bronfenbrenner's *Two Worlds of Childhood* (1970). Americans place a high value on owning a single-family home, on the freedom a car brings, and on being independent of all regulations. It is as if we were trying to make every man and woman an island.

Opportunities for privacy have increased markedly in recent decades. This provides a potentially dangerous context for parent-child relations, particularly in stressful circumstances, such as when a single parent is struggling to earn a living and raise a child. More disturbing to note, then, that in recent decades a single parent has become twice as likely to maintain a separate household rather than move in with another (typically with a household containing a close relative) (Bronfenbrenner, 1975). A single parent living alone may give the parent-child relationship more freedom and privacy but less feedback and nurturance. In Chapter Two we identified the balance of stresses and supports as critical in the matter of child maltreatment. Here we are recognizing that our society has its finger on the scales and may tip the balance over on the stress side through its insistence on autonomy, independence, and privacy. Rotenberg (1977) persuasively argued that because we define dependency as pathological and autonomy as healthy we doom ourselves to a pervasive sense of estrangement and alienation. As always, children in general and poor children in particular pay the highest price.

We yearn to belong and yet seem to do everything we can to thwart the fulfillment of that longing. This is Slater's pursuit of loneliness.

Research on depression (Weissman & Paykel, 1973) and suicide (Paykel, 1976) links overall psychological well-being to involvement in enduring supportive social relationships. Disrupting or terminating these relationships is highly stressful (Fox, 1974). Where does privacy fit into this matrix of stress, psychological distress, and, ultimately, child maltreatment? Privacy provides a fertile medium in which all three grow. What is more, privacy works against natural healing forces and makes it more difficult to deliver help as well as to ask for it. As Elder (1974) noted, a condition of ascendancy to the middle class is the relinquishing of ownership and neighborhood bonds in return for the benefits of privacy. Let us be clear in recognizing that traditional kinship and neighborhood relationships exact psychological costs. The sense of obligation, guilt, dependence, and intrusion weighs heavily on many. There is little privacy.

Family and Kin

One's time and resources are always on call to kin in need. Interpersonal relations and day-to-day activities are under the scrutiny of kin, who have an investment in the nuclear family. Childrearing practices are particularly subject to scrutiny by relatives, since the principal "currency" of kinship is children. Experiences that link the family into the social mainstream of the community, beyond the kinship circle, are essential. Children and parents both need this protection. It appears that kinship lacking this community connection often reinforces rather than counteracts patterns of child maltreatment. Straus (1980) reports that among people experiencing a high level of stress, if the only social network they have is kin, it is likely to mean higher levels of domestic violence. In this as in other matters, diversity and social pluralism are good for children (Garbarino & Bronfenbrenner, 1976). Many people have reacted to the potentially stifling atmosphere of intensive interaction with kin by rejecting intrusive social networks as a matter of both personal and professional policy (Leichter & Mitchell, 1967). They may trade in the intrusiveness of social integration for the privacy of social isolation. We recognize that when it comes to connectedness, too much can be a problem, but we believe the greater danger for most Americans at this point in our history is too little.

Here, then, is the hypothesis emerging from this analysis: as the value of and opportunity for privacy increase, the danger of isolation increases correspondingly. As isolation increases, so does the possibility of child maltreatment. Involvement of families in extensive kin networks (Stack, 1974), natural-helping networks (Collins & Pancoast, 1976), or strong neighborhoods with positive values, organized to implement them (Fellin & Litwak, 1968), can inhibit child maltreatment (Garbarino, Stocking, & Associates, 1980). Such involvement provides both child-care resources and the right to call upon those resources. Both the time and expertise necessary for effective involvement are often lacking in high-risk homes (Gil, 1970). Social connectedness provides access to social and economic resources that can aid the family in times of stress (Garbarino, 1981) and provides personalized observation of the family. It combats family climates that induce depression, anger, helplessness, loss of control, and violence. Without privacy it is unlikely that a pattern of maltreatment can be established and maintained.

Abuse or neglect generally will be inhibited or at least identified at an early stage when families are involved in an active exchange network with prosocial friends, neighbors, and relatives. In her study of domestic networks and kinship in a poor black community, Stack (1974) documented such an intimate and active network of mutual obligation and assistance that granted little privacy. It is illuminating to note that the stresses imposed by racism and poverty seem to be deflected somewhat from children in such a setting. The active involvement of family friends tends to prevent stress from being translated into chronic maltreatment when those "outsiders" themselves are not abusive. We have been persuaded that children can survive maltreatment if they have someone in their social network who provides compensatory acceptance, nurturance, and a positive model for social experience.

Studies of resilient children and our own interviews with victims of maltreatment persuade us of this. Everyone needs someone. If, in the name of family privacy, we isolate the victims of child maltreatment, then we deprive them of a potentially important normalizing influence on their development. They are thus doubly victimized, being denied both prevention and healing.

There are several problems facing traditional kinship networks and their nonfamilial surrogates. First, current levels of geographic mobility bend or break these networks. Mobility stretches the bonds of kinship over long distances. It makes effective feedback and nurturance difficult and in many cases prevents the establishment and maintenance of effective surrogate systems. Strong neighborhoods may counter this, but even they are weakened by transience (Fellin & Litwak, 1968). Second, there is a culturally sanctioned movement to escape the costs of kinship networks. Privacy is valued, and social bonds are opposed as antithetical to individual development. The ascendancy of middle-class norms and practices offers the possibility of freedom, privacy, and individuation to unprecedented numbers of people.

Fewer and fewer families contain adults other than the child's parents. As noted earlier, single parents increasingly maintain separate households (Bronfenbrenner, McClelland, Wethington, Moen, & Ceci, 1996). Housing patterns encourage private residences, and multifamily dwellings, where they are available, increasingly create a ghetto of families with children. The overall development of our culture is downgrading intrusive kinship networks. These trends extend to and in some cases are led by professionals in the field of social services and psychology who often extol the virtues of autonomy and self-fulfillment without an appropriate regard for their costs (Campbell, 1976).

Privacy Sparks Maltreatment

Elder (1974) noted that middle-class observers often were dismayed by the way working-class families shared with kin during the Great Depression. "How could they jeopardize their own marginal economic resources by committing themselves to help?" they asked. Stack's (1974) account of sharing among black kin points out that the typical professional evaluation of such behavior is that it is irrational and self-defeating. In a study of Jewish social workers and clients, Leichter and Mitchell (1967) report some interesting differences in attitudes and values between caseworkers and clients. The more traditional clients and their parents expressed a belief in the rights, wisdom, and obligations of kinship. The more modern caseworkers downgraded kinship networks in favor of personal freedom, autonomy, and privacy.

Campbell (1976) noted the ideological commitment of most modern psychologists to liberation of the individual from collective bonds. In Campbell's view, psychologists who counsel liberation are embarking on a socially dangerous course, a course in conflict with the human need for structure, obligations, and ties that bind. Although the liberation perspective may be strongest among psychologists, it has support from many social-work professionals and from segments of the general public. The allure of privacy is great. It permits individualism to flourish and insulates the family against external meddling by persons who may have their own interests to advance. This protective function seems a major attraction to social workers (Leichter & Mitchell, 1967).

Privacy provides the potential for a quiet atmosphere, whereas kinship intrusion is psychologically noisy. Despite this, privacy may be damaging or even lethal for children when combined with the factors that elicit abusive behavior. Privacy alone is not, of course, sufficient to produce abuse and neglect. But then almost no factor uniformly produces the same effect in different human beings. Each of us is more vulnerable to some conditions than others. In general, however, there are circumstances in which parent-child relations are placed in special jeopardy by privacy. Recent evidence on mothering by gorillas show that these conditions pertain to animals as well as humans.

Young gorilla mothers have been separated from their peers by their human protectors to insulate the parent-child relationship from external interference. The result was a high rate of child abuse and neglect. When restored to the community of apes the abusive patterns were replaced with more healthy behavior (Nadler, 1979). Privacy (as isolation) went against the nature of the apes; they need social contact for healthy family relationships. People do, too. Privacy is a necessary condition that allows abuse to occur when sufficient conditions combine to create a socially critical mass.

When families are exposed to loss of income, excessive work schedules (too much or too little), or other conditions that lead to frustration and tension, the probability of maltreatment is markedly increased. These social conditions interact with the parenting style of the child's caregivers. When the parent is deficient in the ability to empathize with the child, the potential for abuse is heightened. When the caregiver's style is inconsistent, the child is exposed to danger. When the caregiver approves of physical force as punishment, then too the danger is heightened. Caregivers who do not use lower-limit controls on behavior in an effective and consistent manner set the stage for uncontrolled behavior, from both themselves and their child. Caregivers even may violate their own values and rules of conduct when they cannot establish effective control.

As Milgram's (1974) work and Fischer's (1976) studies of arousal imply, in a state of psychological stress many uncharacteristic behaviors by caregivers are possible. Thus one root of abuse is an unstable pattern of parenting, particularly when it includes the use of force in disciplining. A second factor contributing to abuse is the child as a stimulus. Some children are difficult to care for. This may be due to something intrinsic to the child, such as an overly active and nonresponsive temperament, or to something extrinsic to the child, such as its resemblance to a hated person, its position in the family, or its relationship to someone resented by the caregiver.

The characteristics of the child can elicit abusive behavior when the caregiver is prone to abusive behavior because of stress or parenting style. Many families can resolve unstable parenting patterns. Many families can overcome the problems of a difficult child. But to do it they generally require assistance from the outside, and some families do not seek or cannot get the help they need. Lenoski (1974) found that 81 percent of abusive families preferred to resolve their problems without outside involvement, whereas 43 percent of nonabusive families were so inclined. This finding not only reveals the isolation of "abnormal" families but points to the high value "normal" families place on freedom. For a child in a stable and psychologically healthy family, isolation is a limiting factor on development; for a child in a family plagued by stress and parental instability, isolation is dangerous and potentially lethal.

There is little to fear at this point in our history from too little privacy, at least in the sense we have been discussing the term here. The great outcry against Big Brother is really a product of the resentment that comes from impersonal observation and restrictions. Intimate "social smothering," though uncomfortable and even sometimes psychologically oppressive, seems less of a danger than social isolation. Maybe we could advance this issue by redirecting it from a focus on Big Brother—the dominating force—to Big Sister—the nurturing force.

WHAT CAN BE DONE?

What can be done to resist our social excesses in the name of privacy? One way is to resist and even reverse the cultural sanction for privacy in its extreme form. We can recognize the value of kinship systems and their surrogates and nurture their values of mutual obligation, authority, continuity, and accountability. We can encourage helping networks, particularly among populations prone to abuse; that is, those exposed to high stress, socially disintegrating communities, and difficult children.

Another way to do this is to encourage enduring relationships between families and professionals charged with the task of parent education and support. These relationships can begin prior to the birth of the child and can continue through childhood and adolescence. We can enlist the aid and support of the activities of natural helping networks built around central neighbors (Collins & Pancoast, 1976). Finally, we can promote the idea that a primary right of the child is access to the outside world, and a basic right of society is the opportunity to protect the child.

Families do not own their children. They hold them in trust for society. Other societies have developed a clearer concept of what this implies for support systems for families (Bronfenbrenner, 1979). This trust can be fulfilled best when families are not granted so much privacy that they can and do become isolated. Rather, they should be embedded in a web of social relationships that are personal, enduring, and reciprocal. Kinship and neighboring do this naturally. Where they are unavailable or ineffective, social action is needed to create and maintain surrogate networks to support and observe families. The price for privacy should not be paid by the thousands of American children who suffer maltreatment each year.

—◦◦◦—

One further point must be made. This chapter has focused on the costs of privacy. This is not to say that the costs of protecting children are insignificant. Such control involves limitations on freedom and privacy. The Peoples' Republic of China has great concern for children and families (Kessen, 1975), which intrudes into every aspect of the life and mind of the Chinese people. It makes what most people in the United States see as staggering demands for self-sacrifice. It supports the development of children through totalitarian control of social relations. The costs to freedom and individual identity are unacceptably high. We in the United States are faced with the task of reducing the negative aspects of privacy while maintaining the freedom and integrity of the individual. We need a positive concept of dependency (Rotenberg, 1977). Our heritage includes a theme of cooperation and collective identity that can provide a democratic-pluralist alternative to the totalitarian model of caring. We must tap that heritage on behalf of children through a process in which every family is woven into multiple networks of caring.

CHAPTER FOUR

Disturbances in Relationships

Parenting, Family Development, and Child Maltreatment

Kerry Bolger
Marney Thomas
John Eckenrode

~~~

C learly, the social and economic circumstances in which families live are strong predictors of child abuse and neglect. But how do these social and economic forces influence parent-child inter-action and increase the likelihood that maltreatment will occur? Research tells us that economic and social stressors put parents and children at risk for disturbances in personal relationships. Under these circumstances, it is difficult for parents to fulfill their caregiving role, and children are at risk for maltreatment. Some families may be at particular risk for maltreatment because of the developmental histories and personal characteristics of their members. For example, parents who were abused or neglected as children themselves may be more vulnerable to disturbances in relationships. An infant who is irritable and hard to soothe, a toddler who is rebelling against toilet training, or teenagers who are challenging their parents are all going through normal developmental stages that would be difficult for any parent to handle. For some parents these situations create risk for problems in the parent-child relationship. Our goal in this chapter is to identify some of the origins of child maltreatment in the interplay among social and economic stresses, parent and child vulnerabilities, and disturbances in relationships.

SOCIAL CONDITIONS THAT THREATEN RELATIONSHIPS

Economic deprivation is generally recognized as a principal source of risk to children. But how is this risk conveyed to children? The ecological approach to studying human development focuses on how the individual develops interactively with the social environment, defined as a network of interrelated systems. The social riches of a child are measured by enduring, reciprocal, multifaceted relationships that emphasize playing, working, and loving. Therefore, while emphasizing the powerful role played by conditions such as economic deprivation we also must look more directly at the parent-child relationships that are affected by these social conditions.

In recent years, several well-conceived and well-executed studies have shown how economic deprivation can harm children by damaging parent-child relationships. These studies can help us to understand how economic conditions can increase the odds that maltreatment will occur based on their effects on parent-child relationships. One important study, conducted by sociologist Glen Elder, looked at the impact of the Great Depression of the 1930s on the children of that era (Elder, 1974). Elder and his colleagues (Elder, Nguyen, & Caspi, 1985) found that fathers whose income dropped during the Depression tended to become more harsh and punitive in how they disciplined their children. In a more recent study, Lempers, Clark-Lempers, and Simons (1989) found that when families lost their income due to severe problems in the farm economy, parents tended to become more inconsistent in how they disciplined their children. These studies help us to understand how broader social conditions such as economic depression translate into threats to family relationships and put children at risk for maltreatment.

It is important, however, to note that child maltreatment does not occur only among poor families. Although maltreatment is more likely to occur in low-income families, children in higher-income families also suffer abuse and neglect. How do some families living in extremely difficult economic and social conditions maintain healthy, functioning relationships and provide a caring, supportive environment for children? In contrast, why do some families who are living in more secure economic conditions have great difficulty with childrearing? Families in any social class can have serious problems with family conflict or substance abuse. Psychiatric and psychological problems of caregivers can also threaten the development of healthy parent-child relationships. As scholars and practitioners are increasingly recognizing, the maltreatment of children is the product of a multiplicity of factors, not of one influence acting alone. To understand why maltreatment happens across all social classes, we must look beyond approaches that attribute maltreatment only to larger social forces. To understand why maltreatment happens, we must also look within the family system.

BECOMING A PARENT AND CREATING A FAMILY

How is a family created? How does the parent-child relationship begin? Answering these questions can help us to understand the significance of childbirth as a social event in shaping the course of early family development. As natural as families are, they are nonetheless a social creation. By calling childbirth a social event we emphasize that the roles of the participants, and indeed the people participating, have an effect on the outcome. These social factors can play a meaningful part in determining whether or not an infant born to a high-risk parent actually is exposed to a high-risk family and suffers maltreatment.

The Prenatal Period

For most families, the prenatal period is the beginning of psychological family creation. Both systematic and anecdotal evidence document the potential development of a parent-child relationship prior to birth. Physicians have found that women report a perception of fetal activity patterns and even personality in the last trimester of pregnancy. Pediatrician Berry Brazelton speaks of parental "energizing" as birth approaches (Brazelton, 1977). He notes a heightening of anxiety, role disruption, and fantasy, all serving to make the parent emotionally receptive to the newborn. However, parents' responses to the psychological challenges of the prenatal period are influenced by many factors. For example, parents' feelings about this period may be strongly related to whether the pregnancy was planned or unplanned, wanted or unwanted. In addition, factors such as poor maternal nutrition and alcohol abuse during the prenatal period may cause abnormalities in the developing fetus, thus threatening the future of the parent-infant relationship (Sugarman, 1977).

Perinatal Practices

Brazelton (1977) has noted that the dominant Western approach to childbirth is as a disease: "In most of the Western world there is a pervasive attitude on the part of the medical caretakers of mothers and infants which varies little. This attitude is that the birth of a baby must be treated as an illness or an operation—an attitude that creates an atmosphere of pathology, or of curing pathology at best." Although advances in medical technology may produce benefits for infants and parents, the routine use of intrusive medical procedures also carries risks for the developing parent-infant relationship. Interventions such as induction of labor by oxytocic drugs or rupture of membranes, and the use of internal fetal monitors may be deemed medically necessary for some high-risk pregnancies; however, these procedures may increase the stress of the birth process for both mother and infant (Sugarman, 1977). Other more routine procedures can also add to the mother's stress and discomfort. For example, routine episiotomy (incision of the perineum to widen the birth opening); shaving of the perineum; and being moved from one room for labor to another for delivery can add to the mother's physical and psychological distress (Sugarman, 1977).

In contrast, a family-centered approach to the birth process emphasizes the importance of birth as a social event. Using such an approach, a mother's experience of the birth process can be enhanced by factors such as the availability of social and emotional support. A woman in the process of giving birth may feel comforted and less stressed in the presence of a partner, friend, family member, or other supportive person during the birth. Although negative birth experiences alone are unlikely to lead to child abuse, positive birth experiences can and should be promoted and may help to mitigate against the earliest risk factors for child maltreatment.

Postpartum Issues

Stern and Kruckman (1983) have reported that cultures with very low incidence of postpartum difficulties, such as maternal depression, have several notable characteristics in common. In these cultures (in locations as diverse as China, Nepal, Guatemala, Mexico, and Uganda), a new mother during the postpartum period receives social recognition of her new role and status, assistance with her work (such as child care and household duties), social seclusion, and mandated rest. In contrast, the norms of U.S. culture reflect concern for women while they are pregnant (for example, baby showers and prenatal classes) but little support during the postpartum period (Kendall-Tackett, 1994b). In our culture, a woman's husband or partner, if she has one, usually must return to work within a week of the birth, with the new mother often left alone to cope with the many demands of her new role (Kendall-Tackett, 1994b). Mothers who receive adequate social support during the postpartum period are less likely to experience postpartum depression (Kendall-Tackett, 1994a). Adopting some of the practices of other cultures could make this kind of social support more readily available and help to make the postpartum period more positive for parents.

DISTURBANCES IN THE PARENT-CHILD RELATIONSHIP

Most adults competently adopt the role of parent when they create and sustain adequate families. Some do not, however. Why do some family relationships go awry? How can we prevent child maltreatment by strengthening interpersonal relationships? Effective intervention and prevention of child maltreatment depend on our ability to understand how these relationships develop and what role early attachment plays in laying the groundwork for healthy and effective parenting.

Competent Childrearing

A series of studies by Crockenberg and her colleagues (Crockenberg, 1981; Crockenberg & McCluskey, 1986) illustrates the complexity of factors influencing the developing parent-child relationship. In these studies, Crockenberg looked at which factors predicted secure mother-infant attachment. "Securely attached" infants show distress when separated from their mothers briefly but are readily comforted and soothed by the mother upon her return. Overall, Crockenberg found that mothers who had good social support from adults in their lives were more sensitive to their babies than mothers with poor social support. Mothers' level of social support was also the best predictor of secure infant attachment. Moreover, social support was especially important for mothers with irritable babies. Without good social support, mothers of irritable infants were less responsive to their babies; however, mothers of irritable infants who had good social support were able to cope with their difficult infants and respond sensitively to their needs. Furthermore, among mothers who were unresponsive to their infants, social support appeared to benefit infants directly by providing them with responsive substitute caregivers. Thus, mothers' behavior, children's characteristics, and relationships outside the parent-infant dyad all helped to determine the quality of care that a child received. Under the right circumstances, even a difficult child received sensitive care; a less ideal combination (such as an unresponsive mother parenting an irritable child with no social support from others) produced disturbances in the parent-child relationship.

Wolfe (1987) suggests that parenting success depends on the parent's ability to balance the needs of the child with the needs and responsibilities of the parents to provide appropriate boundaries and control. Baumrind (1971) has argued that parents who place age-appropriate demands on their children while still responding warmly to their individual needs both enhance child development and reduce parent-child conflict. In contrast to these prescriptions for optimal childrearing, parents who mistreat their children have been described as individuals who have trouble prioritizing and weighing their needs against those of the child's and receive little support in making appropriate choices (Justice & Justice, 1976). Often these parents present an odd picture of both selfishness and impoverished self-image.

Parent-Child Relationships Gone Awry

Parents' own developmental histories may contribute to difficulties in childrearing. For example, if parents themselves were abused or received inadequate care while they were growing up, they may not have an appropriate model of how a good parent should behave. It should be noted that many people who are maltreated as children do not go on to abuse their own children (Kaufman & Zigler, 1989); however, the existing research evidence suggests that among parents who maltreat their children a substantial proportion experienced child abuse or neglect themselves (Egeland, Jacobvitz, & Sroufe, 1988). Parents who received poor care while growing up may be dismissive of their children's need for care, or they may be unable to see their children as separate, autonomous individuals with their own needs (Newberger & White, 1989; Sameroff & Feil, 1985). Parents whose needs for caregiving have not been satisfied may be so preoccupied with their own needs that they are unable to put their children's interests first. Many parents who have a history of maltreatment as children may also be unable to protect their own children from abuse from their spouse or partner. Incompetence in the role of caregiver, without mitigating personal and social resources, is associated with stress in the parenting role. In terms of its psychosocial consequences, stress without support is a pathogenic influence (Paykel, 1976). Clearly, a parent's experiences of stress must be considered in conjunction with her or his resources for dealing with this stress.

Abuse may be best understood as a process in which initial differences between parent and child are magnified over time. Initially, small asynchronies between child and caregiver, mild control problems, somewhat extreme forms of discipline, and slightly aversive interactions are multiplied over time until they become recognizable as deviant, dangerous patterns. In this way, parents are set up for abuse by the combination of larger social forces and their own special circumstances. "Process" variables such as stress and lack of social support translate social structure into events directly shaping the interaction of family members. The ability to care for a child adequately is, like all forms of competence, situationally determined (McClelland, 1973). Almost no one is completely immune to the role of child abuser if the discrepancy between support and demands is great enough; people vary in the degree to which they are prone to act in an abusive manner.

How do parents' developmental histories, personal relationships, and experiences of stress in daily life influence the quality of care they provide for their children? Egeland, Jacobvitz, and Sroufe (1988) provided some answers to this question in their long-term study of women who had been abused as children. Some of these women went on to maltreat their own children, whereas others did not. Whether or not a woman broke the cycle of abuse depended in part on her current and past close relationships with other adults. Women who did not abuse their children were more likely to have received emotional support during childhood from a non-abusive adult; to have a more supportive, stable, and satisfying current relationship with a mate; and to have participated in psychotherapy at some point in their lives. By forming healthier relationships than might have been predicted by their developmental histories, these women helped themselves to provide better care for their children.

Social Relationships That Support Parenting

The more stressful the social environment, the more the family needs social support. This paradox challenges those who care for families. Those who have the most need generally live in communities that have the least to offer. The unmanageability of the family's stress is the product of a mismatch between the level of stress and the availability and potency of personal and social resources, chief among which are supportive personal relationships. Support systems function through social networks (Cochran & Brassard, 1979; Garbarino, Stocking, & Associates, 1980; Stack, 1974). In recent years, ecologically oriented students of development have begun to adapt the concept of social networks for assessing the support systems for families. Cochran and Brassard (1979) defined four properties of social networks relevant to development: (1) size and diversity of membership; (2) interconnectedness among members; (3) content of activities engaged in; and (4) directionality of contacts. Studying the social networks of families promises to operationalize systematically the concepts of social isolation and social integration. This is an important development because it describes the social isolation, the lack of support systems, of families involved in child maltreatment.

Roles outside the immediate caregiving relationship, such as in the world of work, may be mismanaged or disrupted by social forces beyond the parent's control, such as happens during an economic depression. These events generate the kind of stresses that often result in attempts to assert control through violence or to surrender control through neglect. Linking such role malfunctions together to account for the maltreatment of children is a major and largely unexplored task for developmental research. How does the chain of events that normally supports families and protects children break down? One contributor to this breakdown is isolation from supportive personal relationships, a topic discussed at some length in Chapter Three. Isolation from potent, prosocial support systems places even the strong and competent in jeopardy and often sends the weak or incompetent over the edge when stresses from within and outside the family conspire. Numerous studies have found that maltreating families tended to be socially isolated and to have difficulty in relationships with others. Crittenden (1985) found that friendships of mothers who abused their children were unstable and not reciprocal and that parents who neglected their children had few friends out-side the family. Polansky and his colleagues found that neglecting parents had virtually no one to whom they felt they could turn con-fidently for assistance with day-to-day matters (Polansky, Chalmers, Buttenweiser, & Williams, 1979).

It would be misleading, however, to assume that the fault for social isolation is entirely external to the individual (Thompson, 1995). It is necessary to distinguish between lack of social supports and failure to use available supports. There are many barriers to the effective use of supportive relationships in times of stress, some reflecting the com-petencies and skills of the person in need (Eckenrode & Wethington, 1990). As a preventive strategy, it may not be sufficient to provide par-ents at risk for maltreatment with access to supportive social ties with-out also addressing the issues that may deter a parent from effectively using those resources. Social isolation, like virtually all important hu-man phenomena, is determined by an interaction of the individual and the environment. Social isolation may be a cause of disturbances in relationships or may itself be caused by them. It seems most likely it is both. In the following section we review some of the major threats to the developing parent-child relationship.

THREATS TO THE PARENT-CHILD RELATIONSHIP

The competencies, skills, and behaviors that parents bring to their par-enting role can bolster or threaten the developing parent-child rela-tionship. A damaged parent can hardly be expected to effectively parent a child without significant support from his or her environ-ment. The quality of the relationship parents have with each other also set the stage for their interactions with their children.

Parental Substance Abuse

One serious threat to the healthy development of family relationships and, ultimately, the parent-child attachment, which may protect against child abuse, is parental substance abuse. Rodning and col-leagues at UCLA (1989) studied attachment and play organization in drug-exposed infants who received intensive early intervention. The children of heavy drug users exhibited insecure attachment, disorga-nized play and attention patterns, and an impaired ability to seek and use comfort. These children are often irritable as babies and hyperactive as toddlers and are described as difficult to soothe. In an already stressful family environment with one or more vulnerable and needy parents, this is a prescription for abuse and neglect.

Zuckerman (1994) has argued that the children of drug and alcohol abusers are placed in double jeopardy. First, because of the potential exposure to toxic substances in utero, some children from birth are at significant developmental risk because of prematurity, fetal alcohol syndrome, attention disorders, and mental retardation. Second, even if the child does not incur a biological or neurological disability, parents who are addicted to drugs or alcohol or both are unlikely to provide adequate food, clothing, and shelter and basic supervision for safety, let alone the nurturing attention and cognitive stimulation that facilitates growth and development. In a recent study by Wollack and Magura (1996), parental substance abuse not only had a negative impact on family functioning but also had a direct connection to an increase in repeated reports of child maltreatment. Parental substance abuse of any kind increased the likelihood that a second report of maltreatment would occur, and when alcohol and drug use was combined the effect was particularly strong. Involvement with drugs and/or alcohol also interferes with these parents' ability to form satisfying adult relationships with family and friends that could support them in their tasks of childrearing. As mentioned previously, a strong intimate support network is significantly associated with the prevention of child maltreatment.

Parental Psychiatric Problems

Parental psychological and psychiatric problems can also threaten family relationships. In a study of how parents with a psychiatric disorder interacted with their children, Rutter and Quinton (1984) found that families of psychiatric patients had much higher levels of family discord then families in a control group. Children of parents with a personality disorder were at highest risk: these children were exposed to more hostile parental behavior than other children, and, in turn, they showed the highest levels of emotional and behavioral disturbances. Parents suffering from other forms of psychiatric disturbance are also at risk for problems in parenting. For example, depressed parents appear to be more prone to maltreating their children than parents who are not depressed (Wolfe, 1985). The effects on children of parental psychopathology and maltreatment may interact, putting these children at especially great risk for behavioral and emotional problems (Walker, Downey, & Bergman, 1989). In addition, parents with psychiatric problems (such as depression, schizophrenia, or obsessive-compulsive disorder) may be unable to take care of their own basic needs, let alone the basic survival needs of their children; like those parents caught up in substance abuse, a parent with a significant psychiatric problem is often psychologically unavailable to the young infant and toddler, which impairs the attachment process.

Parental Cognitive Impairment

Cognitive impairment may also make it difficult for a parent to provide a positive childrearing environment or to be able to react to the many tasks of parenting. A caretaker with limited cognitive skills or judgment may overreact to normal developmental stages with excessive discipline or be unable to identify and remove hazards in a child's environment. Some researchers have suggested that child maltreatment may be more common among parents with low levels of intellectual functioning, such as parents with mental retardation. Other investigators, however, have noted that research on abuse and neglect in this population has suffered from methodological flaws, making it impossible to draw firm conclusions about connections between mental retardation and perpetration of child maltreatment. In any case, it seems likely that a parent's cognitive limitations add to the difficulty of providing optimal child care, especially if the family is living in a high-stress environment.

Parents' Relationships with Intimate Partners

A parent's relationship with a spouse or partner may either support or threaten healthy development of the parent-child relationship. The quality of this relationship with a partner may be especially important for parents who are at risk for childrearing problems. Research conducted by Quinton, Rutter, and Liddle (1984) and Pianta, Egeland, and Hyatt (1986) illustrates this point. Quinton and his colleagues examined parenting behaviors among women who had been reared in institutions because of a breakdown of parenting in their families of origin. Some of these women were showing severe parenting difficulties, while others were functioning much more successfully. One important predictor of good parenting was the presence of a supportive spouse. Similarly, Pianta, Egeland, and Hyatt (1986) found that, among a group of women at high risk for parenting difficulties, women who had been involved in numerous unstable relationships with partners were functioning poorly in their childrearing role as compared to women who had been involved in a stable, consistent relationship. Parents' relationships with adult partners may fulfill some of the parents' needs for social, emotional, and instrumental support, enabling them to function more successfully as parents.

Research on domestic violence also highlights the relationship between child maltreatment and parents' relationships with adult partners. Research on the co-occurrence of domestic violence and child abuse suggests that from 45 to 70 percent of battered women in shelters report the presence of some form of child abuse. Stacey and Shupe (1983) suggest that child abuse is fifteen times more likely to occur in families where domestic violence is occurring. Children who witness violence are more likely to exhibit aggressive behavior problems and delinquency and do less well in school (O'Keefe, 1995). Child characteristics such as these create additional stress in families and also increase the risk for maltreatment.

Developmental Challenges

Sometimes, however, the risk for maltreatment may be as simple as a mismatch between the normal stages of childhood and the parent's view of the behavior. Certain parents appear to be less capable, for many of the reasons described earlier, to handle the inevitable challenging behaviors that children from infancy to adolescence present. A colicky baby, an inquisitive toddler, a finicky eater, a shy child who clings to the parent, a nine-year-old who wets the bed, or a teenager who pushes parental limits can elicit dangerous reactions from some parents. Parents attempting to change a teenager's behavior, or silence a crying child, or "teach" an inquisitive toddler not to touch hot items can easily lose control. The fine balance between setting appropriate boundaries, reading the child's cues, and maintaining a calm, flexible manner tests all parents. When stress, drug or alcohol addiction, mental or psychiatric impairment, domestic violence, or lack of emotional and social support are also present, it should be no surprise that the risk for maltreatment increases.

In our view of how parents and children become a family, abuse is truly a system malfunction. A pattern of maltreatment is based on particular kinds of relationships between the victim-perpetrator dyad and others who might be involved. To change a pattern of maltreatment we must understand the factors that threaten family relationships and the development of parent-child attachment. Only then can we design and implement effective interventions to prevent child maltreatment.

PART TWO

Special Issues

CHAPTER FIVE

The Elusive Crime of Psychological Maltreatment

James Garbarino
John Eckenrode
Kerry Bolger

P sychological abuse and neglect is at the heart of the overall maltreatment problem. In Chapter Two we explored Bronfenbrenner's ecological perspective, an approach to human development that looks at both the ever-growing ability to comprehend the world and the content of that understanding. The child's development is measured by the richness and validity of his or her construction of the world. The real crime in abuse and neglect is that the child is taught a false reality, one dominated by negative feelings and self-defeating styles of relating to people. For our developmental understanding of maltreatment to proceed, we must tackle the very difficult problem of psychological abuse and neglect. Psychological maltreatment, or emotional abuse as it is often called, has been addressed in child-abuse legislation, in formal discussions by students of child maltreatment, and by child protective services practitioners in the trenches (Barnett, Manley, & Cicchetti, 1991; Garbarino, Guttman, & Seeley, 1986; Hart, Brassard, & Carlson, 1996). Professionals in the fields of social work, psychology, psychiatry, and law enforcement seem to believe that emotional-psychological maltreatment does exist but have had difficulty reaching consensus in defining it. Psychological maltreatment is truly an elusive crime. Recently, some progress has been made toward defining the phenomenon (McGee & Wolfe, 1991), but a general consensus has not been reached. Our goal here is to describe and add to these efforts to define psychological maltreatment.

THE MEANING IS THE MESSAGE

In 1992 the National Academy of Sciences convened an expert panel to develop an agenda for future research on child maltreatment (National Research Council, 1993). The panel's report illustrates the lack of scientific and professional consensus in defining psychological maltreatment. It described some of the reasons why psychological maltreatment has not received as much attention as other types of maltreatment (for instance, unlike physical abuse, psychological maltreatment does not leave visible marks). The panel's report also described some of the current controversies related to defining psychological maltreatment (for example, whether parents' behavior must have an apparent effect on the child in order to constitute psychological maltreatment). However, the report offered no guidelines for defining psychological maltreatment. Rather, the panel recommended convening more expert panels to establish definitions of each form of abuse and neglect.

Other groups have also been working toward defining psychological abuse. There have been a number of recent attempts to assemble types of parental behaviors that would qualify as psychological abuse or neglect on the basis that these acts may potentially harm children emotionally by making them feel worthless, flawed, unloved, unwanted, endangered, or only of value in meeting someone else's needs (American Professional Society on the Abuse of Children, 1995). For example, Hart, Brassard, and Carlson (1996), revising an early list discussed by Garbarino, Guttman, and Seeley (1986), cite six types of behaviors that fit this definition:

1. *Spurning:* rejecting, degrading hostility
2. *Terrorizing:* placing a child in dangerous situations; threats of harm
3. *Isolating:* placing a child in confinement; severe restrictions on social interactions
4. *Exploiting/corrupting:* encouraging self-destructive, criminal, or deviant acts

5. *Denying emotional responsiveness:* failing to express love, caring, and affection

6. *Mental health, medical, and educational neglect:* ignoring need for treatment; refusing to allow treatment

The last category includes acts that other professionals may want to classify separately. For example, the definitions adopted for the National Incidence Studies include refusal or delay in physical health care as subcategories under physical neglect.

Though such lists of behaviors are valid as composite indicators of psychological maltreatment, they often lack conceptual organization and a clear developmental perspective. The issue of emotional abuse is evident in these behaviors, but it cannot be understood through them alone. Practitioners and researchers alike are stumbling on this issue. Emotional abuse definitely exists in the lives of children, but it is very difficult to establish adequate conceptual and operational definitions that are linked to child development research. What is the problem here? Whenever a problem does not yield to sustained interdisciplinary frontal assault it is time to stand back and rethink the issue. We need this to advance our understanding of psychological or emotional maltreatment and deal with it in theory and practice. As a society, we need such an advance if we are to understand and help abusive families.

A PERSPECTIVE FOR VIEWING PSYCHOLOGICAL MALTREATMENT

Archimedes maintained that if given an appropriate place to set his fulcrum, he could move the world. In the intellectual realm we often lose sight of the power of a theoretical fulcrum to permit progress in solving social problems. Our characteristic orientation is, of course, the pragmatic, positivistic stance reflected in that most American of maxims, "Don't just stand there, do something!" This approach has served us well in many ways and areas, but it has its limitations. Perhaps at this point, having been stymied in the positivist mode, we can profitably turn to another tradition. What is lacking in our attempts to understand emotional abuse, and thus define it in policy and practice, is a suitable theoretical perspective (Shaver, Goodman, Rosenberg, & Orcutt, 1991).

Early students of child abuse adopted a model dominant in clinical work that focused primarily on defective-person theories. Adopting this model may have impaired our understanding of maltreatment as a developmental and social problem. This state of affairs has only recently begun to be rectified in theoretical and empirical work. To understand the emotional aspects of abuse it is likewise necessary to move away from the limitations of a narrow clinical orientation. It is necessary to adopt a perspective emphasizing both developmental and social aspects of the issue. What does this mean in specific terms? Much has been made of the need to consider cultural differences in childrearing as a basis for understanding and dealing with maltreatment. We noted this in Chapter One.

Cultural relativism argues for the need to look at childrearing practices on their own cultural terms as a starting point for complete understanding. When applied simplistically, the notion of cultural relativism in parent-child relations can lead to rationalization for practices that harm children, however. We need to have transcultural principles for evaluating child care. When applied with a more sophisticated understanding of where culture fits into family life, such a relativistic position can illuminate the meaning of behavior and thus can lead to a proper evaluation of it. Is all behavior to be defined strictly by culturally relativistic criteria? Is all behavior developmentally equivalent? Are there any universals that can be applied across and within cultures? To ask these questions is to probe deeply into the meaning of maltreatment. Are there practices that are intrinsically harmful to children? We think there are, and our ecological perspective tells us these practices can be understood only by tackling them through the concept of emotional maltreatment.

One examination of the notion of emotional maltreatment in cross-cultural (and transcultural) perspective is Rohner's study of parental rejection (Rohner, 1975). Using a variety of methods to relate cultural differences in family relationships to psychological development, Rohner concludes that parental rejection has a universal effect on children. His research leads to: "the conclusion that parental rejection in children, as well as in adults who were rejected as children, leads to: hostility, aggression, passive aggression, or problems with the management of hostility and aggression; dependency; probably emotional unresponsiveness and negative self-evaluation (negative self-esteem and negative self adequacy); and, probably, emotional instability as well as a negative world view" (p. 168).

THE DESTRUCTION OF COMPETENCE

When placed in a broad developmental and social perspective, emotional maltreatment is the destruction or significant impairment of a child's competence. The idea of competence as a unifying theme in studying human development has emerged in recent decades (Masten, Morison, Pelligrini, & Tellegen, 1990; White, 1959). We can turn to this tradition for a developmental perspective on emotional maltreatment. The general elements of human competence go beyond adaptivity, as intelligence is conceptualized by Piaget (1952), Binet and Simon (1916), and others. McClelland (1973) argues that *competence* means successful performance in specific social contexts and typically consists of the following abilities:

1. *Communication skills:* the ability accurately to receive and transmit messages verbally and nonverbally

2. *Patience:* the ability to delay one's response in a socially effective way

3. *Moderate goal setting:* the ability to recognize and commit oneself to realistic challenges

4. *Ego development:* a feeling of basic confidence and security about handling day-to-day challenges

McClelland's definition of competence suggests a fulcrum with which to move the problem of psychological maltreatment. It permits us to evaluate parental behavior, parent-child relations, or teacher-student relations in light of a developmental criterion; namely, the contribution those relationships make to the development of competence. McClelland's fulcrum sets goals for the socialization process. To evaluate socialization practices we must know what will be demanded through the life course. This is the key to understanding psychological maltreatment. If we start with this conception of competence as the currency of development, we can proceed toward an understanding of psychological maltreatment as both a scientific issue and a problem for practical solution.

One of the major contributions of the emerging field of developmental psychopathology (Cicchetti, 1989; Sroufe & Rutter, 1984) for understanding psychological maltreatment is that it focuses our attention on the importance of stage-salient competencies as the backdrop for understanding what is normative development and for tracing continuities across stages of development. A definition of psychological maltreatment consistent with this perspective has been offered by Barnett, Manley, and Cicchetti (1991): "Emotional maltreatment involves parental acts that thwart children's basic emotional needs." This perspective is being gradually incorporated into guidelines for assessment and treatment of maltreated children. For example, the American Professional Society on the Abuse of Children (1995) recommends that "an assessment of possible psychological maltreatment should include consideration of the child's developmental level. The caregiver-child relationship should be considered within a developmental framework that takes into account the primary developmental tasks of the child and the related tasks placed on the caregiver" (p. 5).

Such an approach sensitizes us to consider the child's developmental stage when categorizing a parental behavior as psychological maltreatment and evaluating its severity. A particular objective behavior (such as emotional unresponsiveness) may have different meanings for an infant or an adolescent. We must also not forget that, even within a group of children at a particular developmental stage, there will be much individual variability. Each child carries particular strengths and vulnerabilities. A parent's belittling comments focused on the physical limitations of a handicapped child may be particularly damaging to that child's self-esteem, given his or her special vulnerabilities.

PSYCHOLOGICAL MALTREATMENT IN THE LIVES OF CHILDREN

The overall issue of child maltreatment pushes our scientific credibility to its extreme limits. Child maltreatment is not simply less-than-optimal childrearing; it is a pattern of behavior that drastically violates the social, moral, and scientific norms concerning child care. In the United States a parent is free to engage in any and all forms of child care up to the point at which a clear and present danger to the child's welfare arises.

In the opinion of some observers, this point is set far too high. Adults must be held accountable for behavior that is developmentally damaging. Just as it is inexcusable for a parent to maintain that he or she was simply disciplining a child by burning him or her with cigarettes, it is no adequate defense to argue that one is only toughening the child when engaging in emotionally destructive behavior. This highlights the responsibility of educational, health care, and other service institutions to make sure that the acceptable lower limits of child-care activities are communicated clearly to everyone who cares for children. When this responsibility is not met these institutions become accomplices in the abusive pattern.

In law and custom it is the task of society's institutions to guard against violations of the norms concerning minimal child care. Whatever we may think of this lower-limit approach to parental autonomy, it does in fact prevail, in law and in cultural practice. How can we set some lower limits as criteria to be used in acting against psychological maltreatment? How can we operationally define a clear and present danger to a child's developing competencies and needs? This is a pressing task for a policy science of child development.

If we return to McClelland's suggested components of competence listed earlier, the task becomes one of identifying dangers to communication skills, patience, moderate goal setting, and ego development. Whether scientists like it or not, the actual decision on whether or not the danger is real will be made on the level of family life by a variety of medical, child-care, police, social work, and legal personnel. Can we offer these helpers something that will stand up in court, the overarching criterion for people in the field? We certainly can direct their attention to specific outcomes, such as a child with a nonorganic communication disorder, an impatient youngster who cannot cope with everyday frustrations, a student who is wildly inappropriate in his goal setting, or a child with disablingly inadequate self-esteem.

There are two problems with such an approach. First, we must be able to specify when a parent is culpable for the psychologically damaged child. This means there must be evidence that the parent is directly contributing to the child's maladaptive condition. There are many nonparental and nonculpable causes for such failures. In fact, it is common for a child's aversive idiosyncratic behavior to act as a stimulus for abnormal parental behavior, as in the case of a colicky infant or a preschooler's oppositional tantrums (Patterson & Reid, 1970). Second, we need to be able to intervene before the damage is done, or at least before it is permanently debilitating. Here again we face a problem of determining causation. These issues exactly parallel those faced in working with physical abuse, where both unequivocal diagnosis of risk and preventive intervention are often impossibly difficult tasks.

As others have recognized, with respect to the issue of emotional abuse, there are always two interests to be served by the process of diagnosis (Giovannoni, 1991). First, in theory and in practice, diagnosis serves the function of identifying a need for service. Second, diagnosis provides a basis for invoking the coercive resources of the state when provision of service alone is not enough to meet the protective needs of the child or when the parent refuses to accept the services offered. Both aspects of diagnosis are designed to produce evidence of maltreatment that serves to legitimize action by the state.

Because of the adversarial nature of the legal proceedings required to invoke intervention by the state—such as court-ordered participation in parent-education programs or removal of the child-victim to foster care—the criteria for diagnostic proof in such cases are much more procedurally stringent and require more extensive documentation than do efforts to offer services on a voluntary basis. Although prevention is always preferable to treatment in dealing with child maltreatment, we must make progress in defining criteria for psychological maltreatment to ensure that families are restored to healthy functioning and that children are protected. We need to recognize the importance of individual differences and the impact of the child's temperament in shaping the outcome of parent-child relations as a last qualifying condition before beginning the task of specifying criteria for psychological maltreatment.

Whereas in the case of physical abuse there are at least some universals—a broken bone is a broken bone is a broken bone—in the matter of psychological maltreatment there are few. As developmental psychologists have recognized, the impact of any specific parental behavior is to some degree dependent upon the child toward whom it is directed. Temperament and experience produce a context in which parental behavior acts upon development, and some children seem to be almost invulnerable.

TOWARD A DEFINITION
WE CAN ACT UPON

Using competence as the criterion, we have seen that rejection of the child and her or his normal behavior stands at the heart of psychological maltreatment. Once we take this point of view many existing data are brought into focus. For example, the frequently reported finding that abusive families reject their children even during early days of life now can be seen not only as a predictor of future physical abuse (which it may well be) but as an act itself of psychological maltreatment. Polansky's extensive work on neglect focused on the apathy/futility syndrome (Polansky, Chalmers, Buttenweiser, & Williams, 1981). Characteristic of this syndrome is a systematic rejection of the child as evidenced by failure to offer adequate care. Work on the childrearing implications of maternal depression augments this view (Weissman & Paykel, 1974). The principal developmental threat of parental depression is the rejection that it implies. The observational studies conducted by Burgess and Conger (1978) further document this point. The principal conclusion of these studies is that parents involved in maltreatment characteristically ignore positive behavior in their children, have a low overall level of interaction, and emphasize negative behavior. Burgess and Conger's results are quite consistent with Rohner's notions of rejection. Coopersmith's (1967) work on developing self-esteem in children suggests that a loving, involved, and actively contributing parent produces high self-esteem in the child, whereas a passive, neglecting, and uninvolved parent produces low self-esteem. Research has also shown the damaging effects of both psychological unavailability and psychological intrusiveness for children's development. In the Minnesota Mother-Child Project, a longitudinal study of high-risk families, young children whose mothers were psychologically unavailable showed serious social and emotional difficulties, such as being angry and noncompliant both with their mothers and in preschool (Egeland, Sroufe, & Erickson, 1983). Children whose mothers had an intrusive style of caregiving during infancy (that is, they interfered inappropriately with their children's activities and were inconsiderate of their wishes) had significant academic, social, emotional, and behavioral problems when they reached school age (Egeland, Pianta, & O'Brian, 1993).

These findings also may be interpreted in light of the rejection hypothesis. These parenting behaviors impinge on the development of competence. In parents' relations with infants, broad concepts such as rejection are translated into concrete and specific behavior. First, there is rejection of the child's natural prosocial actions, of the normal instinct to engage in social interaction. This rejection includes lack of parental or caregiver response to the infant's vocalizations, smiles, and attempts to initiate eye-to-eye and bodily contact. A study by Tronick and his colleagues (1978) involved an experimental manipulation in which the normal feedback that infants received from their mothers in face-to-face interaction was distorted. Mothers faced their infants but remained facially unresponsive. The infants reacted with intense wariness and eventual withdrawal. This experimental treatment approximates maternal rejection by providing a demonstration of the operational meaning (and presumably the consequences) of emotional maltreatment.

What are a child's rightful claims on a parent or other caregiver? As always, we must employ a mixture of culture and science, community standards and professional expertise, in answering this question. Briefly, we think we can establish that a child has a rightful claim to a parent (1) who recognizes and responds positively to socially desirable accomplishments; and (2) who does not inflict on the child his or her own needs at the expense of the child's. Thus an emotionally abusive parent may reject the infant's smiling, the toddler's exploration, the schoolchild's efforts to make friends, and the adolescent's autonomy. An emotionally abusive parent demands that the infant gratify the parent's needs ahead of the child's, that the child take care of the parent, and that the adolescent subjugate himself or herself to the parent's wishes in all matters (including perhaps sexual relations). How can we hope to define emotional abuse? We must specify some absolute standards for parental behavior within a developmental context. The idea of necessary information on and within parent-child relations presented in Chapter Three can be applied here.

The information necessary for parents consists first of both general knowledge of appropriate norms, expectations, and techniques concerning childrearing and regular feedback on parent-child relations. Second, adequate information depends upon three factors: day-to-day regularized observation and discussion of parent-child relations; informal folk wisdom based on extensive, historically validated firsthand experience; and formal, professional expertise, particularly in the areas of solving behavior problems. Third, the need for information is a direct function of situational demands that are both internal and external to the parent-child relationship. As these demands increase, so does the need for information. Fourth, formal institutions can become effective sources of information insofar as they are linked actively to the family's social network, either directly through the parent or indirectly through the parent's relationship with some other person.

FOUR ASPECTS OF PSYCHOLOGICAL MALTREATMENT

Evidence of psychological maltreatment comes directly from applying the general principles on the development of competence to specific family systems. This requires getting sources of information both from and to the family. To advance our understanding of emotional maltreatment we need to study these mechanisms. Applying general principles to specific children requires observation and evaluation by both informal sources such as family, neighbors, and friends and by formal, professional family support systems. With reference to the model of competence noted earlier, four principles of psychological maltreatment emerge. Each refers to a significant aspect of emotional abuse because it presents a clear and present danger to the child's developing competence. It thus represents behavior, first, as a basis for initiating service and, second, as a basis for legal coercion.

• *Principle One:* Punishing positive, normal behaviors such as smiling, mobility, exploration, vocalization, and manipulation of objects is psychological maltreatment. Research from a variety of contexts has demonstrated that caregiver behavior can have a direct impact on the performance of these building blocks of human development. Human beings possess an operant drive to mastery or motive to be effective in the world. To punish this drive and its accompanying behaviors is a clear and present danger to the child's development of competence.

• *Principle Two:* Discouraging caregiver-infant attachment is psychological maltreatment. Caregiver-infant attachment has emerged as one of the central issues in child development. Disruptions in early attachment has been linked to physical abuse, failure to thrive, and a variety of deficits in competence. Researchers who have examined the impact of insecure attachment in infancy on the development of preschoolers have noted two major signs of emotional damage: (1) an overconcern with dependence/security issues and (2) an underconcern with competence/effectance issues (Aber, Allen, Carlson, & Cicchetti, 1989). Systematic efforts to discourage early attachment therefore pose a direct threat to adequate development and are grounds for diagnosing emotional abuse.

• *Principle Three:* Punishing self-esteem is psychological maltreatment. Self-esteem is the positive valuing of one's characteristics, a positive identity. Self-esteem rises and falls in response to the behaviors of others, and it is linked to a variety of prosocial characteristics. To discourage self-esteem is to attack a fundamental component of competent development. It is emotionally abusive.

• *Principle Four:* Punishing the interpersonal skills necessary for adequate performance in nonfamilial contexts, such as schools and peer groups, is psychological maltreatment. Burgess and Conger (1978) observed that families involved in child maltreatment do not provide positive reinforcement for important interpersonal behaviors.

Others have noted that abusive parents typically discourage normal social relations for their children, including the formation of friendships outside the home. In developing a set of principles to define psychological maltreatment, we can therefore include systematically discouraging behavior needed for competence in nonfamilial settings. As a matter of primary prevention, parents should be steered away from each of the behavior patterns just mentioned. They result in pervasive emotional deprivation and the destruction of ego and self-esteem that leads to a variety of emotional deficits, among them inadequate empathy, which is a precursor to trouble with interpersonal relationships in general and parenthood in particular.

—⁓—

Psychological maltreatment conveys the developmentally dangerous message of rejection. When put this way, we can see that when it comes to defining emotional maltreatment, the meaning is the message. When informed observation identifies grounds for suspecting that this message is being given, there is prima facie evidence that the child's competence is being undermined. These become grounds for offering services and ultimately for initiating coercive action if the offer of services is not successful. The key, of course, is having access to the family and thus being able to provide the appropriate assessments to uncover psychological maltreatment.

The pressing need is for appropriate procedures to gain valid lay and professional testimony concerning the character of parent-child interaction. Once again, social isolation emerges as a dangerous risk factor in the lives of families. When families are cut off from caring support of and observation by others, the necessary flow of information to and from the family dries up. A healthy family is a well-connected one. The elusive crime of psychological maltreatment can be grasped, both conceptually and practically, only if this is understood. We saw this when we looked at the community context of child maltreatment, in the neighborhood where concepts such as social impoverishment were defined in daily experience. We see it again when we examine sexual abuse in the next chapter.

CHAPTER SIX

Family Sexual Abuse

Marney Thomas
John Eckenrode
James Garbarino

———ᔕᔕᔕ———

In Chapter Two we discussed some of the historical developments that led to the current concerns with this once-hidden form of maltreatment. In the past decade, many of the myths about sexual abuse of children have been debunked. While the popular press and even milk cartons advertise the dangerous stranger, we now know that strangers make up a very small percentage of sexual offenders. We have also learned that parents and parent substitutes are not the only family offenders. We now recognize that the developmental nature of childhood and adolescence explains much about the risk of sexual abuse for children and the ways different offenders approach them. Children are at risk for many types of victimization, especially sexual abuse, because of their dependency, which varies according to age and level of development. Sexual offenders often take advantage of these developmental differences in children.

> If I was alone with my dad, he would touch me and kiss me. I would try to please him in little ways because it was confusing to me. Then he came into my room one night. I was real scared, but he told me to relax, and he wouldn't hurt me. It did hurt, but there were moments I

remember enjoying. I mean, I was the ugly one and this was the closest thing I had ever experienced to love. The only affection I can remember were those times with my father. He told me he would kill me if I told, so l never told my mom. I still don't know if she knew.

Child protection statistics differ from adult retrospective studies in estimates of who is sexually abusing children, with the retrospective studies showing that intrafamily perpetrators constitute less than half of the total sexual abuse of children. We need to acknowledge the importance of acquaintance perpetrators, especially neighbors, teachers, coaches, religious leaders, and peers. Community surveys of adults who have been sexually abused as children or adolescents indicate that 30 to 40 percent of the offenders were peers (Finkelhor, Hotaling, Lewis, & Smith, 1990; Saunders, Villeponteaux, Lipovsky, & Kilpatrick, 1992). Such statistics differ from studies that rely on child protective records, which show a higher percentage of intrafamily offenders, because these agencies typically deal only with maltreatment by family members and caretakers. Although our emphasis in this book is on families, and we will not consider in detail issues such as date rape in adolescence, we must recognize that nonconsensual sex with an older, more powerful peer is for many children their first and perhaps only experience of sexual abuse. And the future role of incestuous father, stepfather, or uncle may be preceded by a history of sexual exploitation in the role of peer. Many child sexual abusers are adolescents, and many adult offenders have a history of adolescent offending (Becker, 1994; Sgroi, 1982).

FAMILY SEXUAL ABUSE: A SPECIAL CASE?

In this chapter, because of our emphasis on understanding abusive families, we will be concerned specifically with sexual abuse within the immediate family. This particular type of sexual victimization is worth major consideration, because there is good reason to believe that sexual abuse within a family is more damaging than is exploitative contact with a stranger (Kendall-Tackett, Williams, and Finkelhor, 1993). One researcher believes that even though violence by a stranger is surely terrifying, it is less destructive than incest, because at least the violence from a stranger can be dealt with directly.

Family life is intimate. Within the homes of many cultures (including our own), people live in crowded quarters, share common beds, and are regularly exposed to each other's nudity. Humankind always maintained some sort of incest taboo to protect us from the natural attraction and sexual arousal that can easily occur in such close quarters between people already bound by powerful relationships. Many who have studied the phenomenon most closely believe the urge to commit incest is deeply rooted within us all. Society's strongest sanctions are needed to forbid it. Every culture upholds this taboo in some form, though specifics vary greatly from place to place, particularly among traditional folk societies. Both violence and sex are inevitable issues for families because when people with strong attachments are locked in together the most powerful human forces always surface. Our increasingly mobile society, which increases separation from extended family networks and decreases community supports, cuts families off from the outside world and accentuates the degree to which members of American nuclear families have only each other. For this reason we must come to terms with domestic sex just as we must deal with domestic violence.

DEFINING SEXUAL ABUSE

The National Center on Child Abuse and Neglect (NCAAN) defines sexual abuse of children as "contacts or interactions between a child and an adult when the child is being used for the sexual stimulation of the perpetrator or another person when the perpetrator is in a position of power or control over the victim"(1978, p. 2). In addition to adult-child sexual abuse, sexual contact by older children or teenagers may also be abusive depending on age, size, and developmental differences. The sexual activity can include various forms of sexual abuse ranging from sexual penetration, fondling, and other sexual touching to noncontact sexual abuse such as exposure and voyeurism. It also may include involving the child in pornography or prostitution. Regardless of the form, placing misuse of power at the heart of the matter is a sound decision, in our opinion. Here, as elsewhere, exploitation is the hallmark of the perpetrator-victim relationship.

Indeed, although sexual acts constitute our common definition of sexual abuse, issues of power, control, sadistic pleasure, and displaced anger are often what motivates the abusers. Finkelhor (1979) highlighted this issue when he stated that adult sexual contact with children is intrinsically wrong because children are not in a position to give informed consent, be it due to their limited understanding of sexuality or the coercive context in which they must inevitably operate, given the dimensions of adult power and authority. The coercive nature of much sexual abuse is reflected in the fact that force, threat, and the inducement of fear in the child often accompanies the sexual acts themselves (Briere & Elliott, 1994).

Whether or not it involves actual incest (sexual intercourse between two people too closely related to marry), sexual abuse by family members or acquaintances of the child (friends, teachers, coaches, baby-sitters) is both inappropriate and damaging. We will refer to all incestuous and nearly incestuous activity as *family sexual abuse,* to differentiate between that which goes on within the family life and that which goes on outside it. (Only when we are reporting the work of other researchers who have investigated actual incest will we use the term *incest.*) Some studies attribute harmful psychological effects not to the sexual acts themselves but to society's reaction and intervention. We maintain that it does not matter. One cannot function apart from society; society will not be ignored. Whether or not incest would damage people in the best of all possible worlds is not the issue here. Some cultures permit sexual contact between adults and children under certain circumstances, as in certain religious and coming-of-age ceremonies (Korbin, 1987). However, in this culture, at this time, the sexual abuse of children presents a serious problem, and it is this culture that affects the children and adolescents with whom we are dealing.

INCIDENCE AND PREVALENCE

Given the shamefulness and secretiveness of the acts involved, it is little wonder that estimates of the incidence and prevalence of sexual abuse vary. There have been three main sources of information about the scope of this problem in the United States. Perhaps the best source of information comes from the three federally funded National Incidence Studies as reviewed in Chapter Two. The most recent study, involving 5,600 professionals in forty-two counties, estimates that 300,000 children were sexually abused in 1993 (4.5 per 1,000 children).

A second source of national statistics comes from the National Child Abuse and Neglect Data System (NCANDS), also cited in Chapter Two. The statistics represent officially reported cases that have been substantiated after an investigation. In 1993, there were approximately 135,000 substantiated reports of sexual abuse nationally, a figure understandably lower than the NIS study because many children suspected of being sexually abused are not reported to child protection agencies, and, of those reported, only about half are substantiated. Sexual abuse represents about 14 percent of all reports of child abuse and neglect substantiated by child protective agencies (National Center on Child Abuse and Neglect, 1995).

Both NIS and NCANDS data are likely to underestimate the actual amount of sexual abuse, because they represent only acts that came to the attention of some professional. Many acts of sexual abuse remain hidden. The NIS and NCANDS studies are also limited to telling us the number of incidents that occurred during that year—which does not reflect the cumulative risk over an entire childhood and adolescence.

A third source of information provides some clues of the lifetime prevalence of sexual abuse among children and also helps document acts that remain hidden from professionals. Several researchers have conducted surveys with adults, asking questions about childhood experiences that would be considered sexual abuse. Although studies have used different definitions and have asked different questions of respondents, the general view has emerged that approximately 20 percent of adult women in North America have experienced sexual abuse as children or adolescents, while most studies reveal that between 5 and 10 percent of males report sexual abuse (Finkelhor, 1994).

As reported by the third National Incidence Study and supported by other clinical studies and population surveys, we know that most sexual abuse is committed by adults or peers who are known to the victimized children. However, unlike cases of physical abuse and neglect, biological parents only constitute approximately one-fourth of the perpetrators. Stepparents and parent substitutes constitute another one-fourth of the cases, with the remaining perpetrators being persons not in a parental relationship with the child. There has also been recent concern with the increasing reports of older children and teenage offenders who may be within the family unit and are not parental figures. As we shall see later, many of these juvenile offenders may have been victims themselves. Contrary to the popular press and media hype, strangers account for only a small proportion of sexual abuse (6 to 16 percent) although often the most violent and sensational cases (Briere & Elliott, 1994).

In analyzing the results of these various studies and looking at the characteristics of the families, one is led to question whether children in particular types of families are more vulnerable to sexual abuse. One controversial topic pertains to the socioeconomic background of families where sexual abuse occurs. The 1993 NIS study shows that children in families with incomes under $15,000 are eighteen times more likely to be sexually abused than children in families with incomes over $30,000. This suggests that income is a major risk factor for sexual abuse. On the other hand, surveys with adults about childhood experiences are much less convincing about the link between income and sexual abuse. About as many middle-class and affluent people report being sexually abused as do low-income people in these studies (Finkelhor, 1994). It may be that sexual abuse, when it does occur, is much more likely to be detected by community professionals in lower-income families. Families with financial resources can maintain their privacy to a greater degree than poor families. Families with financial resources can also seek alternative forms of help outside the publicly financed systems of care (such as private therapy). But it may also be that poorer families are less likely to be recruited into community surveys by academic researchers (because of greater mobility, fewer telephones, lower literacy rates) or are more wary of strangers asking personal questions. This could result in an underestimation of the role of socioeconomic conditions as a risk factor for sexual abuse. We also do not know if socioeconomic status of the respondents in these surveys may be related to the likelihood of recalling sexual abuse. In an intriguing study, Williams (1994) did interviews with women who had a documented history of sexual abuse as children. A substantial proportion of these adult women (38 percent) did not recall the abuse that had occurred seventeen years earlier.

Although some amount of *detection bias* is probable (that is, poor people are likely to be under more scrutiny by public agencies), it is unlikely to entirely account for the increased risk to poor children shown in the NIS studies. First, such an explanation is less plausible in the case of more visible forms of maltreatment, such as physical abuse and some forms of neglect, where the NIS findings also point to a higher risk among lower-income children. Second, much of the sexual abuse that comes to the attention of professionals often co-occurs with other more visible forms of maltreatment. While sexual abuse can occur in isolation in an otherwise well-functioning family, it is more likely to occur in families where other problems exist, including problem marriages, high levels of conflict, substance use, and emotional disturbances, and where other forms of abuse or neglect are also occurring (Finkelhor, 1994).

CHARACTERISTICS OF FAMILY SEXUAL ABUSE

We have set sexual abuse apart from other types of abuse because its dynamics are different. While it may be accompanied by the use or threat of physical abuse and may grow out of a neglectful situation as well as lead to future refusal to provide care, it is not any of these things alone. The issues are not entirely the same as physical abuse, but they do bear a resemblance. Physical abuse with young children is often triggered by challenging developmental stages that evoke over-reaction in parents (excessive corporal punishment or attempts to control crying, reduce temper tantrums, or toilet train). Physical abuse also occurs through injury due to lack of supervision in unsafe environments coupled with an overwhelmed or stressed parent (Schmitt, 1987). When physical abuse begins with the onset of adolescence, it usually centers around issues of adolescent autonomy and independence. Sexual abuse seems to spring more directly from dysfunctional interpersonal relationships within families and in the history and background of the perpetrators. As in the case cited at the beginning of this chapter, it may be the only sign of acceptance a child or youth receives. While physical or emotional abuse may explode from conflict, sexual abuse is a misuse of power and a failure to live up to the protective responsibilities implicit in the caregiver role, either by committing the sexual abuse or by not protecting the child from sexual abuse.

One review described peak vulnerability for sexual abuse of both boys and girls to occur between the ages of seven and thirteen (Finkelhor & Baron, 1986). It is likely, however, that sexual abuse under the age of six is undercounted because the younger children are less likely to disclose and may also not recognize that it is occurring. Some authors have also suggested that younger children may not remember the abuse.

Sexual abuse has a variety of patterns. Girls are the largest group of victims and are more likely to be abused by family members, while boys are abused at one-third to one-half the rate of girls, are less likely to come to professional attention, and are more likely to be abused by nonfamily members. Boys are also more likely to be abused by females

(Faller, 1989). Asian children tend to be older at victimization, while African American children tend to be the youngest victims. Hispanic and African American children are more likely than Asian and Caucasian victims to experience penetration offenses (Rao, DiClemente, & Ponton, 1992). Children who have a psychological or cognitive vulnerability may also be at increased risk for sexual abuse. The incidence of sexual abuse among children with a disability is 1.75 times the rate for children with no disability (National Center on Child Abuse and Neglect, 1993).

Most sexual victimization of children, particularly within the family, occurs in the context of an ongoing relationship. Children who have been sexually abused (by both familial and nonfamilial offenders) describe the process as moving from nonsexual (bathing, massaging, snuggling, wrestling) to sexual (fondling, masturbation), and then increasing to more intrusive forms of sexual activity (oral and anal sexual activity, intercourse) (Berliner & Conte, 1990). This progression of slowly sexualizing the relationship over time is referred to by professionals as a "grooming process." It has an insidious effect on the child above and beyond the actual sexual acts, because it sets the child up to believe in her or his own complicity in the activity and makes it harder for the child to tell. Despite this gradual approach to the victim—combining emotional coercion and rewards while misusing adult authority—as the child gets older and becomes more aware of what is happening, many initially nonviolent offenders will resort to force, threats, or fear to maintain the relationship and prevent reporting. Younger children are not able, by virtue of their developmental status, to recognize that taboos are being violated and that their experience is not normal. In this view it is only at adolescence that children are capable of becoming sharply aware of the norms and expectations of the culture beyond their immediate family (Finkelhor, 1995).

There have been many changes in our knowledge around sexual abuse within the family, particularly around who is abusing children. With that increased knowledge comes a corresponding change in our understanding of the dynamics. While poor communication, rigid sex roles, stress, misuse of drugs and alcohol, and marital distress and conflict certainly contribute to familial sexual abuse, they cannot explain why so many families in which all of these conditions occur never become involved in sexual abuse despite being at high risk for physical abuse and neglect. One part of the explanation may lie in the childhood histories of the offenders. There is increasing interest in looking at the characteristics of the offenders in terms of their own childhood maltreatment and victimization, which may be linked to early onset of offending and a lack of impulse control. Earlier studies seemed to indicate that there were clear distinctions between those who abused children within the family structure and those who offended against children outside the family. It was also widely believed that there was a clear distinction between those who used exhibitionism and voyeurism versus those who used bodily contact. There is growing evidence that child sexual abusers offend across all these categories, both in and outside the family (Becker, 1994).

Considering the current rates of divorce and remarriage in this country, reconstituted families form a sizable demographic group. Additionally, the U.S. Census Bureau estimates that half of today's children will spend some of their first eighteen years in single-parent homes, a family characteristic considered to place children at increased risk for sexual abuse, especially when combined with poverty and substance abuse. Stepparents or other parent substitutes such as mothers' boyfriends, while not biologically related, fill roles that are similar to those of biological parents, which provides the kind of access and privacy that allows sexual abuse to occur. For the new American family, then, we will define sexual abuse in terms of the role the perpetrator plays in the family rather than in bloodlines. Thus the stepfather-stepchild relationship may be particularly risky because it combines the authority and opportunity for exploitation that parenthood brings without the natural inhibitions of consanguinity (Russell, 1984).

Sexual abuse is frequently but not always a symptom of family dysfunction. Often the individuals involved suffer from limited personal resources (cognitive, developmental, psychiatric, or psychological impairments) that warp interpersonal relationships as well as diminish access to social resources, and the combination results in a high-risk environment for children. According to those who counsel them, members of many sexually abusive families tend to have diffuse boundaries and unclear separation of the parental, spousal, and child roles. The family may not allow individuals to develop normally and consume everyone's energy just trying to stay together. This may help to explain a victim's extreme fear of leaving the home, for to be without a family in this situation is to be without identity. The families may be socially isolated or surrounded by other extended family networks that are equally chaotic and dysfunctional. Many are made up of destructive relationships characterized by hate, jealously, and immaturity. Members often function within rigid sex roles (Alexander, 1990; Madonna, Van Scoyk, & Jones, 1991). There seems to be a high incidence of early economic deprivation among sexually abusive fathers and a marked history of emotional impoverishment. Many of them were deserted by their own fathers in their formative years. Often they are angry with their wives or at women in general.

Occupying the maternal position in a sexually abusive family is also a difficult task. Coping with incest would exceed the personal resources of most women. Mothers in some sexually abusive homes have been viewed as complicitous in the incest, either because they are not exercising appropriate supervision, are indirectly contributing to it by virtue of their own history as victims of sexual abuse, or refusing to take protective action when the abuse is discovered (Faller, 1989). Some mothers choose to ignore, deny, or rationalize the sexually abusive situation. Some former female victims who were sexually abused as teenagers report that the inaction by their mothers hurt them as much as their father's abuse. Many remain just as angry at their mothers as at their fathers, if not more so.

Contrary to earlier reports, however, most parents believe their children and take some protective actions (Briere & Elliott, 1994). In particular, mothers who believe and support the child can decrease the negative impact of intervention. It is impossible to know how many women are actually aware of sexual abuse and what their real feelings are when it occurs in their own homes. Some women may have a history of emotional deprivation or sexual victimization themselves and are ill equipped to protect their children. Others are helpless under the threat of domestic violence or loss of financial support. However, it does seem to be clear that the lack of maternal support once disclosure occurs has been linked with more damaging effects and less positive outcomes for children.

Sexual abuse is often attributed to a poor marital relationship and poor communication, perhaps complicated by substance abuse and/or isolation of the family from traditional social networks (Berliner & Elliott, 1996). Some of the individual psychological factors mentioned earlier influence whether the family becomes sexually abusive or not, but it is the relationships between the parents or the parent substitutes that are by far the most important factors. Other contributors such as emotional crises, unemployment, death or separation of a spouse, and illness are thought to precipitate the event. However, if everyone's needs were being met, and appropriate social controls were in place, there would be no incentive to break such a strong taboo. As is so common in human behavior, we see an interaction effect, where the combination of personal vulnerability and social conditions gets people in trouble.

The power balance in a child sexual abuse relationship is so unequal that physical force is rarely necessary to initiate sexual abuse. For the child, there are many reasons for compliance. Children need love and affection, and familial sexual abuse often involves the gradual sexualization of the relationship, leaving the child unable to distinguish between acceptable and exploitative behaviors. Even when the child realizes the inappropriate or violent nature of the acts, their options are limited. Leaving home is not an option for younger children and may be risky, frightening, and even illegal for adolescents. They may also be ambivalent toward the offending parent, relative, or older sibling and may be especially needy of the love and affection that the abuser offers them if others in the child's life are rejecting (Finkelhor, 1995). This concept of being especially vulnerable is supported by research that identifies certain risk factors for sexual abuse. Thus neglect by one parent may set the stage for abuse by the other. The child may wish to remain loyal to a father or mother who has been a source of support during childhood. Simple childhood respect for authority loads the deck. The child may want to express anger about a chaotic home life or defy a nonsupportive or rejecting parent. The child may even comply in exchange for special privileges. If the child derives any sensual pleasure out of the sexual interaction (despite its moral repugnance), feelings of self-blame may result.

Family members who know about an incestuous relationship often deny it. This denial may cause the child to doubt his or her own senses, wondering why no one mentions the topic or seems to even be aware of the sexual abuse. This kind of denial appears frequently in the recollections of victims. If the child wants to tell, they may be threatened with physical harm for disclosure. Even if the child does tell, they are often not believed, at least initially. If the child reports sexual abuse to others, they face the real possibility of breaking up the family to which she or he is bound. Traditionally, children have rarely ended incestuous relationships through official means. Instead of reporting sexual abuse, most children choose to leave home as soon as possible through early marriage or running away. This course of action compounds the normal problems that the sexually abused child may have in establishing sexual relationships outside the home, particularly given the pool of sexually exploitative adults waiting to capitalize upon the child's vulnerability.

EFFECTS OF SEXUAL ABUSE

As noted earlier, it is difficult to differentiate the adverse effects of sexual abuse from those of the disturbed family environment in which it occurs. This parallels the problem of determining the effects of physical abuse. Different children and adolescents react differently, of course, but there are several indicators that seem to determine the severity of damage that sexual abuse will cause. In general, the closer the relationship between the aggressor and the victim, the more damaging the abuse will be. Other considerations include the age, sex, and developmental status of the victim; the type and duration of the sexual abuse; the use or lack of violence; the degree of shame or guilt the child feels; and the reactions of parents and professionals (Conte & Schuerman, 1987). Recent studies (Hunter, Goodwin, & Wilson, 1992; Mannarino, Cohen, and Berman, 1994) report that most children do not blame themselves for the abuse but do see themselves as very different from their peers and are likely to blame themselves for other negative events. Where the victim does not have access to a network of supportive relationships, the risk is substantially increased (Briere & Elliott, 1994; Kendall-Tackett, Williams, & Finkelhor, 1993). Social isolation here as elsewhere is a threat to development, particularly in abnormal or unhealthy families.

It is useful to divide the potential effects of sexual abuse into three areas: (1) initial or short-term effects; (2) adjustments that are made to ongoing abuse; and (3) long-term consequences on psychosocial development (Briere & Elliott, 1994). The short-term adjustments to sexual abuse may serve to help the child deal with his or her emotions and understand why this is occurring but may also be detrimental to the development of healthy social relationships and an integrated sense of self.

There is evidence that children who have been sexually abused display more fear and anxiety than nonabused children (Kendall-Tackett, Williams, & Finkelhor, 1993). This may be a sign that some of these children are experiencing Posttraumatic Stress Disorder (PTSD) (McLeer, Deblinger, Atkins, Foa, & Ralphe, 1988). Although PTSD as a diagnostic category arose initially as a way to describe symptoms experienced by combat veterans, it has been used more recently to describe the experiences of sexual abuse victims, particularly those who were repeatedly or violently abused.

Some sexual abuse is not perpetrated in the context of violence and intimidation but under the pretext of love and affection. Or it begins in this way, adding elements of threat and fear-inducement when the child is old enough to understand that the behavior is inappropriate or potentially dangerous. This is part of a unique psychological challenge for the child: how can an act presented as part of love and affection be reconciled with the secrecy, the shame, and the negative reaction of others when the secrecy is broken? In a natural search for meaning in these circumstances, children may develop, understandably, certain cognitions that help them cope with the ambiguous or negative emotions they are feeling.

One explanation is self-blame. Although many children do not blame themselves for the sexual abuse, some do, with this attribution often reinforced by abusers who degrade the child as a way to bolster their dominance in the relationship. Self-blame is one precursor to low self-esteem, which is also prevalent in these children and in adult survivors of sexual abuse (Oates, Forest, & Peacock, 1985). Low feelings of self-worth also are consistent with the higher rates of depression observed among adults who have been sexually abused (Browne & Finkelhor, 1986).

COPING WITH SEXUAL ABUSE

Efforts of children and adults to cope with the pain of sexual abuse may take many forms. The coping repertoire of young children may be limited to certain self-soothing behaviors and to seeking the attention of nonabusive attachment figures such as a mother or sibling. As children grow older, other responses become possible, such as running away, which may well expose the child to increased risk of further victimization (Powers & Jaklitsch, 1989). Many self-destructive behaviors observed in adolescents and adults molested as children can be classified as avoidant forms of coping (Briere & Elliott, 1994). These include various forms of dissociation (such as amnesia, emotional numbing), the abuse of alcohol or drugs, and suicidal thoughts. As with many stressful experiences, these coping strategies serve to numb the pain and keep away unpleasant thoughts, but they rarely are associated with positive life course development.

Sexual abuse strikes at the heart of the child's developing sense of social relationships and, as such, is likely to have an impact on these areas of functioning. Sexually abused children and adolescents may have problems developing close, mutually reaffirming relationships or end up with partners that confirm their worst suspicions about themselves. It is also logical to expect dysfunction related to sexual behaviors and intimate relationships, although sexual dysfunction is by no means a universal long-term outcome of sexual abuse. Children who have been sexually abused are somewhat more likely than nonabused children to display sexualized behaviors, such as sexual play with dolls, excessive masturbation, or age-inappropriate sexual knowledge (Kendall-Tackett, Williams, & Finkelhor, 1993). Adults who have been molested have also been reported as being at a higher risk of remaining single, getting divorced (Finkelhor, Hotaling, Lewis, & Smith, 1990), or reporting problems with sexual intimacy (Briere & Elliott, 1994).

Our brief review suggests that sexual abuse can be a serious threat to the developing child and adolescent. Some symptoms associated with sexual abuse, such as low self-esteem and depression, are also common with other forms of maltreatment and likely reflect the stressful nature of growing up in a dysfunctional family environment. Others, such as sexualized behaviors in young children, appear to be effects more linked to this form of child maltreatment. The same factors that protect children from the adverse effects of other forms of maltreatment, such as family support, also are crucial to recovery and treatment of sexually abused children and adolescents.

TREATMENT

Two major bodies of thought dominate the issue of treatment of sexually abused children and their families. One approach advocates primary intervention by the criminal justice system to protect the children, while the other advocates greater reliance on the mental health system in conjunction with child protective supervision. The dilemma is real and reflects genuine differences and goals at different points in the service needs of families involved in sexual abuse. While some point out the trauma of a trial for children who must testify against their parents, other relatives, or siblings in the presence of outsiders, others see the result of the process (prison for the offender) as the only sanction severe enough to protect the child and to force the family or offender into therapy.

After a child reports sexual abuse, she or he will often have to repeat the story to strangers and will be asked to describe the incidents in graphic detail. The vast majority of incidents of sexual abuse against children cannot be substantiated by medical or physical evidence, and rarely are there eyewitnesses. These circumstances make the child's testimony critical for both prosecution of the offender and protection for the child. Not surprisingly, considerable controversy has arisen over the truthfulness of children who report sexual abuse, their ability to accurately report on past events, and their susceptibility to suggestion in investigative interviews. Confronted with the pressure to maintain the family's integrity, protect the perpetrator, solve a custody dispute, or testify in a court setting, the child may present a confusing picture, first disclose then retract the complaint, or label the initial report a lie—thus contributing to the controversy surrounding child witnesses. Younger children may be unable to provide enough information to determine the specifics of a case, while older children and teens may be accused of deliberate manipulation. Involvement in the criminal justice system puts the family into an adversarial relationship in the courtroom and into financial jeopardy whatever the outcome, but particularly if the breadwinner is imprisoned.

This concern with the intrusiveness of the intervention itself, regardless of good intent and the disruptive impact on families, prompted one anonymous physician to ask, "If the public sector deals with the problem in a destructive way, is the therapist ever justified to bypass the system and provide needed care to all members of the family, while at the same time putting an end to the sexual exploitation?" This spokesperson attributes the lack of cooperation by many professionals with reporting laws to this suspicion.

Most treatment for child sexual abuse victims and their families offers a wide range of treatment services such as individual and group psychotherapy, play therapy, family counseling, support groups, marital counseling, crisis intervention, and allied services such as alcohol and drug counseling. (See Friedrich, 1991; Gil, 1991; and Keller, Cicchinelli, & Gardner, 1989, for an extensive review and description of programs.)

However, the efficacy of various forms of child sexual abuse treatment programs is difficult to determine due to the limited data available. Small samples, limited outcome measures, and generally absent comparison groups make it almost impossible to say anything definitive about which types of treatments work best and for which children, offenders, and families. Complicating the issue for understanding treatment options is the fact that there is no single or specific pattern of symptoms or problems that arise from a common history of child sexual abuse. The effect of sexual abuse for some children is devastating but not uniform. A surprising number of children appear to cope, survive, and even thrive in spite of child sexual abuse. In addition, given that the known etiology and the effects of sexual abuse as described earlier are so varied and the characteristics of the offenders and family units so different, treatment must focus on a wide range of problems. "The process of treatment may be as simple as educating parents to supervise and set appropriate limits" (Berliner & Elliott, 1996, p. 63).

Therapy and counseling need to address such diverse areas as sexual behavior problems, communication breakdowns, social isolation, depression, PSTD, and cognitive distortions. The appropriate treatment choice for each child and family is highly specific. Although there are few well-controlled treatment outcomes studies that match treatment type and duration and control for different effects and family constellations, there are anecdotal, retrospective, and clinical data that suggest that effective programs have four general therapeutic aims: (1) relieving and managing symptoms; (2) destigmatizing the abuse for the victim; (3) increasing self-esteem and mastery; and (4) controlling and changing the environment by separating the child from the perpetrator(s). Additional treatment consists of providing counseling and support to the nonoffending and offender members of the family so that appropriate behaviors are learned or relearned, and appropriate monitoring systems are in place. Offender treatment, whether court-mandated or voluntary, relies heavily on the offender taking responsibility for the sexual abuse, apologizing to the victim, and actively participating in both individual counseling and family therapy.

Providing immediate crisis support for victims and families, involving all members of the family system in the treatment (regardless of the particular theoretical framework), and providing opportunities for support groups and longer-term monitoring and follow-up are advocated for better treatment outcomes (Beutler, Williams, & Zetzer, 1994).

FOR THOSE ON THE LINE

Sexual abuse, like other types of abuse, is an expression of family dysfunction. Many therapists tell us these families present some special problems. Often it is a challenge to convince these families they need treatment, particularly when they cannot be compelled by law to attend counseling sessions. Sexually abusing families are reported as less cohesive, more disorganized, and frequently suffering from the compounded effects of substance abuse and isolation and lack of personal and social resources. All these problems can be draining to the professional who encounters them. As one clinician put it, "No one is immune from the outrage, righteousness, morbid curiosity, sexual arousal, resentment, hostility, despair, helplessness, omnipotent rescue fantasies and to countless other surges of conflicted feelings that the incest family elicits in the would-be helper." Like those who counsel families involved in other types of abuse, the clinician working with sexual abuse needs special support. We will return to this issue (helping the helper) when we deal with programmatic issues in our concluding chapter.

CHAPTER SEVEN

Child Maltreatment in Loco Parentis

Michael Nunno
Martha Holden
Brian Leidy

————

W hen child abuse and neglect received public attention in the 1960s, the discussion was focused on maltreatment within families. In the 1970s the concept was expanded to include institutions and society in general (Gil, 1975). Although families have the primary responsibility for the care and safety of children, in the normal course of children's lives almost all children spend time with and are cared for by others such as preschool, elementary, and high school teachers and, for a growing number of children, day-care providers. In other circumstances, when families cannot or will not properly care for their children, children will often be placed by the courts in foster homes, group homes, or residential facilities that are designed to meet a child's care, security, and developmental needs. The concept of *in loco parentis* is a legal term that means "in the place of the parents." It is a term that can apply to teachers, school personnel, day-care providers, foster parents, residential child-care workers, and others not in a familial or a parental role who have some state-sanctioned rights and responsibilities for children in their care. It does not apply to baby-sitters, scout masters, clergy, or family members as potential perpetrators.

In this chapter we will focus on the maltreatmentoof children by those adults who are in loco parentis with children in their care. This covers maltreatment within residential facilities that provide twenty-four-hour care to children, such as hospitals, shelters, detention facilities, centers for special needs children, and foster homes. We will also examine maltreatment within community-based organizations, such as elementary and high schools, preschools, family day care, and day-care facilities for the entire range of a community's children.

ABUSE IN LOCO PARENTIS: WHAT IS IT?

When an agency or an institution accepts the responsibility to provide for the care of children it is held to a higher standard than parents. The acceptable range of parental behaviors with children is wider than the range of behaviors of out-of-home care providers. For instance, parents can spank their children, take them to fast food restaurants three times a week, let their children sleep in the same bed, and send them to whatever schools parents choose. Out-of-home providers must adhere to the strict rules and regulations that govern these parental prerogatives. Maltreatment in out-of-home care includes acts of omission, commission, or permission perpetrated by the staff and/or the administration of schools, juvenile justice facilities, mental health hospitals and centers, and child welfare organizations that violate a child's rights to basic care, safety and growth.

Decisions determining culpability for child maltreatment in out-of-home care are often based on the foreseeability of the incident or the circumstance. For example, should the organization have predicted or foreseen that this child would harm himself and taken measures to prevent it? The responsibility for the incident or the circumstance often extends from the individual child-care worker to the administration and management of the facility and on to the placing agency. Therefore, an incident or an environment that created or contributed to an incident would be considered maltreatment if it (1) endangered or had the potential for endangering the protection, security, and/or safety of the child; (2) prevented the child from obtaining basic care and satisfying basic physical and emotional needs; (3) placed obstacles in the way of the child's development or severely restricted the developmental opportunities available to the child; or (4) prevented the child from participating in the special care and treatment that he or she needs for adequate developmental progress.

MALTREATMENT IN RESIDENTIAL CHILD-CARE FACILITIES

Although estimates can vary widely on the number of children living in out-of-home care, there is general agreement that the numbers have increased throughout the spectrum of child welfare, mental health, and juvenile justice facilities through the 1980s and early 1990s in North America. Lerman (1994) estimates that 1 to 1.4 million U.S. children under the age of eighteen, or between 1.5 and 2 percent of that population, lived in out-of-home care placements during 1987. Through the 1990s these figures have risen in the United States, with children placed in juvenile justice facilities leading the way. Children are placed for a combination of reasons: familial abuse, lack of appropriate alternative family resources, meager community services to meet a family's and a child's needs, or the community's judgment that such placement is necessary to protect itself from these children. Upon placement, the community assumes that the care and conditions within the facility meet or exceed state standards; yet child abuse reporting rates for out-of-home care are often double or triple the rates of familial maltreatment (Rindfleisch & Nunno, 1992).

When maltreatment is discovered in facilities designed for the care and protection of children, it is often met with public outcries for reform by child advocates, politicians, and concerned citizens. Maltreatment in child care facilities can take a variety of forms, ranging from violations of specific state regulations, such as denying a child a home visit or withholding food, to more heinous acts, such as prolonged isolation, physical injury, and involvement of staff and children in sexual activities (Brannan, Jones, & Murch, 1992; McGrath, 1985–1986; Nunno & Motz, 1988; Rosenthal, Motz, Edmonson, & Groze, 1991).

At the extreme end of the spectrum, some facilities develop institutional control procedures such as "beatdown"[1] (Seely & Craig, 1993) and "pindown"[2] (Levy & Kahan, 1991). The sole purpose of these activities is to subjugate a child's aggression with adult and peer counteraggression. These conditions and practices have called into question the effectiveness and safety of residential care (Miller, 1987; Schwartz, 1991; Thomas, 1990), and some have suggested that the most effective prevention strategy might be reducing the placement of children in out-of-home care facilities (Lerman, 1994). Yet, mental health and child welfare professionals see residential care as the last best hope for some children who are products of high-risk families living in high-risk neighborhoods and who need a controlled environment to break the cycle of violence and aggression in their lives (Goldstein & Glick, 1987).

The Residential Care Environment

Even under the best of circumstances, working conditions in residential facilities can be extremely difficult and stressful. Structural supports are essential if the facility is to provide quality care. The structural components consist of the facility's organizational culture, its human resources, its technology, and its treatment methodologies. These include the quality and quantity of staff, staff supervision, education levels, qualifications and appropriateness of staff, and services for the children in care (Donabedian, 1980).

Leadership and the Culture of the Facility

Sundrum (1984) suggests that institutional abuse is caused by an organizational culture enforced from the top that permits "self-sealing circles" that prevent detection and correction. Facility leadership is responsible for holding the children in high regard, opening communications, and setting clear expectations for staff behavior. The top administrative or executive officer of a facility sets the tone for the facility and accepts responsibility for the environmental factors, conditions, and actions of subordinates (Thomas, 1980). Further, in a survey by Dodge-Reyome (1990) of executive directors' perceptions of maltreatment within their facilities, directors identified administrative issues (such as the lack of clear policy and procedures on the interaction between caretaker and child) as one of the most important factors affecting maltreatment within their facilities.

System of Care

The lack of a well-integrated educational, psychosocial, and physical care system promotes maltreatment in residential facilities (Daly & Dowd, 1992). The adherence to a single treatment methodology and a lack of competence within the facility to deliver alternative methodologies is an identifier of a high-risk environment (Thomas, 1990). Lerman (1994) argues that maltreatment occurs when any child is in a placement not consistent with that child's developmental, health, and safety needs.

Supervision and Staffing Patterns

Lack of supervision of staff who care for large numbers of difficult children is associated with a higher incidence of child maltreatment (Spencer & Knudsen, 1992). Supervisors can mediate the stresses and pressures that child-care workers feel on the job, set clear expectations of how children in care should be treated, and be responsive to the needs of caregivers. The supervisor is also the linchpin between the workers and the administration and has a role in identifying environmental factors that may place children at risk (Blatt, 1990). Lack of close supervision of caregivers and the supervision of other residents is also a variable positively correlated in child-to-child sexual abuse and adult-to-child sexual abuse episodes (New York State Commission on Quality of Care, 1992; Rosenthal, Motz, Edmonson, & Groze, 1991).

Minimal supervision of children in care can result in higher rates of maltreatment among residents (Spencer & Knudsen, 1992). In a study of facilities for the mentally retarded, 57 percent of the reported incidents occurred while the children were engaged in free time or in activities of daily living such as eating, bathing, or dressing. The most vulnerable times for institutional child abuse and neglect allegations are when direct care staff are left alone, without planned activities (New York State Commission on Quality of Care, 1992).

The Caregivers

Direct line staff who have the most contact with children often have the least training and experience. Newly hired staff are quickly immersed in the work and directed to carry out the duties of full-time staff without adequate training, orientation, and supervision. This leaves new workers, who lack experience and training, unprepared to handle the difficult and explosive situations with the provocative youth they are likely to encounter (Powers, Mooney, & Nunno, 1990; Snow, 1994).

Rosenthal, Motz, Edmonson, & Groze (1991, p. 259) note that direct care staff "frequently lack skills in preventing crisis from occurring and in de-escalating crises without resorting to physical force." This lack of training in crisis management and other child-care skills is cited as a risk factor for maltreatment by a number of studies (Blatt, 1990; Daly & Dowd, 1992; Dodge-Reyome, 1990; New York State Commission on Quality of Care, 1992) and is the rationale for a variety of residential child care training programs (Budlong, Holden, & Mooney, 1993; Edens & Smit, 1992).

Status and Attitude

When staff seldom or never participate in the decisions of the facility, the use of force with children may increase (Rindfleisch & Baros-Van Hull, 1982; Rindfleisch & Foulk, 1992). Child-care workers who are powerless, in professional isolation, and told to do difficult jobs with little training or incomplete knowledge can make children the targets and outlets for this powerlessness (Blatt, 1990; Mercer, 1982; Sundrum, 1984). The more restrictive the facility the harsher the crisis and control methods utilized. Rindfleisch and Baros-Van Hull (1982) associate the level of a child-care worker's resentment toward children with an increased use of force. McGrath (1985–1986) connects the interaction between the alienated child-care worker and the new care worker to the depersonalization of children that results in maltreating behavior.

Job Stress

Studies cite the relationship between job stress and burnout behavior on the part of staff (Freudenberger, 1977; Mattingly, 1977; McClelland, 1986) with the corresponding influence on the interaction with and depersonalization of children (McGrath, 1985–1986). Garbarino, Guttman, and Seeley (1986) also cite job stress and burnout as critical factors associated with child maltreatment in facilities, while general life stress levels were high among populations of child-care workers involved in adverse events (Rindfleisch & Foulk, 1992).

Child Factors

Children who tend to be maltreated are a subset of youth who are placed because of mental retardation, emotional problems, substance abuse, and/or previous familial maltreatment, and they are likely to emerge from aggressive, hostile, or disorganized communities and families (Garbarino, Guttman, & Seeley, 1986; Lewis, Mallouh, & Webb, 1989). Youngsters who were subjects of institutional maltreatment reports were perceived as more difficult for facility staff to work with; that is, more likely to be assaultive, suicidal, violent and dangerous, and in greater need of one-on-one supervision in comparison to the other children in care (Blatt & Brown, 1985). They were also more likely to have run away from the facility, destroyed property, or set a fire. Rindfleisch and Foulk (1992) identified residents' characteristics such as mild or moderate disturbance and the relative isolation of a child from his or her family (more than 150 miles) to be predictors of adverse events between themselves and the adults in the facility.

MALTREATMENT IN SCHOOLS, PRESCHOOLS, AND DAY-CARE FACILITIES

As we look at the role of schools in child maltreatment, we have to be concerned with not only maltreatment as a result of acts of abuse but also with the ways schools perceive and fulfill their responsibility of providing for children's basic, developmental, and safety needs.

Are schools culpable as perpetrators of maltreatment? A large part of this issue revolves around the definition of maltreatment. Using the narrowest possible definition—intentional bodily harm that violates community standards—schools are rarely culpable as perpetrators. Using a broader definition—*abuse* being any violence or force used against children and *neglect* being any refusal to provide needed services—many schools are directly culpable for maltreatment.

In many countries, corporal punishment of school children continues to be an officially or unofficially sanctioned form of discipline. Continuing support for the use of corporal punishment is related to the following factors: (1) widely held beliefs regarding the effectiveness of corporal punishment; (2) lack of awareness of problems resulting from the use of physical punishment; and (3) a lack of knowledge about effective disciplinary alternatives (Dubanoski, Inaba, & Gerkewicz, 1983). The use of corporal punishment as a prerogative of school officials has been maintained by the U.S. Supreme Court, to the acclaim of many educators. Some states have limited its use by restricting when and how it may be used. At the same time, there is evidence that, until prodded (or even forced), many schools have refused to provide service to children and youth who are educationally handicapped, exhibiting antisocial behavior, or deviating from the normal in some other way. Using the broad rather than the narrow definition, schools are culpable for maltreatment.

By the same token, schools engage in various forms of psychological or emotional maltreatment. A teacher who ridicules and humiliates students when they give incorrect answers; a coach who taunts smaller, frailer children and encourages other children to hurt them; a teacher who use sarcasm and verbal put-downs, screams at children, or shows inconsistencies toward children may leave vulnerable children with self-doubts, lowered self-image, and negative perceptions of school.

Perhaps most disturbing of all developments in U.S. education is the apparently growing sense that schools are getting out of control. How do school professionals respond to difficult or special children? In many cases they resort to behavior that parallels the behavior of families: they respond with coercion or neglect, if not abuse, toward children who are socially, psychologically, and physically deviant. In this, schools are both victim and victimizer. In a society that demands at least minimal academic competence, we cannot afford to permit children to experience such institutional neglect.

CHILD DAY-CARE SETTINGS

Child day-care settings include center care, family day care, and child care provided in the child's own home by someone other than the primary caregiver. Unlike school, day care is not a universal experience. However, a significant number of children are cared for by someone other than their primary caregiver for part of the day. For this reason, the same questions raised about the school's role in child maltreatment need to be asked about child-care settings. Although children are more likely to arrive at the care setting having been abused than to be abused while in care, in recent years there has been greater concern about the potential for children to be abused by their caregivers. At the same time, research suggests that those who experience out-of-home abuse are no less traumatized than those who experience familial abuse (Browne & Finklehor, 1986; Ehrenshaft, 1992).

Margolin (1990) argues that caregivers who abuse do so because the child acts in a difficult, unresponsive, and unmanageable way that threatens the caregiver's self-image and control over other children. The caregiver's abusive behavior toward the child often has the parents' support. Parents permit the use of corporal punishment and overlook the child's complaints or fears of the caregiver. Children who are abused frequently have behavioral problems, so it may be that children who are abused by caregivers come to the care situation already having been abused by family members. Durkin (1982) suggests that the victims and perpetrators of abuse in child-care agencies are in many significant ways similar to the victims and perpetrators of intrafamilial abuse. In both cases the victims are difficult children requiring special care, while the abusers are often isolated individuals who lack a support system and are overworked, underpaid, and overstressed.

Another way to look at abuse in child-care settings is offered by Korbin (1991), who considers child maltreatment in cultural terms. She notes that abuse is less likely to occur in cultures that value children as economic resources, as carriers of family lines and cultural heritage, or as sources of emotional satisfaction. This same sense of valuing may or may not occur on an organizational basis between a child-care staff and a group of children or on an interpersonal basis between an individual caretaker and child. Caretakers may take license to treat children in an abusive manner because children are not seen as able to contribute in any important way.

Both paradigms for considering abuse in child-care settings—stress and isolation for the caregiver versus devaluation of the victim—can be seen in studies of differences between male and female perpetrators. Margolin (1991) examined the social context in which sexually abusive child-care providers came into contact with children and parents. She found that female perpetrators were generally teenagers hired to come into the home and provide care on a regular basis. Male perpetrators represented a wide range of ages and committed sexual abuse over a significantly broader range of situations than female caregivers. Abuse by females more typically occurs in isolated stressful situations, while abuse by males is more likely to involve devaluation of the victim.

Regardless of the reasons for abuse in child care settings, community reaction is often quite strong. Spencer & Knudsen (1992) found that children in day-care homes, day-care centers, and schools were less likely to be maltreated than those in foster homes, residential homes, or state institutions and hospitals. Although the likelihood of abuse is lower in child-care situations, public response tends to be distorted for various reasons. Bybee & Mowbrary (1993) found that certain aspects of child-care center sexual abuse complicate public response to allegations: (1) the victim witnesses are very young; (2) the number of victims and perpetrators may be large; (3) the abuse is likely to be serious, and the means of coercion extreme; and (4) the incident may involve extraordinary elements that are hard to believe, such as female perpetrators and pornography production.

Because of the way the public perceives abuse in child-care situations, it is especially important that day-care providers be proactive in preventing abuse and neglect within their programs. Atten & Milner (1987) found that workers in day care had the lowest potential for child abuse as clarity of job expectations and overall job satisfaction increased. Screening of employment applicants is also important. Haldopoulos & Copeland (1991) found that when infant child-care applicants were administered an open-ended screening interview that assessed past history, child-care knowledge, and individual personality dynamics, 10 percent were high risk for potential child abuse, even though all those who were screened saw themselves as good candidates for providing care.

Our society's legal and child welfare system holds agencies and institutions to a higher standard of child care than the standard held to families. The community assumes that these organizations will meet this standard, yet the reporting rates for abuse in facilities exceed the reporting rates for familial maltreatment.

Unfortunately, the children who are abused in child-care settings are often the same children who are abused within families. Familial maltreatment often results in children with more difficult, unmanageable behavior, which in turn leads to more stress for the caregiver and increases the likelihood that the cycle of abusive behavior will continue in the child's life. Maltreatment is also associated with a devaluation of children. When children are not seen as having significant worth or making an important contribution, caregivers may feel at greater liberty to exploit them. It is important for those in charge of child-care programs to minimize abuse and neglect by attending to the job and personal factors that lead to stress and a devaluation of the children in their care.

Even under the best of circumstances the provision of quality out-of-home care to meet a child's developmental needs and society's expectations can be extremely difficult and stressful. Children who emerge from aggressive, hostile, or disorganized communities, neighborhoods, and families (Garbarino, Dubrow, Kostelny, & Pardo, 1992) are higher risk for maltreatment in out-of-home settings. These children often exhibit difficult, unmanageable behaviors which lead to more stress for the caregiver. Working with children in these settings is a task that requires sophisticated organizational programming and activities and experienced and accomplished practitioners. Without adequate training and programming, caregivers are at risk for reinforcing violence with the violence that characterized the youth's family, neighborhood, and community life.

Notes

1. *Beatdown* is described as a process of staff encircling a youth in an isolated area of the facility and yelling at him, listing all the things that he had done wrong. After the list of wrongs is exhausted, a staff person begins to push the youth from one person to another. The pushing escalates to punching and kicking.
2. *Pindown* has four basic features: (1) isolation in a special unit; (2) removal of ordinary clothing and enforced wearing of shorts or night clothing; (3) earning privileges; and (4) allowing attendance in the facility school in ordinary clothing but returning to night clothes upon return to isolation.

PART THREE

Adolescent Maltreatment

CHAPTER EIGHT

The Maltreatment of Youth

James Garbarino
John Eckenrode
Jane Levine Powers

F or all its importance, the issue of abuse passing from generation to generation is not the only pertinent developmental consideration in looking at the maltreatment of youth. A more sophisticated developmental approach proceeds to investigate changes in the causes, correlates, and effects of mistreatment as development and maturation proceed. We began to see this earlier, when we looked at the role of the schools in child maltreatment. The issues for school-age children are somewhat different than those for infants or even for three-year-olds, for that matter. The infant can do virtually nothing to protect itself from abuse and is totally defenseless against neglect. The battered baby is victimized in direct proportion to the parent's impulses and the presence of outside constraints (which are typically few). The infant experiences neglect in exact proportion to the parent's failure to provide care, thus being liable to nonorganic failure to thrive. Additionally, the infant's capacity to signal its plight to others is limited and unconscious.

School-age children, on the other hand, have better resources. They can adapt to the parent to minimize abuse by assuming whatever role will mollify the parent: being extremely compliant, innocuous, or responsible. They can counteract neglect by fending for themselves to some degree. Their ability to communicate their plight is greater, as is their opportunity to do so, for example, in school. Finally, they are likely to have larger independent social networks from which to draw nurturance and support.

ADOLESCENCE IN THE LIFE COURSE OF MALTREATMENT

This kind of developmental perspective is still more important when we turn to a comparison of child maltreatment and adolescent abuse. In the latter case, there are myriad developmental grounds for anticipating differences in causation, correlates, effects, and effective intervention strategies. At its heart, the matter of being a parent to an adolescent (and adolescent to a parent) is substantially different from the parent-child relationship in several ways:

1.   The adolescent's cognitive abilities are likely to be much more advanced than are the child's. Adolescents reason much more like adults, and this injects a new element of complexity into the parent's task.

2.   The adolescent's power is much greater than the child's. This includes both physical power (implying the capability of effective physical retaliation if assaulted by a parent) and the power to stimulate and influence family conflict, to leave the family situation, to harm self and others, to embarrass the parent, and to compare the parent with other adults. Conversely, the adolescent also has the power to provide help to him/herself and others.

3.   The adolescent has a broader field of other significant individuals with whom the parents must come to terms. Autonomous relationships with other adults and with peers increase, including sexual relationships, which many parents perceive as volatile.

These factors (and many more) come together to shift the boundaries around appropriate behavior in family relationships. Some forms of parents' behavior that were appropriate (if not particularly wise) in childhood may become abusive in adolescence. For example, the psychological connotations of spanking a three- or four-year-old are quite different from those of spanking a fifteen-year-old. Efforts to exert a high level of control over every detail of a four-year-old's daily existence may be acceptable, while the same intrusiveness with a teenager would be entirely inappropriate. Likewise, some types of affectionate touching and other intimate physical contact may be quite appropriate between a father and his infant daughter but inappropriate between the same father and his teenage daughter.

In some ways, parents have more latitude in their dealings with young children than in their treatment of adolescents. The latter have a broader base of experience with which to compare the parent's actions. If abused, teenagers are more likely than young children to perceive the deviance of their treatment.

Adolescents have the cognitive equipment to better understand flaws in parental reasoning and moral character. They typically demand a more nearly equal role in family decision making. These factors, combined with differences in the way our culture views adolescents (with suspicion) and in our institutional treatment of them (with a mixture of compassion and toughness), predict that the phenomenon of adolescent abuse will differ markedly from child maltreatment, not merely in nature but also in means of identification and, ultimately, treatment.

Abuse has many roots. Families with adolescents experience pressure from inside and from without. Internally, the changes that midlife for the parent and puberty for the child bring to the parent-child relationship pressure the family to adapt. Externally, stresses such as financial pressures, geographic mobility, and youthful frustration at the lack of an acceptable outlet for their energy no doubt leave their mark. Any sort of family dysfunction is a cumulative result of some combination of external (environmental) stress and internal (interpersonal) vulnerability.

For long-term abusing families, the situation is obviously different than for families that abuse children for the first time in adolescence. If an inability to accommodate to the changes of puberty is the catalyst for abuse that begins in adolescence, it must certainly exacerbate long-term child abuse. In our view, adolescent abuse is rooted in both our culture's inadequate provision for adolescence and in the inadequacies of individual families. The two feed upon each other, and no complete understanding of adolescent abuse can neglect either part of the problem. While the inadequacies of parents are easily recognized, society's deficiencies are often harder to see. The developmental agendas that individual family members pursue independently can complicate their own lives and those of people around them. We now examine the issues surrounding the development of adolescents and their parents and the culture that affects them both. This will help us understand how some parents come to mistreat their teenagers; how circumstances victimize parents, who in turn victimize their offspring. To understand the mistreatment of youth we must understand the human ecology of adolescence.

HUMAN ECOLOGY OF ADOLESCENCE

Most of us have mixed feelings about our own adolescence. We probably remember it as better and worse than it really was. More than any other period in life, the adolescent years have been alternately romanticized and feared. We hear that children today are disrespectful, idealistic, irresponsible, generous, or dangerous, depending upon the motives of the speaker. This ambivalence and confusion is not new.

Historically, adolescents have always been held in low regard. In the 1800s, young men were described as giddy, romantic, and harebrained. Youth was thought of as not merely the opposite of old age but as a period of prolonged immaturity and lamentable irresponsibility (Hawes, 1828). The ancient Greeks could have written the pop classic, "What's the matter with kids today?" G. Stanley Hall, one of the first psychologists to consider adolescence as a scientific issue, described it as a period when the individual reenacts humanity's passage from savagery to civilization. In his view, any attempt to end adolescence prematurely by imposing adult values and rules was doomed to failure, because it would only lead to the expression of savage propensities in adulthood. As we shall see, society's view of adolescence today has not moved very far from Hall's depiction. Erik Erikson defined adolescence as "a period of rapid change: physical, psychological, physiological, and social; a time when all sameness and continuities relied upon earlier are more or less questioned again." (Erikson, 1963, p. 26).

Many definitions of adolescence emphasize the issues of change and autonomy, and it is these two issues that have the greatest effect upon the way teenagers interact with their parents and siblings. Adolescence is also a time when one learns adult roles, and that process requires some testing that may also affect life at home. All these learning processes take place in adolescents who are undergoing the fundamental biological, intellectual, and social changes that define this stage of life. While a complete review of our knowledge about adolescent development is beyond the scope of this book, we will point out some aspects of the physical, social, and psychological changes of puberty that put the phenomenon of maltreatment in context.

Physical and Sexual Development

The biological start of adolescence is the growth spurt that signals the beginning of puberty and is followed by the maturation of the sexual organs (ovaries in girls; testicles and penis in boys) and later by secondary sex characteristics (facial hair and lowering of the voice in boys; breast development and broadening of the pelvis in girls; and the appearance of pigmented pubic and auxiliary hair in both sexes). All this growth is stimulated and accompanied by hormonal changes that may precipitate mood swings. These biological changes are really less important for our purposes than are their social implications, because the social factors have a greater influence upon family dynamics. There is a great deal of variability in the timing of the growth spurt and sexual maturation. The sexes differ, as do the individuals within them. Boys may begin their growth spurt as early as ten-and-a-half or as late as sixteen years old. Girls may begin their growth spurt as early as eight and as late as eleven-and-a-half. (Historically, the age when puberty begins has become ever younger, though the trend seems to have leveled off. For service professionals, this has meant an ever-younger clientele.) The typical adolescent tends to be self-conscious about these changes, especially when he or she develops early or late. It seems that early-maturing girls and late-maturing boys have more psychosocial problems later in life than their friends who developed along with the majority (Weatherly, 1963). Menarche (the onset of menstruation) for girls and nocturnal emissions for boys are tangible proof that one is growing up. And depending on the context in which they occur, these sure signs of maturation can themselves generate either apprehension or pride both in teenagers and their parents. Parental reaction is thought to be one of the primary determinants of the psychological impact of menarche (Konopka, 1966). Parents are often surprised by and uncomfortable with the emerging sexuality of their offspring, perhaps because they fear that sexuality can become a vehicle by which the adolescent challenges adult authority and power.

In our society, authority and sexuality are both withheld from youth until they "pay their dues"; that is, until they accept the cultural ground rules for sexuality. Some teenagers no doubt see sex as a way to separate from the adult world as represented by their parents or to define themselves as distinct, powerful individuals. Sexual experience is now often equated with general life experience by adolescents themselves (Blos, 1979). Needless to say, the issues surrounding sexuality—including curfews, dating activities, and choice of friends—are a powerful force in the lives of teenagers and adults. Unseen and therefore difficult to dictate, adolescent sexual behavior can inflame families that seek, with variable success, to exert a high level of control over the teenager's social life. Parents are left to trust their teenager to uphold their wishes, to abdicate choice to the youth, or to quarantine her or him from social contact. Whenever values as sacred as chastity, trust, and independence are involved, emotions run high, and the time is ripe for abuse.

Intellectual Development

If sexual maturation and the growth spurt are the primary factors in physical development, the emerging ability to think abstractly is the salient aspect of intellectual development. With adolescence comes a significantly increased ability to deal with hypothetical problems, mathematics, philosophy, and ethics. Adolescents are also able to think abstractly about their own behavior, their families, their schools, and about society in general. Unlike children, teenagers can ponder alternative points of view and can independently evaluate the motives of others. This means that they are better able to discuss family problems and that they can have a much more objective view of their parents' motivation than ever before.

While educators welcome increased cognitive capabilities because they permit more sophisticated academic work in the classroom, parents quickly realize that these new intellectual tools can also be turned toward social and interpersonal matters. Most teenagers change their focus, becoming more introspective and analytical than their former childhood selves. They are typically preoccupied with defining their own individual identities and with reconciling the enormous physical changes they are undergoing with their social experiences. Their thoughts may shift from the real to the possible, absorbing them in the pleasure of thinking for thinking's sake. Psychologist Paul Osterrieth (1969) notes that while these intellectual developments open new vistas for the youngster, they, like all opportunities, contain the seeds of trouble and conflict as well as those of harmony and improved relationships. Finally, since they can take alternative points of view, adolescents for the first time have the ability and the inclination to take the side of the underdog. This new ability causes teenagers to side with victims of oppression, and they may even include themselves in this group.

Although teenagers may use myriad techniques for gaining power within their families, they remain largely powerless politically, economically, and socially. In our society, adolescents are generally outsiders, and if their views reflect that position they may encounter grave differences with their parents, especially with parents who are well established in the society's economic and social life. Heated discussion of social and political issues has never been known for its soothing effect. Realistically, however, most intrafamily disputes do not evolve from such ethereal realms. As we shall see, the routines of daily life generate much more conflict than does ideology.

Expanded cognitive abilities and the exploration these abilities encourage have some important implications for the way teenagers act. As self-assured adults, we tend to approach new situations with some degree of confidence and also with caution, usually knowing that, based upon our past experiences, our behavior will probably be acceptable. Adolescents need reassurance and may therefore try to imitate the behavior of competent people they know. Their behavior may try parental patience, as parents at times face living replicas of pop singers, screen idols, sports figures, and other heroes and heroines. Although this identity sampling no doubt accounts for much of the perceived erratic behavior of adolescents, it seems to be a necessary step toward developing a stable sense of self and generally does not threaten an underlying affiliation with parents and their basic values in most families.

Social Development

Partly as a result of their need to separate from their parents, adolescents appear to be preoccupied with their peers. Peers become the primary influence on many daily activities and may compete with parents. Because peer influences are likely to be strong over highly visible aspects of lifestyle, it is easy to overemphasize their long-term significance. The dichotomy between parental values and peer demands may be exaggerated (Hill, 1980). However, teenagers who enter the world of their peers, perhaps unconsciously swearing allegiance to a new set of values (particularly if they seek to dramatize peer affiliations), see adults realistically as outsiders whose authority is to be mistrusted. In the modern world of the United States, teenagers lead much of their day-to-day lives segregated from other age groups in high schools that are a sort of youth ghetto (Bronfenbrenner, 1970). They have created their own distinct subculture in many ways. The values and norms of this youth subculture, divergent from the adult world and uniform unto itself, constitute the context in which teenagers practice interpersonal relationships with friends, dates, and acquaintances. The personal egocentrism we noted in individual adolescent mental development extends to absorption with other teenagers. Few adults penetrate this world and feel comfortably accepted in it. Those who do can be a bridge between youth and adults and may serve as a vital link between adolescent victims and services, because abuse victims are likely to have few people to whom they may turn. These youth also tend to be wary of reaching out to anyone for help.

Developmental Tasks

Many of the internal changes that teenagers undergo have a direct effect upon their attitudes about the world in general and their families in particular. The tasks that adolescents must accomplish in order to mature are not always pleasant to experience or even to observe. One important task is that of separating from one's parents. It is a normal process; indeed, we worry more when it does not occur. To accomplish the task of separating from one's parents, teenagers must believe that their parents are not the perfect people they had imagined them to be, after all (Offer & Offer, 1974). For children, idealization of the parent is reassuring because it makes them feel safer and more secure.

At adolescence, it is time to leave this security behind in favor of establishing an independent identity. Some teenagers, especially those most dependent upon their parents, need to work harder to make the separation (Steirlin, 1974). They need to launch out further and with more force than other adolescents. A dependent youth may be angered by his or her own feelings of dependency as he or she seeks to make the separation, and this anger may be directed back at the very parents to whom the teenager feels so strongly attached. To separate, the teenager may feel the need not only to take his or her parents off their pedestals but to go further, to the point of denigrating the powerful authority figures who have always controlled his or her life. This pattern may be a common one for U.S. youth, who often seem to have extreme ambivalence about dependency once they reach adolescence (Kandel & Lesser, 1972). This normal adolescent task (individualization) is probably made more difficult by our culture's obsession with independence and our unresolved feelings about dependency (Rotenberg, 1977). Compounding the task is adolescent dogmatism. Perhaps this is partly the result of the role model experimentation we spoke of earlier. Osterreith (1969) describes the process by which adolescents defer their opinions with a melodramatic flare that indicates their need to assert their own identity as much as it reflects a genuine difference of opinion.

It could also be that since the adolescent is examining so many new concepts for the first time, she or he is likely to have little capacity for entertaining alternative points of view. In any event, teenagers do seem to have a surprising capacity for fervent adherence to simplistic ideologies and beliefs. In the home setting this can mean, for example, that parents who are average individuals and who were once exalted are suddenly denounced as weak hypocrites. And, naturally, dogmatism can make the job of providing services to adolescents more difficult. Beyond that, the whole setting of adolescence is one of ever-widening unfamiliar circles to be tested. These new situations are threatening, albeit alluring. Adolescents tend to retreat sporadically to the security of the home, even though they might be quite independent at other times. This swinging from independence to dependence and back again can frustrate parents who misinterpret it as simply wanting to have one's cake and to eat it too (which may be true in some cases, because the existence of a legitimate need does not preclude the use of that need for manipulative purposes).

Furthermore, U.S. families may be particularly prone to trouble with independence. In this country, most parents ascribe to a strong belief in early autonomy, yet they don't socialize their children accordingly. This practice makes for a prolonged period of dependency (Kandel & Lesser, 1972). Parents who view the situation from their own perspective without considering their teenager's needs may begin to feel that they are being used. Empathy, putting one's self in the place of another, is a primary skill for being an effective parent, particularly when one's offspring reaches adolescence (Jurich, 1979). Without it, many daily crises that adolescents experience must seem trivial and annoying. And in a society where there is little support for parents, empathy may become still more important. If parents take too much responsibility for a youngster's dress and appearance, their feelings of success or failure may depend upon the ability to control the preferences of their youngsters.

This need to control may stem from the parent's own lack of confidence about authority and can also lead to inconsistency and the use of developmentally inappropriate forms of control. Moreover, a parent's unthinking threat to control private behavior can bring out the righteous, dogmatic indignation of a teenager intent upon protecting his or her privacy. This vicious cycle can occur when a parent has not given out responsibility gradually, as the child learns to use it. This can cause problems in adolescence. Because adolescence usually brings independent mobility, it is simply impractical for parents to monitor their teenager's actions away from home. Thus overcontrolling parents may end up relying upon emotion-charged interrogations in the absence of firsthand data, because parents have no mechanism at this point for observing many of their children's behaviors. Such scenes can easily lead to abuse. Indeed, one study found that most adolescent-abuse cases involved mild to severe "acting out" behavior of the adolescent as an antecedent to physically abusive incidents (Libbey & Bybee, 1979).

CHILD VERSUS ADOLESCENT MALTREATMENT

Although the problem of child maltreatment has become an extremely high-profile social issue in the United States today, the main focus of the concern and public outcry has been on young children, not on adolescents. Prevailing belief has it that adolescent maltreatment is less serious, less pervasive, and less damaging than maltreatment involving younger children. Few researchers have focused on understanding the unique causes and consequences of adolescent maltreatment. Perceptions of child versus adolescent victims influence the recognition and treatment of this problem (Garbarino, Schellenbach, Sebes, & Associates, 1986; Fisher, Berdie, Cook, Redford-Barker, & Day, 1979). On a basic level, young children evoke sympathy; teenagers do not. Understandably, most adults see children as far more vulnerable to maltreatment and in greater need of help and protection than adolescents. To be a child connotes defenselessness and inability to self-protect or seek help because of limited access to adults outside of the immediate family. Children are innocent of any wrongdoing and are not to be blamed. Adolescents, on the other hand, do not evoke images of innocent victimization. Not only can they take care of themselves, run away, and seek help but their greater size and enhanced cognitive and physical abilities mean that they can protect themselves or avoid abusive situations (Gelles & Cornell, 1990). Negative stereotypes of teenagers as provocative, difficult to handle, and unruly contribute to the perception that they are responsible for and deserving of the maltreatment they receive. The fact that some adolescents respond to parental abuse with mutual assault further contributes to the perception that they deserve the maltreatment (see for example, Kratcoski, 1985). It is easy to sympathize with parents who can't cope with their teenagers, and it may be easier for society to view adolescents as perpetrators rather than as victims.

Public and professional bias leads to an assumption that adolescents are responsible for their own abuse and get what they deserve. This may lead adults to overlook signs of abuse and forego reporting when they do see it. At a deeper level, unconscious forces may lead adults to defend against their own experiences of adolescent maltreatment in a self-protective fashion (Miller, 1984). This also may contribute to the lack of interest from child welfare agencies in dealing with abused adolescents (Fisher, Berdie, Cook, Redford-Barker, & Day, 1979).

The lack of attention to adolescent maltreatment is particularly disconcerting given its association with developmental risk and damaging consequences that have been documented in existing research. The range of health risk behaviors and serious social problems among maltreated youth is staggering: premature pregnancy and parenthood, depression, suicidal ideation and behavior, chronic anxiety, confused sexual identity, substance abuse, adjustment and acting out problems, academic difficulties, and delinquency (Browne & Finkelhor, 1986; Polit, White, & Morton, 1990; Berenson, San Miguel, & Wilkinson, 1992; Gardner & Cabral, 1990; Farber & Joseph, 1985; Lewis, 1992).

The ramifications for society are also disturbing. A growing body of research indicates that youth who have been abused (as children or as teenagers) are more likely to be future perpetrators of family violence (Straus, Gelles, & Steinmetz, 1980; Wiehe, 1990; Kratcoski, 1985; Corder, 1976; Widom, 1989). Further, links have been found between maltreatment and subsequent criminal behavior (Widom, 1989). A high prevalence of abuse has been found among youth in the juvenile justice system (Straus, 1988). Family backgrounds of severe abuse have been found among adolescents who are runaways or homeless (Burgess, Janus, McCormack, & Wood, 1986), prostitutes (Seng, 1989), or have AIDS (Zierler, Feingold, Laufer, Velentgas, Kantrowitz-Gordon, & Mayer, 1991). The long-term consequences for a healthy adulthood are also at stake: adolescent maltreatment may significantly interfere with the negotiation of key developmental tasks and predispose an individual to develop mental health disorders in later life (see Cicchetti, Toth, & Bush, 1988; Wolfe, 1987; and Wyatt & Powell, 1988, for reviews).

Scope of the Problem

Research evidence suggests that adolescent maltreatment is no less serious, pervasive, or damaging than the maltreatment of children. Several national surveys have found that at least one-fourth of the officially reported cases to child protective service agencies involved youth between the ages of twelve and seventeen (National Committee on the Prevention of Child Abuse, 1996; U.S. Department of Health and Human Services [USDHHS], 1996; American Humane Association, 1988). Data from the National Child Abuse and Neglect Data System (NCANDS) (see Chapter Two for a description) also show that age trends in official reports of maltreatment vary by type of maltreatment. Although only 16.7 percent of neglect cases nationwide involved youth between the ages of twelve and seventeen, 33.4 percent of physical abuse cases, 36.4 percent of sexual abuse cases, and 32.8 percent of emotional maltreatment cases involved adolescents. Smaller statewide investigations report even higher percentages of adolescents in official reports of child maltreatment. In Minnesota, Blum and Runyan (1980) found that 42.3 percent of all confirmed cases of child maltreatment involved adolescent victims. In a representative sample of official reports of maltreatment drawn from New York State, Powers and Eckenrode (1988) found that adolescents represented over one-third of all victims of child maltreatment.

Data from the second National Incidence Studies of Child Abuse and Neglect (NIS), previously described in Chapter Two, indicate that adolescents constitute a substantial proportion of all the maltreatment cases known to professionals, approximately 44 percent. The rates of maltreatment (number of maltreatment victims per 1,000 children) were also higher for adolescents than for younger children: adolescents experienced maltreatment at a rate of 28.5 per 1,000 children, as opposed to younger children, whose rate was 19.4 per 1,000. This pattern of higher rates of maltreatment for adolescents held across all types of maltreatment.

Recently released results from the third National Incidence Study (NIS), reporting the maltreatment statistics for 1993, suggest some changes in these age trends in the seven years since the second NIS. The rates of adolescent maltreatment has shown a modest increase over time, especially for younger adolescents (ages twelve to fourteen). Maltreatment rates increased at an even greater rate for younger children, however, resulting in rates of maltreatment for children and adolescents that are more similar than observed in the second NIS. Further analyses of the NIS data will be needed to explain these changes.

Case Characteristics

National data indicate that while young children and adolescents who suffer maltreatment are predominantly from low-income families, adolescents are more often from families with average incomes. Olsen and Holmes (1986), in analyses of the first NIS data collected in 1980, report that while only 11 percent of maltreated children under age twelve were from families with incomes over $15,000, 26 percent of youth ages twelve to fourteen and 39 percent of youth ages fifteen to seventeen were in the higher-income families. Only one in six families with a maltreated adolescent were receiving public assistance, while one in three families of maltreated children under twelve years of age were receiving aid. Additionally, these data indicate that parental unemployment is less common for adolescent than child cases, and the portion of mothers and fathers graduating from high school was higher among adolescent cases. In sum, the socioeconomic measures suggest that adolescent-maltreatment cases are drawn more evenly from the general population, while child-abuse cases are drawn primarily from families of lower socioeconomic status. Since parents of adolescents are generally older than parents of young children, the age difference can partly account for any differences of income and education favoring the older group and for all else that greater age implies for income and education.

Data from the National Incidence Studies also make it clear that the victims of adolescent maltreatment tend to be females. Olsen and Holmes (1986) report that in the first NIS, while 46 percent of maltreated children under age twelve were female, 60 percent of the twelve- to fourteen-year-olds were female, and 65 percent of maltreated adolescents fifteen to seventeen years old were female. Our own analyses on the second NIS (1986 national data) show that while this effect is partly due to the fact that nearly three-fourths of adolescent sexual abuse victims are female, females outnumbered males in every other category of maltreatment also. The largest age difference involved physical abuse, where 65 percent of adolescent cases involved females, whereas only 45 percent of cases involving children under twelve involved females.

In many respects, then, adolescent cases of abuse do appear to differ from cases involving young children. In general, the adolescent cases seem more representative of the general population in terms of socioeconomic factors, while the child cases are more concentrated among high-risk groups—single parents and the poor. This suggests a hypothesis for us to pursue in subsequent discussions of the sociology of adolescent abuse; namely, that families with young children are more likely to be victims of socioeconomic and demographic stresses, and that the day-to-day care of a young child is more heavily dependent on the material circumstances of life than is caring for an adolescent. Put another way, adolescent abuse may well be a more interpersonal problem than is child abuse, which is more closely tied to the quality of socioeconomic and demographic life. This is the principal developmental hypothesis generated by our review of the national data on reported cases. We also must be sensitive to the fact that girls may be more at risk for many types of maltreatment in adolescence than boys, a phenomenon that may be tied to their increased vulnerability to certain types of maltreatment (for example, sexual abuse), their roles in the family, and the options for coping with dysfunctional family relationships.

With these data as a starting point, we are in a position to move forward with our analysis, confident of our developmental hunch concerning maltreatment: namely, that the issues in the behavioral equations relating parent to child and family to environment shift as a function of age. What is more, we now have some leads to pursue: the hypotheses that adolescent abuse is less tied to material impoverishment than child maltreatment; that it touches a wider range of social contexts; that it is more psychological and less physical; that it is more likely to involve complex negotiations among parent, victim, and society over placement.

I skipped out of school a day and my dad found out and he really gave it to me with his razor strap. I had bruises all over my legs. So that Friday I just ran away.

They hit me with a meat cleaver. I was broiling hamburgers one night and I burned them and my mom grabbed the knife and she cut me. They don't do it all the time, only when they're mad. I've gotten a lot of bruises and strap marks since I was a little kid. I never left because I deserved every one of them.

One of these teenagers left home when she was first abused. The other tolerated years of severe mistreatment. Their stories illustrate one of the major points of this chapter: that the experience of abuse differs from individual to individual and may have quite different effects when it begins in adolescence as opposed to childhood. An adolescent who suffered abuse starting in early childhood lives in different circumstances than someone who is abused for the first time as a teenager. Earlier, we contrasted adolescent with child abuse. Here we further examine different types of adolescent abuse. These types are defined upon the basis of the child's age when abuse began.

FOUR ABUSIVE PATTERNS

Based on a limited research base, we identify four patterns of adolescent abuse.

Pattern One: Abuse Begins in Adolescence

Presumably, this type of abuse occurs because the level of conflict rises until it reaches dangerous proportions, primarily over issues unique to adolescence itself, or perhaps adolescence injects some new element into the situation. Some investigators believe this pattern is most common in families in which children have been indulged by their parents. This indulgent pattern causes parents to expect excessive dependency and compliance from their offspring, and that expectation in turn elicits frustration, resistance, and anger in adolescents as they begin to mature and resent their infantilized state. The behavior that characterizes a dependent teenager striving for autonomy is precisely the behavior that will enrage an indulgent parent (Steirlin, 1974). There are many other reasons that adolescence can spark conflict in a family, including the synergistic effect of parents' and teenagers' developmental states, a characteristic economic squeeze during the children's adolescence, and the ambiguities of adolescent privileges in society. In our own research (Garbarino & Gilliam, 1980) we conducted a small-scale study and found that about half of the reported cases of abused teenagers had no prior childhood history of abuse. Other researchers have reported a higher proportion of such cases: Lourie (1977) reports that 90 percent of seventy clinical cases involved adolescent onset; Libbey and Bybee's (1979) small study of twenty-five adolescent abuse cases revealed that 80 percent of them began in adolescence; a study of thirty-three adolescent abuse cases by Pelcovitz, Kaplan, Samit, Krieger, & Cornelius (1984) reports 57 percent had adolescent onset. Other studies (Berdie, Berdie, Wexler, & Fisher, 1983) show smaller percentages. Although the precise number is not yet known from these small-scale studies, we are confident that a distinct phenomenon of adolescent-onset abuse exists.

Pattern Two: Abuse Has Coincidental Link to Adolescence

Here abuse simply continues mistreatment begun in childhood. The mistreatment is nothing new to the family and has nothing in particular to do with the victim's age or developmental stage. One may wonder how it is possible for abuse to continue throughout childhood into adolescence without outside intervention, but, unfortunately, it happens quite a bit in the real world. Often abuse is not discovered during childhood, and, even if discovered, it may continue. Success rates among abusive families that receive treatment typically are between 40 and 60 percent. Particularly when the problem does not reach life-threatening proportions, chronic abuse may continue unabated as long as the child remains in the home. We hope this pattern will be a declining residual category that will continue to shrink as early identification and treatment become more widespread and effective. But in our small study this pattern accounted for 40 percent of the cases.

Pattern Three: Mild or Moderate Corporal Punishment Becomes Abuse

It is hard to distinguish this pattern from Pattern One; indeed it is perhaps better conceived of as a subvariety of it, since only at adolescence does corporal punishment, a practice widespread throughout the childhood population, become statistically deviant. The youth who was slapped or spanked as a child may be beaten or otherwise abused as an adolescent.

This pattern may characterize restrictive or rigid parents who find themselves losing control as the child's strength, size, confidence, and independence increase (Williamson, Borduin, & Howe, 1991). As a result, the parents feel more force is necessary to punish and control. It may also represent an escalation of conflict, whereby early inept discipline practices by the parent lead to increasingly hostile reactions by the child, resulting in a cycle of violence that gets more severe over time (Patterson, 1986). This escalation of force may reflect a last-ditch effort to save the family from the real or imagined disgrace that a disobedient son or daughter could bring. Authoritarian methods of childrearing keep youngsters from internalizing values and self-control. This lack of internal control shows up as a propensity for irresponsible behavior and may lead parents to feel they must use more force. (The thought that "he's now too big to spank" can mean a shift to more psychological discipline or to an escalation of force.)

These confrontations can be brutal and may involve reciprocal assault. This pattern accounted for a small percentage of the reported adolescent abuse in our own study, but since it is difficult to document retrospectively, it may well be more common than these data indicate. Indeed, given the prevalence of low-level violence against children, it may actually represent a finding contrived by the measures used. No doubt most of the abused youth in Pattern One also were disciplined with corporal punishment as children.

Pattern Four: Abuse Represents a Return to Earlier Behaviors

Many investigators comment on the parallel between adolescence and the "terrible twos," and several studies of abuse noted that these two periods are times of heightened risk. In both these stages of the life cycle, parents and children are often at odds over expectations, dependency, autonomy, and social control. Parents who have difficulty with these issues when their offspring are toddlers may experience the same difficulties, perhaps in a more intense fashion, when the child reaches adolescence. The issues are the same: autonomy and independence. About 5 percent of the reported cases fit this pattern in our study.

Conceptually, this pattern falls somewhere between the two major types of adolescent abuse.

Two Contrasting Sets of Circumstances

We will look closely only at Patterns One and Two: abuse that begins in adolescence and abuse that continues a pattern begun in childhood. These two categories account for most of the cases, and, as we have shown, they may easily subsume the other two categories. Our research (see Garbarino & Gilliam, 1980) suggests that families from the two major groups differ on nearly every gross measure of home life. In other words, it looks like very different things are happening in these families, and for very different reasons. In general, we found that families that became abusive for the first time during their off-spring's adolescence appear to be more settled and stable than are those who have been at it for years.

In fact, parents who started abusing their children when they were young appeared similar to the classic multiproblem child-abusing family who is characterized by unmanageable life stress and inadequate coping resources. This is no surprise, since they were probably the very same families who continued to be abusive into the child's adolescence. We found that parents of teenagers who abused their children for the first time at adolescence were much more likely to be married than were long-term abusers. They were also much less transient than long-term abusers. We also found that when social agencies helped families involved with short-term abuse, predominantly both victim-oriented counseling and mental health–related services were provided, in contrast to the predominance of life-management services provided to long-term abuse families.

This complements the finding that emotional abuse is cited three times more often among first-time abuse cases than in long-term cases. Parents in long-term cases had lower incomes (less than half that of the parents who did not mistreat their youngster until adolescence). Parents who abused their teenagers as children were also somewhat more likely to themselves have been victims of abuse as children or to have a history of spouse abuse.

While mothers were more likely than fathers to abuse young children, that trend reversed itself for adolescents, where fathers were more often reported as perpetrators, in part, it would seem, because of the level of sexual abuse. Mothers who abused their young children were more likely to be single, poor, transient, and unemployed. Among those who were married, it is possible that sex roles may have dictated that they alone would be charged with caring for the child (Gil, 1970). Mothers were the ones who lashed out when caught in the squeeze between their deficient social skills and their children's imperfect behavior (Gray, 1978). Fathers (including stepfathers) play a larger role in rearing adolescents and thus a larger role in abusing them.

The fact that fathers are more likely to abuse their teenagers points to the different issues that adolescence itself brings to the picture. Normal teenage developmental changes such as striving for independence, sexual maturation, and the ability to think abstractly require adjustments by parents and can create substantial conflict (Hill, 1980). In normal families, both mothers and fathers may alter their behavior in response to the teenager's challenge (Steinberg, 1977). Traditional paternal dominance dictates that the father's role include asserting authority over the children. This puts him at the apex of potential abuse (Straus, 1980). In most families, fathers are also more likely than mothers to let their own needs dominate their responses. Thus a father is more likely to try to physically or verbally control a teenager's behavior in this period of normal change than is the mother. Some fathers use methods that are inappropriate and damaging.

Much of the profile we have drawn is an elaborate way of describing the differential patterns and types of abuse as class phenomena. The marital instability, transience, and unemployment we have described in long-term abuse families are all problems associated with poverty. Poor people are greatly overrepresented among the abusers of young children.

We do not know how much of this is due to differential patterns of reporting as opposed to the stresses that poverty brings. Previous research suggests that any class bias in reporting is neither so large nor so simple as conventional wisdom suggests (Garbarino & Crouter, 1978a; Garbarino & Kostelny, 1992). Leroy Pelton has gone so far as to refer to the "myth of classlessness" in child abuse, as a way of countering the suggestion that class differences in reported cases are invalid (Pelton, 1978). He argues that the reported differences reflect actual differences. The class difference makes sense when one considers the act of hitting an infant compared with hitting an adolescent. Assuming that infants are less capable of deliberately angering their parents, child abuse is mainly a result of the other environmental factors, especially stresses, surrounding the parent. Poverty limits the healthy venting of frustration in almost every conceivable way, from the amount of square footage each person is allowed to the ability to pay for diversion and baby-sitting to the lack of residential stability.

Outside its tangible limitations, poverty has another pernicious effect: many poor people begin to internalize the values and opinions that the dominant society holds about them. If they feel that they are to blame for their underprivileged condition, the loss of self-esteem they experience can be crippling. Low self-esteem can trigger aggression if a person terrorizes others as a self-validation of potency. Once abuse has occurred, the parent loses further esteem by confirming his or her failure in the parental role. Previous chapters dealt with the social origins of child and adolescent maltreatment. Those origins are painfully clear. However, there are many factors that influence the quality of life that have nothing to do with social class. Abuse beginning in adolescence does not appear to have any particular link to poverty. Rather, it is spread across the community.

The differences in the class backgrounds of the two categories of adolescent abuse have important implications for service professionals. Those who work with youth are likely to notice striking differences between adolescents from the two groups, particularly once workers are made aware of these differences. In general, the later abuse began, the more whole the victim will be. One reason is the amount of development that was permitted without disruption. Another is the likelihood that the short-term abuse victim will come from a less impoverished environment, an environment that does not itself retard development.

We will discuss service implications later. Based upon this class difference, it appears that the remedies for child abuse are in many respects simpler to identify but harder to implement than those for adolescent abuse. The most obvious primary remedy to child abuse is to ensure that the basic economic structures of life are equitable, that the gap between rich and poor is as small as possible. Currently in the United States this gap is large and growing. For example, whereas in Canada the top 10 percent have four times the income of the bottom 10 percent, for the United States the figure is six times (for Sweden it is about two times). Meeting the goal of reducing the income gap would require nothing less than a major redistribution of wealth. In contrast, victimization of adolescents is a more complex phenomenon than child abuse, harder to understand but, paradoxically perhaps, simpler to solve. The capabilities of adolescents themselves form the basis for approaching the problem through relatively inexpensive services, some of which address the family, others that exclude it in favor of the youth. The resources necessary for such services are minuscule when compared with those required to totally remedy child abuse.

This is not to pit the needs of one age group against another. Indeed, it is unchecked child abuse that accounts for half the problem in adolescence. Child abuse has been recognized much longer than has adolescent abuse. Both are significant problems. It is true for adolescent abuse, much more than for child abuse, that awareness goes a long way toward resolution of the problem.

CHAPTER NINE

Youth in Trouble Are Youth Who Have Been Hurt

John Eckenrode
Jane Levine Powers
James Garbarino

> They wouldn't have beat me if I didn't deserve it. They just wouldn't have done it.
>
> *—Marcia, age fifteen*

Children come into this world without any frame of reference. They have no inherent scale upon which to judge their worth; they must ascertain their value from the messages they receive. Parents largely determine the ratings that children give themselves, at least until they enter school and begin to reevaluate themselves based upon the feedback they receive there. It is no wonder that youth whose parents show signs of emotional pathology have trouble making value judgments, especially when it comes to assessing their own personal worth (Tucker, 1976). Considering the impact that parents have upon the lives of their children, it is also not surprising that maltreatment can have devastating consequences that may show up years later in the form of self-destructive and antisocial behavior: when a vulnerable youth suffers maltreatment, the result can be physical damage, low self-esteem, anxiety, lack of empathy, poor social relationships, drug or alcohol abuse, suicide, delinquency, or homicide.

PATTERNS OF EFFECTS

In Chapter Eight we organized our thoughts around two groups of mistreated teenagers: those for whom maltreatment began in adolescence and those who are child maltreatment victims grown to adolescence. As we discuss the effects of maltreatment, it is logical to assume that abuse may affect these two groups differently. While the base of evidence is growing, we still know relatively little about the developmental course of maltreatment. Except for what we can infer from general studies of troubled youth, we do not really know a great deal about the educational or career success of former abuse and neglect victims or even their marital or social adjustment. What is more, we know almost nothing about how different individuals react to these patterns of abuse. Still, from the fragmentary evidence available, it seems that both the abuse itself and the environmental context in which it occurs are quite different for people in the two groups.

Based on the preliminary study cited previously, we believe the two groups of victims differ in their social class and family stability (Garbarino & Carson, 1979a). We assume that the psychological effects of long-term abuse are not the same as those of relatively short-term abuse. We assume that years of abuse during early childhood do more damage than does maltreatment that begins in adolescence. One small sign that adolescents who have no history of abuse are psychologically stronger than those who have such a history is the fact that the former report themselves as victims nearly twice as often as the latter (22 percent versus 13 percent in our study). We suppose that teenagers who were not abused as children are not accustomed to mistreatment, and they do not expect it. All the other pertinent studies support this hypothesis. For example, Hershberger (1996) found that once abused kids had been through a treatment program that educated them about appropriate and inappropriate parental behavior they could reevaluate their own families and see maltreatment where they had not before (Lourie, 1977; Libbey & Bybee, 1979).

Reporting oneself as a victim of parental abuse requires recognition that such treatment is intolerable and undeserved. It also requires personal initiative and the ability to communicate. Long-term abuse tends to undermine such capabilities, so we would interpret the lower rate of self-reporting among long-term victims as a sign of psychological damage. Clinicians tell us that abused teenagers who have a childhood history of abuse tend to be more crippled emotionally than those who do not. These adolescents also tend to have extremely strong dependency needs. Many youths who were abused from infancy or early childhood and were subsequently removed from the home never get a chance to deal with the abuse they suffered and, in fact, may idealize their parents and be eager to return home (Friedman, 1978). This has serious implications for the foster-care system.

We are addressing the issue of differential effects partly because we will be drawing links between maltreatment and delinquency. We believe youth from the two groups will have very different motivations for becoming delinquent. A middle-class teenager who has recently been sexually abused is likely to commit different sorts of offenses than her poverty-stricken counterpart who has always been beaten and who feels forced to acquire her spending money by stealing it. We cannot ignore the effects of the impoverished environment from which long-term abuse victims are likely to come (Elmer, 1979). Indeed, growing evidence points to the critical importance of impoverished social environments in damaging kids already made vulnerable by parental mistreatment (or other risk factors) (Garbarino, 1995). It is as if some environments are themselves abusive (Martin, 1976).

In a racially defined ghetto, for example, much delinquent or disturbing behavior, such as hustling, gang membership, and audacity in sexual exploits, may serve as alternative modes of attaining competence because legitimate ones are closed off (Smith, 1968). Whether or not the problems that an abused adolescent suffers show up as delinquency probably has as much to do with the demands and expectations of his or her social situation as it does with any predisposition of personality. We do not know enough about the differential effects of the two types of abuse upon delinquency apart from the settings in which they occur.

This should come as no surprise when decades of research on delinquency in general have failed to resolve many basic issues of causation and consequence. Social class also affects the destiny of an abused adolescent. In 1997 we sat with the directors of a secure youth detention facility as they reviewed the background of the kids incarcerated there. A student asked about the social class background of the inmates. The assistant director rolled his eyes. "These aren't any rich kids here," he said.

This effect extends beyond violence and delinquency, however. Status offenses are acts legal for adults but disallowed for minors. Poor parents are more likely to file status offense petitions against their teenagers than are those who can afford to send a child to boarding school or some other private out-of-home placement. In a family setting, parents sometimes petition the state to assume responsibility for a child they cannot control. The poor have less access to psychiatric services and are therefore less able to get professional help for their problems. There are many other ways that poverty places a family in a double bind by both causing problems and preventing their successful resolution.

Social service and criminal justice systems may react less favorably to victims from these families than to more affluent youths. This differential treatment may be partly a function of class bias as well as a response to more severely impaired psychological health among long-term victims. The differences between the two types of adolescent-abuse cases require a differentiated response in some ways, and we will discuss some of these in the next chapter. On the other hand, the developmental damage experienced by the victims is probably more similar than not. The principal difference is one of degree: low social class and long duration of mistreatment exacerbate the problems. That said, we will deal with abused adolescents as a single group for the rest of the chapter because, for all their differences, the two groups face the same developmental tasks, societal rules, and parental abuse. What is more, we simply do not have the knowledge base necessary to differentiate between the types of damage youth in these two groups may experience.

—◦◦◦—

There are a few basic essentials that human beings need in order to grow into competent adults. While many psychologists have offered alternative models of these basic needs (such as Maslow, 1954) they tend to contain similar themes. For example, kids need to feel powerful, that they can affect the world around them. They need identity, to know who they are and with whom they belong. They need acceptance from their parents, an unconditional regard that allows them to experiment and make mistakes. They need consistency in order to believe that the world is predictable. They need to feel worthwhile. They need affection. Parents who supply these essentials tend to have competent children. As we are using the term, competence includes effective communication, ability to adapt socially, patience, high self-esteem, social responsibility, and empathy (McClelland, 1973). An authoritative style of childrearing (in contrast to both a permissive and an authoritarian style) tends to produce these secure, happy people (Baumrind, 1979).

Authoritative parents combine support with limits, grant reasonable autonomy, and explain the rationale behind their decisions. Parents who encourage their children, who pay attention to the child's contribution in the decision-making process, and who are concerned with the child's own accomplishments tend to have competent children (Bee, 1967). In fact, the amount of support as opposed to severe punishment that parents give their children is directly related to the social and intellectual competence of those children (Kelly & Drabman, 1977). In adolescence, the essential ingredients of effective parenthood include a gradual meting out of responsibility and privilege to the child, a handing over of more power within the family.

One major determinant of teenagers' mental health is whether or not they feel respected and liked by their parents (Harris & Howard, 1979). Those who believe their parents think positively of them are more likely to hold prosocial value systems and to care about their own social images. Older teenagers whose parents grant them a lot of freedom tend to feel close to their parents, enjoy activities with them, ask them for advice, want to be like their parents, and fight with their parents infrequently (Kandel & Lesser, 1972). Adolescents who are autonomous, who make their decisions independently of parents and peers, tend to come from homes with high levels of support and moderate levels of control (Devereux, 1970). Youth who enjoy positive relationships with their parents and other adults are motivated to avoid antisocial and self-destructive acts, because they recognize the value of their social investments. It makes sense that adult disapproval would be ineffective in discouraging such acts among people who have never experienced the approval of their parents. In abusive homes the process of socialization tends to work to the child's detriment.

PROCESSES OF DAMAGE

The good news about kids is that they can adapt to anything. The bad news about kids is that they can adapt to anything.

Perhaps the most amazing characteristic of the human being is its flexibility and adaptability. Children can learn to live with a wide range of circumstances. The price that children pay for this adaptability is often developmental damage if they must adapt to unhealthy circumstances. Those who live in abusive and neglectful environments learn to accommodate the hurtful things they experience. There are several normal processes through which they are damaged. These processes have been described and observed by many clinicians, theoreticians, and researchers and may be described in the specialized language of the psychodynamic, cognitive-developmentalist, and behaviorist approaches to behavior and development.

We believe there are two key processes of damage relevant to understanding the consequences of abuse and neglect. The first involves children or youth imitating and identifying with their parents. Through imitation, victims learn to be socially deficient. The second involves children or youth rationalizing family dynamics and the hurtful consequences of those dynamics. Through this process, they learn a negative self-concept.

There are many technical terms for these processes, most of which are related to particular theories of personality and psychological development. In the interest of providing the most practically useful discussion we have chosen to focus on the behaviors involved, linking those behaviors to some of the classical psychodynamic concepts. One way that damage occurs is through identification and imitation. By and large, children learn to become the people they "belong" to.

Children learn to be like their parents (in greater or lesser degree) because they are emotionally tied to and spend their formative years with their parents. This process involves both the accumulation of specific behaviors, habits, and characteristics (modeling) and the development of a more general identity (identification). Modeling, or setting an example, is an efficient method of teaching since it includes much more than words. A person who models a behavior is giving information through body language and voice inflection. Through modeling, children grow to become like the people who matter to them and to whom they are important.

Thus, these processes (modeling, imitation, and identification) are the natural avenues for social and personal development. Without them, the process of becoming human would be almost impossible, because adults could never specifically teach children every detail of personhood. By identifying with their parents' prohibitions in order to avoid punishment, children develop consciences and become effectively socialized (Hall, 1954). However, the processes of identification and imitation also mean that children will absorb whatever reality is defined for them, even if it is a warped and violent one.

One expert describes the process of identification this way. The child says, in effect, "If I make my image of you part of my image of me, I can control you. Then you cannot hurt me as much" (fear of aggression), or, "Walk away and leave me" (fear of loss of love). Ironically, the higher the level of violence or the more intense the threat of loss of love, the stronger the child's inclination to emulate the parent. This seems to say that abusive homes can be powerful producers of damaged human beings because they generate strong identification with people who have many negative lessons to teach.

Children are motivated strongly to imitate their parents' social incompetence. Behavioral evidence suggests they do (Burgess & Conger, 1978). If children identify with parents who are aggressors, they will incorporate those parents' hostility. Thus by attempting to gain the favor of a potential enemy, the victim may become his or her own enemy. In cognitive-developmental terms, the child's concept of self is defined in large part by the day-to-day experience of reality in the family. In an effort to gain some measure of self-protection and mastery over his environment, the child may identify strongly with the aggressor and develop a deeply set pattern of discharging aggression against the outside world in order to manage internal insecurities (Steele, 1970).

Cognitive Consistency

Human behavior is largely a product of emotion screened through intellect. In encounters with other humans, intellect is often expressed as social skill. A competent person possesses both a range of social skills and a positive emotional life to motivate and regulate the effective use of those skills. Just as abuse seems to undermine the necessary social skills for effective and gratifying interpersonal relationships, so it also seems to produce a negative emotional life. Children learn to value themselves (to develop self-esteem) by being valued. Rejection (through mistreatment) directly tells a child he or she is not worth much. Through the process of striving for cognitive consistency, a person always seeks to reconcile reality with feelings.

Because of this process, there is always the possibility that a child will justify parental abuse by downgrading himself or herself. As one young victim put it, "There must have been *some* reason they beat me. Otherwise, why would they have done it?" In addition to this downgrading of self, there is likely to be anger, rage, frustration, hatred, fear, and pain. It is impossible to fully reconcile oneself to a horrible existence. Some victims avoid their situations by compartmentalizing their emotions or by letting go of reality through drugs, alcohol, or insanity. Others simply end up with strong negative emotions that work against them.

It is little wonder that the emotional life of an abuse victim is in jeopardy; "walking on thin ice" is the way one of the victims we interviewed put it. The process begins early. Abusive parents help their young children less and show less approval than other parents. The children reciprocate by showing much less affection to their parents and expressing less pleasure in life generally than nonabused children (Herrenkohl, 1977). When a child repeatedly encounters extreme punishment or the withholding of affection by a parent, the natural reaction is likely to be one of open hostility or withdrawal (Katz, 1967).

In light of the processes involved, it is difficult to imagine a child surviving abuse—let alone surviving unscathed. Fortunately, it does happen, and for all we know it could even be the rule rather than the exception, simply because the human psyche is so adaptable. The fact that children survived life in World War II concentration camps relatively intact psychologically is testimony to this phenomenon (Freud & Dann, 1951). We really do not know how many victims of maltreatment survive psychologically and socially (Garmezy, 1977). We know some do.

There is a small group of extremely competent children who accommodate their parents' faults in a healthy way and who may even thrive. They are called *resilient,* and they usually have some special personal and social resources to call upon: they are well-armed and well-armored against adverse parental influences (Haggerty, Sherrod, Garmezy, & Rutter, 1994). But many mistreated people are not so fortunate. They are negatively affected by the mistreatment; many grow up with substantial emotional problems. We will describe the more common problems that abuse victims carry, then examine the actions those problems precipitate, actions that often mean harm for others.

Physical Damage

It didn't matter if I did right or wrong. Sometimes she would beat me for nothing, and then say it was for "in case you did anything." My mom used to hit me really hard—not just a swat—and for nothing. She even cut me a couple of times with a knife.

Adolescents are unlikely to die at the hands of their parents. Studies (such as McClain, Sacks, Froehlke & Ewigman, 1993) show that only about 10 percent of abuse-related fatalities involve children over four years of age. Although physical injury is not the overriding problem for abused adolescents that it is for infants, it cannot be ignored. Size can actually work against teenagers in this regard. Because they are harder to physically subdue than children, they are more often assaulted with weapons. One study found that only preschool males were more in jeopardy of physical attack than teenage girls (Alley, Cundiff, & Terry, 1976). Nonetheless, adolescents are better able to defend themselves when compared with young children, and most experience only minor injuries. While there is always danger of permanent damage, especially to the central nervous system, the most common danger of physical abuse remains its psychological consequences. This is evident in the informal reports we have received from victims.

Low Self-Esteem

> My mom, see, she has hit me with furniture, and my dad has beaten me with his belt, hit me with his fist, and everything else. . . . I took it for five years. I don't blame them for doing it because I deserved every bit of it.

Self-esteem is the value we place upon ourselves, the way we rate ourselves. It is one of the crucial determinants of our response to life (Coopersmith, 1967). People with high self-esteem feel the world is a better place because they are in it. Researcher Stanley Coopersmith studied self-esteem and formulated internal monologues of people with high and low self-esteem as a way to describe the concept. In his view, someone with high self-esteem might think, for example, "I consider myself a valuable and important person and am at least as good as other people of my age and training. I am regarded as someone worthy of respect and consideration by people who are important to me. I can control my actions toward the outside world and have a fairly good understanding of the kind of person I am" (Coopersmith, 1967, p. 4).

Parents who instill a high level of esteem in their children give them lots of attention and praise while maintaining high standards for the children's behavior. Children with high self-esteem are better equipped to take on challenges, can better express their creativity, and are more competent than those with lower self-esteem. In contrast, Coopersmith writes that an internal monologue by someone with a low self-esteem would sound something like this: "I don't think I'm a very important or likable person, and I don't see much reason for anyone else to like me. I don't expect much from myself, now or in the future. I don't have much control over what happens to me, and I expect that things will get worse rather than better" (Coopersmith, 1967, p. 5).

A person with low self-esteem is in an impossible situation when faced with adversity, apt to think, "After all, how could such a worthless person as myself solve my problems?" People with low self-esteem are more likely to manifest deviant behavior patterns, including destructive tendencies toward inanimate objects, anxiousness, and psychosomatic symptoms. Between these two extremes we find people with moderate levels of self-esteem, who were raised in families that provided moderate levels of support. For victims of maltreatment, the task of convincing themselves they are actually worthwhile individuals after having been told and shown for so long that they are not is probably the most common problem. It is natural to believe the opinions of parents and other significant people, so when such adults express a low opinion through their words or actions, it is difficult not to believe them.

We believe that one's evolving conception of the world and one's place in it—the "social map"—is the essence of development (Garbarino & Associates, 1992). All the evidence that abuse presents a victim is negative. According to Coopersmith, constant parental criticism "not only reduces the pleasures of the present, but it also serves to eliminate realistic hopes for the future. The corrosive drizzle of negative appraisal presumably removes the joy of today and the anticipation of tomorrow" (Coopersmith, 1967, p. 130).

Coopersmith regards the overall climate as a more important determinant than outstanding events: "It is possible that by their repetitive occurrence, less severe or dramatic occurrences might well have a more depressing effect than might more isolated, dramatic episodes" (Coopersmith, 1967, p. 158). This supports our belief that it is the abusive climate that does the most damage. Domination, rejection, and severe punishment—all different expressions of what we label abuse—result in lowered self-esteem. Under such conditions, adolescents have fewer experiences of love and success, and tend to be generally submissive and withdrawn, though occasionally they veer to the opposite extreme of aggression and domination. They simply have not been provided a basis for believing themselves to be secure. They have no practice in being competent. The world does not feel safe. Children and youth reared under such psychologically crippling circumstances have little hope of seeing the world realistically or being effective in their everyday functioning, much less of realizing their full potential.

What happens if, despite maltreatment, some adolescents are able to develop and maintain a positive sense of self, perhaps because they had access to at least one supportive adult relationship? Evidence suggests that such adolescents may be protected against some of the psychological damage of maltreatment. In one study (Moran & Eckenrode, 1992), maltreated adolescent girls who had average or high levels of self-esteem were no more depressed than their nonmaltreated peers with similar levels of self-esteem. Alternatively, maltreated adolescents with low levels of self-esteem were particularly vulnerable to depression. Consistent with our earlier discussion of patterns of adolescent maltreatment, this study also found that when the maltreatment began in childhood, self-esteem was more likely to be compromised than if it began in adolescence.

Anxiety

A problem closely related to low self-esteem is anxiety. Because abuse victims tend to think of themselves as not being worthwhile, they may be overly dependent upon the opinions of others. They are therefore very anxious about the cues they send out. This high level of anxiety also causes real problems to become even larger than they might otherwise be. Anxiety is a significant reason for school failure and lack of achievement. People learn best when their minds are clear, when they feel good about themselves. Low-achieving students are more self-critical than high achievers. This self-criticism is self-protective, because it reduces anxiety. It prefaces every action with a negative appraisal and thus eliminates the hearer's option to devalue the act. Low school achievement, anxiety, and self-devaluation are interrelated, and each is in turn related to a predominance of negative reinforcement from parents, low parental interest and acceptance, and high parental punitiveness (Katz, 1967). Severe punishment or abuse in the past creates anxiety about the future, especially if that punishment or abuse was unpredictable (Feshbach, 1973). Anxiety about aggression can even drive a person to violence. People with a high degree of anxiety over aggression will respond more aggressively than those with low-aggression anxiety. All in all, maltreatment increases most youngsters' uncertainty about themselves and their place in the world. Neither they nor that world is reliable. This anxiety is often compounded by a genuine inability to read people and social situations accurately—by a lack of empathy.

Lack of Empathy

> That old man thought he was tough or something. Wouldn't give me his wallet, so I had to cut him up. He shouldn't be around when I need money if he doesn't want to give it to me.   "

Empathy is taking the role of the other, feeling what another person is feeling. Empathy plays a major role in making human society more humane. Children as young as six have chosen to give an adult pleasure rather than receive candy themselves in laboratory tests. They have shut off a painful noise that another child is experiencing after hearing it themselves (Aronfreed & Paskal, 1969). Empathy acts as a strong motivator for social responsibility. Young children behave more morally when the consequences of their behavior are explained in terms of the effect upon others than when they are punished or simply told the behavior is wrong (Hoffman & Saltzstein, 1967). An empathetic person will work to help another person, even when the receiver cannot know or find out who is giving help (Berkowitz, 1957).

Empathy is so central to mental health and maturity that it is considered by some to be the key to socialization, which one researcher defines as "largely the ability to put oneself in the position of others while keeping one's own position in mind. . . . If understanding others is the essence of social interaction, to do so successfully means that one is able to differentiate between self and others. . . . Increasing differentiation is the process by which the mind develops what is loosely called maturity" (Coser, 1975, pp. 256–263). Empathy has some other positive effects and is part of the general pattern Goleman (1995) calls emotional intelligence.

A child who has strong emotional intelligence will be much less aggressive than one who has little (Feshbach, 1973; Miller & Eisenberg, 1988). Empathy can provide the basis for altruism, sympathy, and help. It is the very foundation of morality (Berkowitz, 1957). Not surprisingly, youth who are empathetic see their parents as being more supportive. Conversely, those with little empathy see their parents as severe (Keller, 1975).

One of the most disturbing effects of abuse is that those who have suffered it tend either to lose their ability to empathize or to not develop it in the first place. They reenact the lack of empathy their parents showed them while growing up. Mistreated teenagers tend to respond to children in a manner reminiscent of the way their own parents responded to them, with an inability to be empathetically aware of a child's needs (Bavolek, Kline, McLaughlin, & Publicover, 1979). Parents who lack empathy are liable to become abusive when exposed to social and economic stress (Gray, 1978). This suggests the need to retrain mistreated youth to help them avoid a chronic pattern of unsuccessful social relationships.

Poor Social Relationships

It's hard for me to give up part of myself to somebody and have them take it because I'm afraid they're going to take it and go "crunch"— you know, wring it and throw it back at me.

Teenagers who have been mistreated are often sadly ill equipped for meaningful relationships with other people. Low self-esteem is a major root of this difficulty. People with low self-esteem are grateful that anyone speaks to them, no matter what is said or how it is said. By devaluating their own worth, they place themselves beneath the value they assign to others. They feel responsible for everything that goes wrong. They feel they owe everyone gratitude and would not think of asking anything for themselves; after all, who are they to ask (Satir, 1972)? Victims of mistreatment are thus naturally set up to become lifelong victims. Feelings of worthless can have another effect: aggression. Persons with low self-esteem may attempt to convince others that they count for something by making others obey their wishes or fear them. We know that if teenagers become aggressive, they fare less well with everyone, including their peers (Bandura & Walters, 1959).

Research found that rejected children do not perform well socially (Rohner & Nielsen, 1978). They face the future with less confidence and are more confused, discouraged, and insecure than children reared with parental acceptance (Symonds, 1938). And it is not just in early life that rejection hurts. Parental rejection in adolescence following the establishment of earlier attachments tends to produce antisocial behavior and increased dependency upon peers and other adults (Wolberg, 1944). It is only natural for people to seek support wherever they can find it; when it is not forthcoming from their parents, youth look elsewhere.

The desperate need to fill a void, combined with the insecurity that results from being made to feel unworthy, causes abuse victims to be extremely vulnerable to the people around them and to the larger forces of social toxicity (Garbarino, 1995). Take, for example, these words from a perceptive runaway: "It's terrible. Someone just has to reach out and I'm waiting for any person who walks by and will hold my hand and be my friend. They can hurt me just as much as anyone else." The most slavish peer conformity happens in adolescents whose parents are either extremely permissive or authoritarian (Devereux, 1970). Extending the scale even further to include neglect (on the permissive side) and abuse (on the authoritarian side) can only have even stronger effects.

Despite the need to belong, the abused adolescent is also at a disadvantage in forming healthy relationships with peers. In part this stems from the way in which these youth tend to think about relationships. One longitudinal study with elementary school children has found that abuse leads to deficits in the way children process social information (Dodge, Pettit, Bates, & Valente, 1995). Abused children are more likely to be overly sensitive to hostile cues in their social environment, tune out nonhostile social information, and attribute hostile intentions to others more readily than other children. Because they have already learned an aggressive set of behaviors at home, these cognitions reinforce aggressive behaviors in otherwise benign social situations involving mild disagreements or conflict with peers. These children will tend to affiliate with other children with similar cognitive and behavioral characteristics and become isolated from other less aggressive and antisocial peers.

This is one reason why victims of abuse in the home seem to be so vulnerable to abuse from strangers. Abusive families tend to be socially isolated in the sense of being cut off from prosocial support systems. We know that most neglectful parents were themselves isolated as teenagers (Polansky, Chalmers, Buttenweiser, & Williams, 1979). As parents, they tend to isolate their children by discouraging friendships. Children reared in abusive homes tend to follow a self-perpetuating course of social behavior that leads to social isolation. They probably have not learned how to deal successfully with other people. Since they fear dependence, they mistrust signs of love and esteem and thwart friendly relations by quick displays of aggression (White & Watt, 1973). One long-term victim described it like this:

> You get too used to being beat up where, if you're not beat up, you don't know what the hell to do. And when I would find somebody that would not hurt me, I'd do something very fast in order to get some-thing negative to come out of them. And then I could walk away and say, "I told you so, you don't care about me." You can't trust everybody. That's a fact. It's not just a paranoid statement, it's a fact.

Coming full circle, social isolation can even make young teenagers more vulnerable to abuse. For one thing, they will spend more time at home alone. With a smaller world, they may be enmeshed in the pathological dynamics of their families. Finally, they will have no place to turn for advice on alternative ways to survive (Fisher, Berdie, Cook, Radford-Barker, & Day, 1979). If, as a result of inadequate social skills, youth find themselves cut off from social contact and support, their isolation itself is a self-perpetuating problem. They are thus deprived of opportunities to learn the skills they would normally learn from regular social contact.

The problems that mistreated youth sustain tend to reflect the type of mistreatment they suffered. A neglected teenager will not neces-sarily have the same problems as one who is sexually abused. Girls who are sexually abused tend to experience problems relating to men. Children raised by overly restrictive parents who foster dependence upon adults are likely to themselves grow into overcontrolling adults (Hill, 1980).

We should therefore expect immaturity from those who have never been allowed to mature. Children from overcontrolling, authoritar-ian homes have been found to fight and quarrel more, to be more inconsiderate and insensitive and less popular. Clinical studies report that those who were also punished severely show little affection, are hesitant to express themselves verbally (Radke, 1946), and are extremely submissive (Newell, 1934). Submissiveness around an over-powering adult is nothing more than a survival technique, a natural outcome of domination.

One early researcher stated it this way: "The authoritarian parent who uses his age status as a naked assertion of power over his children gets dependence and passive resistance; maybe, if he is lucky, revolt"

(Newell, 1934, p. 400). Another maintains, "the undercontrolled individual may be responsible for numerous acts that are antisocial, but the chronically overcontrolled person is much more dangerous in the long run" (Johnson, 1972, p. 127).

Many people who are extremely assaultive; that is, who have committed homicides, assault and battery, and related offenses, were chronically overcontrolled as children. These offenders appear to be profoundly repressed individuals who, though outwardly controlled, are inwardly alienated and potentially capable of extremely violent, antisocial acts (Megargee, 1971). More than one infamous murderer has been described by his neighbors as "quiet—kept to himself, mainly. Never heard a peep out of him. He was a good tenant."

The psychological problems that rejected children suffer are too numerous to explore in detail here (Rohner, 1975). Abuse and neglect are both evidence of rejection; even overcontrol is rejection because it expresses disapproval of the youth's independence. Briefly, clinicians have found rejected children to be sadistic, nervous, shy, stubborn, noncompliant (Radke, 1946); restless, apathetic, indifferent, impulsive, antagonistic, compulsively dependent, detached, emotionally immature (Wolberg, 1944); less stable and more aggressive than accepted children (Newell, 1934). Rejection is a malignant force in human development (Rohner, 1975). As one physician put it, "The character strivings to overcome [the victim's] sense of helplessness produce distortions in attitudes, values, and goals that engender pathological relationships with the world and with people" (Wolberg, 1944).

SUICIDE: ESCAPING THE PAIN

Most people try to avoid pain. Those who find the whole world most excruciatingly painful tend to try hardest to escape it, either permanently through suicide or temporarily through drugs or alcohol. Although not all studies report greater overall alcohol use among runaway and abused youth, there is some evidence of more socially disastrous problem drinking (Houten & Golembiewski, 1976). The demonstrative presence of love from both parents helps to protect teenagers from becoming involved in the abuse of drugs. Conversely, its absence is a reliable predictor of drug and alcohol abuse.

Researchers have reported a connection between the misuse of drugs and impaired family relationships, particularly in father-daughter and mother-son dyads (Streit, 1974). The more desperate children try to kill themselves. Of course, most of what we know about suicide victims comes from research done with those who made unsuccessful attempts:

> I took some pills and tried to kill myself. I had been through it so many times, I just didn't want to live. It felt that bad, the way my mom treated me.

Most children who commit suicide do so because of neglect, abuse, or bereavement (Duncan, 1977). Lack of family harmony, marital conflicts, isolation in the parent-child relationship, and sibling hostility have driven some youngsters to regard suicide as the only escape from acute emotional pain (Paulson & Stone, 1974).

Adolescent suicide is often preceded by a sequence of events, including a long-standing history of problems from childhood, that mount into a chain reaction that dissolves any meaningful social relationships (Teicher, 1973). Many (but of course not all) suicidal adolescents come from families in which a destructive cycle of anger is established between parents and children (Toolan, 1975). Parental alcoholism is common among those who attempt suicide, as are extremes or inconsistency of parental control and expectations, hostility, depression, parental rejection, and extreme parental reactions to the child's behavior.

One study found clear differences between teenagers who had attempted suicide and those who had not, even though both groups had experienced similar stress, including parental divorce, problematic stepparents, and economic deprivation. Hostility, indifference, and overt rejection by the parent was the rule for the suicidal subjects and the exception for the controls (McIntire, Angle, & Schlicht, 1977). Attempted suicide is often intended as a plea for help rather than as an act of self-destruction. Many abused youth no doubt use self-destructive behavior to manipulate other people, hoping that those people will gratify their wishes (Kreider & Motto, 1974). It may be a way to rectify a parent-child role reversal within the family.

The suicide attempt reclaims the child's right to induce the parent to meet his or her dependent needs. This drastic step certainly removes the youth from the situation, possibly even permanently through placement outside the home (Kreider & Motto, 1974). One major difference between those who attempt suicide and other troubled youth is that, while neither group communicates especially well with parents, the nonsuicides at least have maintained contacts with peers and other adults (McIntire, Angle, & Schlicht, 1977). Because of their poor social skills, victims of maltreatment are set up for social isolation (Francis, 1978). Many youth who try to kill themselves do not have even one person they feel they can turn to in times of trouble. Finally, many adolescents who choose to die or to try to die feel utterly helpless and hopeless.

Very few adolescent suicide survivors say they have perceived a significant change in their parents' attitudes (McIntire, Angle, & Schlicht, 1977). The decision to attempt suicide is often the result of a rational decision-making process (Teicher, 1973), attempted only after alternate solutions to the problem have failed. This is a damning indictment of the community's willingness and ability to help these youth.

TROUBLING BEHAVIOR

Life with the psychological problems we have just chronicled is not easy. People who have them tend to have a hard time fitting into normal society. Adolescents who are having such problems tend to have trouble coping with the constraints of any environment. We often label such youngsters as troubled, at risk, alienated, antisocial, or wayward. Their role incompetence expresses itself in all sorts of disturbing behavior: truancy, poor school performance, substance abuse, and sexual promiscuity. Besides endangering healthy adolescent development, these behaviors can cause problems that imperil the youth's future. Truancy and poor school performance can lead to low occupational mobility. Drug and alcohol abuse can become addictive. Sexual promiscuity can produce unwanted pregnancy, venereal disease, and AIDS. All can lead to contact with the criminal justice system.

Each of these behaviors can disrupt an adolescent's life, and, collectively, they may predict an antisocial personality in adulthood. Yahares (1978) found that theft, incorrigibility, running away, associating with other delinquent children, staying out past the hour allowed, discipline problems in school, being held back in school, fighting, recklessness, slovenliness, enuresis, lying for no apparent gain, failure to show love, and the inability or unwillingness to show guilt over disturbing behavior were all predictors of antisocial personalities. He found that the number of symptoms evidenced was a better predictor than any one particular symptom.

THE LINK BETWEEN ABUSE
AND ANTISOCIAL BEHAVIOR

Even if all maltreatment were prevented, we would not predict an end to conduct problems, antisocial behavior, and juvenile delinquency (terms with overlapping clinical, scientific, and legal meanings). There are numerous causes of delinquency; some are situational, while others are tied to the adolescent's personal history (Loeber & Dishion, 1983). However, abuse and neglect are closely related to delinquency for three reasons (Garbarino, Schellenbach, Sebes, & Associates, 1986): (1) maltreatment victims tend to display traits characteristic of pre-delinquency; (2) both abuse and delinquency spring from common environments; and (3) abuse and aggression go hand in hand. It is hard to imagine an experience that would weaken a personality more than parental abuse and neglect.

Furthermore, since the nature of a parent-child relationship is a good predictor of future delinquency, maltreatment makes teenagers prone to become delinquent. If violently assaulted, they may carry the heavy weight of barely suppressed rage. If sexually or emotionally abused, they may be looking for some way to compensate or gain revenge for their feelings of self-contempt and resentment. Children who believe their parents are unaware of their whereabouts are more likely to have committed delinquent acts (Hirschi, 1969). Neglected adolescents fall into this category, of course. In general, if a child is alienated from a parent, she or he will be less likely to have a feeling for moral rules or develop an adequate conscience (Nye, 1959).

The scientific literature is consistent in implicating hostile or rejecting parenting as a cause of antisocial behavior (Yoshikawa, 1994). Indeed, social factors such as family instability and poverty, often linked to antisocial behavior, appear to do their damage because they compromise parenting behaviors (Loeber & Strouthammer-Loeber, 1986). Efforts to document the link between child abuse and violent juvenile delinquency has a long history. When Kempe first identified the Battered Child Syndrome (Kempe, Silverman, Steele, Droegemueller, & Silver, 1962), Curtis (1963) hypothesized that children who were subject to severe mistreatment would "become tomorrow's murderers and perpetrators of other crimes of violence" (p. 368).

Mistreatment and delinquent behavior are often to be found in the same family environments. In one study, nearly half of the families reported for child abuse and neglect had at least one child who was later taken to the court as ungovernable or delinquent (Alfaro, 1976). Moreover, the way that families of delinquents communicate tends to be different from the communication of families without delinquent children. The members of deviant families deal with each other much more defensively and less supportively than other families (Alexander, 1973). In this, their behavior resembles that found in studies of abusive and neglectful families. These abusive families have been found to be dysfunctional, multiproblem families that do not fit into the normal lives of their communities. Children from these families who have been abused or neglected are five times as likely to be delinquent or ungovernable as those from the general population (Alfaro, 1976).

Several studies have demonstrated an association between the degree of violence expressed by a delinquent and a history of abuse (Alfaro, 1981; Welsch, 1976) and have shown that abused children are more aggressive and disobedient in general (Kent, 1976; Reidy, 1977; Lewis, Shanok, Pincus, & Glaser, 1979). Although most abused children do not become violent delinquents, clinical studies and retrospective statistics have demonstrated that both male and female juvenile delinquents and adult criminals have a much higher rate of reported abuse as children than the general population (Lewis, Mallouh, & Webb, 1989; Vissing, Straus, Gelles, & Harrop, 1991). Furthermore, statistics from the Department of Justice found that 49 percent of women who were convicted of violent crimes were the victims of abuse ("Women report past abuse," 1991).

A series of studies carried out by Widom and her colleagues (Widom, 1989; Maxwell & Widom, 1996) have helped shed light on the specific nature of the relationship between child maltreatment and delinquency. These researchers identified a large number of children who had been maltreated between 1967 and 1971 and a matched group of nonmaltreated children. Then arrest records were examined when these children grew into adolescence. The study confirmed that maltreatment was associated with an increased risk for delinquency (26 percent among the maltreated children versus 17 percent among nonmaltreated children) and also showed that maltreated children began their criminal careers earlier than nonmaltreated children.

Indeed, timing becomes an important issue when considering the lifelong risks to adolescents engaging in antisocial behaviors. Many adolescents will at some time be involved in some form of delinquent or antisocial behavior—indeed, such behavior may be considered normative. Most adolescents, however, desist from such behavior once they reach young adulthood. There is a subgroup of delinquents who begin early and whose delinquency persists beyond adolescence, becoming translated into adult offending. Moffitt (1993) labels these patterns as "adolescent-limited" and "life course persistent" (p. 674).

This parallels our discussion of different patterns of adolescent maltreatment, one that begins in childhood and continues into adolescence, and one that begins in adolescence. There are a host of reasons why conduct problems in maltreated children may persist into adolescence as antisocial behavior and into adulthood as criminal offending. These sources of continuity are routed in both the environment and the individual (Caspi & Bem, 1990). There is good reason to believe that maltreatment may make it more likely that such destructive continuities take place for a child.

Moffitt (1993) proposes two major types of interactions between persons and their social environments that promote continuity in antisocial behavior: (1) failing to learn conventional prosocial alternatives to antisocial behavior; and (2) becoming "ensnared" in a deviant lifestyle by crime's consequences. Maltreatment undermines the psychological resources children need to view themselves and their social world in a positive and affirming way. Once a child and then an adolescent then begins to turn to antisocial behavior, the consequences of such behavior further erode their life chances. The earlier such a process starts and the more chronic the pattern becomes, the more resistant it is to intervention. This is another reason, of course, to begin prevention programs early with maltreating families and their children.

Clinicians report that male victims of mistreatment are more likely to become aggressive while females tend to become self-destructive. This sex-typed pattern is consistent with that found in deviant behavior in general. Boys are much more likely to be officially reported for delinquent acts and to admit to delinquent acts in surveys (Elliott, Huizinga, & Menard, 1989). FBI statistics indicate that in 1992 between 80 and 85 percent of juvenile arrests for property crimes involved males, while 90 to 95 percent of violent crimes involved males (Snyder & Sickmund, 1995). However, female arrests have increased at a greater rate over time than male arrests: females arrests for property crimes increased by 27 percent between 1983 and 1992, while increasing 7 percent for males.

Historically, we had a picture of adolescent girls encountering the juvenile justice system in this country for basically self-destructive acts, things such as vagrancy, running away, curfew violations, drunkenness, drug-abuse violations, and prostitution. Traditionally, fewer than 2 percent of those arrested are charged with violent crimes (U.S. Federal Bureau of Investigation, 1978). This is changing, however, as traditional sex-role stereotypes have released the rage of victimized teenage girls, and the general desensitization to aggressive behavior has progressed. While boys continue to commit the bulk of violent crimes, the pattern of caseloads in juvenile courts is now quite similar (Snyder & Sickmund, 1995), with boys and girls showing roughly the same proportion of property, person, drug, and public order offenses. Widom's (1991) research also showed that while maltreatment was associated with an increase in property crimes and status offenses for both boys and girls, it was associated with an increase in violent offenses only among girls. Such findings need to be replicated with other studies, but they do suggest that the traditional stereotype that maintains that girls will always respond to maltreatment with nonviolent or self-destructive behaviors may be changing.

Unfortunately, the aggression of some youth turns into murder. The numbers are sobering. Between 1976 and 1991, nearly twenty-three thousand youth under eighteen years of age committed homicide in this country, and the number of known juvenile homicide offenders has doubled between from 1984 to 1991 (Snyder & Sickmund, 1995). In a sadly odd confluence of statistics, the number of juveniles known to have committed murder in 1991 (2,202) is roughly the same number of children known to have died from abuse at the hands of their parents and caretakers that year: the victims and the victimizers.

YOUTH VIOLENCE AND DOMESTIC VIOLENCE

When we consider the ultimate form of violence, namely homicide, the link with abuse becomes even clearer. From the moment we accept the fact that kids who kill were not "born" killers but became killers, we must ask, What makes a child become a killer? And, why do some kids from the same families turn their backs on violence?

Here is the story of Leo and Tony—two brothers growing up in a family dominated by domestic violence, two boys who witnessed their mother being abused repeatedly and who are thus at high risk for learning to become violent men.

• Leo is an eighteen-year-old accused of first-degree murder. He killed a rival gang member in a street confrontation in his own neighborhood. Leo's was a story of accumulating risk factors— absent father, drug-addicted mother, poverty, discrimination, and community violence. Growing up amidst community violence, he had been shot at more than once and stabbed in the months prior to the crime for which he is being tried. What path could be more natural for Leo than to end up as a "foot soldier" in his neighborhood gang? Is it surprising that defensiveness and aggression dominate his view of the world?

Leo has a twenty-year-old brother, Tony. The eldest in the family, Tony also never saw his father. Leo and Tony were raised by their mother, a single parent with a history of alcoholism who provided for her family by alternating between periods of employment at low-paying jobs and welfare. During most of their upbringing, Tony and Leo saw their mother involved with men who mistreated her psychologically and physically. Violence in the home was a daily reality. As a result, the boys spent as much time as possible outside the house on the streets, where violence also reigned. Five years ago Leo shot another kid in a confrontation over drug-dealing territory. Within four years of this act of severe violence—for which Leo served time in a state youth facility—Tony had turned his life around. He learned to read, became a high school track star, and subsequently made the move to a college campus. He is now in his senior year and will graduate in the spring.

Why did Leo end up caught in a web of violence, while Tony ended up in college? Both were raised in an atmosphere of domestic violence, but one brother turned off that path, while the other progressed from early acts of violence to juvenile homicide. Why? Why do some boys who grow up living with violence against the most important woman in their lives end up incorporating that violence into their own interpersonal style, while others find a path away from violence and toward a more positive way of living?

What differentiates Tony and Leo? What will Leo do now that he is serving prison time for his act? Will he ever have an opportunity to succeed in life? And what of kids from the same background of family deprivation and community violence who never walk down the path of violent crime at all?

Violence Against Women and Children

Society reacts to murders committed by children and youth with shock, anger, and confusion. It is difficult to imagine that a young person is capable of willfully and deliberately taking the life of another human being. At the same time, many of us have a human need to make sense of the violence in our world, including the extreme violence displayed by young murderers. An increased understanding of the root causes of violence may be our only hope for long-term solutions, solutions that can reclaim youth before their lives become locked in violence. There is a growing scientific interest in describing alternative "pathways" of development (Rutter, 1989) and deepening our understanding of the development of extremely aggressive behavior in children and youth and in those who commit murder. What experiences lead a child down a violent pathway that culminates in murder? What is it about our society that breeds this lethal behavior in children and youth? And why can some kids reject that path?

Today, thousands of young children in U.S. cities and in other urban centers around the world are growing up amidst a worsening problem of community violence—from petty crimes on the street, in the schools, on buses, and in the subway system to shootings and stabbings on the street (Garbarino, Dubrow, Kostelny, & Pardo, 1992). For many children violence does not only exist "out there"; they are witnesses to or victims of violence within their homes. In a study of a low-income community conducted by Osofsky, Wewers, Hann, and Fick (1993), 91 percent of the children had witnessed firsthand some form of violence—either at home or in their community—and more than half had been victims of violence.

From widespread awareness of murders and other serious assaults within a community to participation in gang activity, young children are enmeshed in the problem of community violence in many ways, particularly if they live in poor families lodged within poor neighborhoods. They are witness: by age five, most children living in the inner cities have had encounters with shootings. By adolescence, most have witnessed stabbings and shootings, and one-third have witnessed a homicide (Bell, 1991). They are also victims: in 1991, about twenty-two hundred kids under the age of eighteen were murdered (Allen-Hagen & Sickmund, 1993). Finally, they are perpetrators: in 1992, thirty-three hundred children and youth were arrested for murder or manslaughter (U.S. Department of Justice, 1992). The number of juvenile homicides and the rate at which juveniles kill have been steadily increasing over the last several years (Ewing, 1990).

Childhood Experience with Violent Trauma

Domestic violence plays an integral part in the problem of youth violence in many ways. One is its role in the etiology of violent juvenile delinquency, as described earlier in this chapter. The relationship of physical abuse to homicidal behavior has been of special interest. The literature is full of statistics and anecdotal evidence regarding the extremely high incidence of child abuse among juveniles who kill. As early as 1940, Bender and Curran noted that child and adolescent murderers had histories of early and severe physical abuse. According to Lewis, Pincus, Feldman, Jackson, & Bard (1986), among the fourteen juvenile death row inmates they studied, twelve had been brutally physically abused during their childhood. Other studies support this finding (see for example, King, 1975; Lewis et al., 1985; Sendi & Blomgren, 1975).

Childhood: The Foundation for Violent Behavior and Beliefs

By age eight, patterns of aggression have become so well established that they become predictive into adulthood—*if there is no intervention to short-circuit them* (National Research Council, 1993). It is during adolescence that we see the crystallization of childhood patterns of thinking, feeling, and behaving (Garbarino, Schellenbach, Sebes, & Associates, 1986). Thus, adolescence is the critical period in the human life course for the expression of aggression in the form of violent crime (James & Krisberg, 1994), just as childhood is the critical period for its causation.

Studies of violent juveniles, especially those who eventually commit murder, indicate that a history of abuse is part of the picture of violence within families of aggressive youth. In addition, high levels of domestic violence frequently characterize the families from which violent delinquents were raised (King, 1975; Corder, 1976; Lewis et al., 1985; Sendi & Blomgren, 1975). Thus, understanding the impact of risk and resilience factors in the socialization of boys living in abusive families is crucial in understanding the larger issues of youth violence.

MALTREATMENT AMONG HOMELESS AND RUNAWAY YOUTH

I don't remember much about my childhood other than the beatings. My father was an alcoholic and would come home drunk and be very loud, aggressive, and violent. He'd pick up things and throw them across the room. He would hit my mother. I remember many times I just would sit in the corner and cry because he would hit my mother. Then he began to hit me. He would hit me with his fists and also with belts. He hit me anywhere he could. He sometimes beat me up four or five times a week. He scared me for a long time. I just silently lived with it. Then one day, I decided I had had enough. So I ran away from home. I had no money, and I had no place to live. I started pulling tricks. The money was easy, and the money was good. I was doing pretty well. I was drinking every night—I used to drink a fifth of Southern Comfort a day. I started drinking probably about nine o'clock at night and continue until I passed out. Then I would get up, pull some tricks, and go out and start to drink all over again (Carrie, a fifteen-year-old runaway).

Adolescents leaving home, living on the streets, and being exploited is by no means new. Throughout history, young people have chosen or been forced into this form of exile. Since the late 1960s, however, the problem of runaway and homeless young people in the United States has increased in volume, scope, and visibility. Recent attempts to measure the extent of the problem suggest that each year in the United States at least a half-million (Finkelhor, Hotaling, & Sedlak, 1990) to one million (U.S. Department of Health and Human Services, 1984; Solarz, 1988), and perhaps as many as several million youth between the ages of ten and seventeen, are living on the streets, in abandoned buildings, or in "welfare" hotels (National Network of Runaway and Youth Services, 1988). These numbers are alarming in view of the lethal risks associated with life on the street and the degree to which the lives of young people are jeopardized and their futures cut short. Ill-equipped to survive on their own, homeless adolescents are easy targets for victimization and exploitation. In order to secure food and shelter, increasing numbers of street youth resort to prostitution, the drug trade, and other forms of criminal activity (Janus, McCormack, Burgess, & Hartman, 1987). The vast majority of homeless teens are at high risk for self-destructive behaviors such as substance abuse and suicide, mental health problems, and physical health problems, including AIDS (Mundy, Robertson, Roberts, & Greenblatt, 1990; Robertson, 1989; Shaffer & Caton, 1984; Solarz, 1988; Yates, MacKenzie, Pennbridge, & Cohen, 1988).

Service providers who work with today's runaway and homeless adolescents deal with a very different population than the youth of the

1960s who ran away in search of new lifestyles, in a gesture of political protest, and in rebellion against their parental value system. Today, young people often run not to something but from something—very typically, intolerable home conditions (Janus, McCormack, Burgess, & Hartman, 1987). Increasingly, evidence shows that an alarming percentage of runaway and homeless adolescents are currently on the streets because they have been physically abused, sexually abused, or "pushed out" of their homes by their parents (Farber, Kinast, McCoard, & Falkner, 1984; Garbarino, Wilson, & Garbarino, 1986).

There is a growing body of empirical evidence suggesting a link between maltreatment, running away, and homelessness. Researchers have demonstrated that a violent home life can lead to runaway behavior (Gutierres & Reich, 1981). Farber and Joseph (1985) found that 75 percent of the 199 runaway young people in their sample had been subjected to severe maltreatment in the year prior to running. These investigators concluded that violence in the home significantly contributed to the youths' runaway behavior.

Several studies have shown that in comparison with the general population, runaways exhibit a much higher rate of childhood sexual abuse, including incest (Burgess, Janus, McCormack, & Wood, 1986; Adams-Tucker, 1982; Young, Godfrey, Mathews, & Adams, 1983). A recent survey reports that on a national level, 61 percent of all runaways have been maltreated (National Network of Runaway and Youth Services, 1988). Other studies provide supporting data and indicate a high incidence of maltreatment among samples of runaways (Powers, Eckenrode, & Jaklitsch, 1990; Shaffer & Caton, 1984; Nilson, 1981).

Unfortunately, all too often, the maltreatment of runaways is not recognized, reported, or treated. "Acting out" behaviors such as criminal activity, prostitution, and drug abuse bring these youth to the attention of the courts, emergency rooms, and law enforcement systems, yet the maltreatment histories remain hidden, and appropriate services are rarely provided. Many adolescents who are channeled into the juvenile and criminal justice systems are sometimes thrown into adult jails or other facilities that expose them to people involved in more serious criminal behavior. Although federal and state legislation has attempted to address this issue by, for example, instituting policies that separate minors from adult criminals, many young victims continue to be inappropriately served.

ADOLESCENT ABUSE AS A SOCIAL ISSUE

Despite the grim facts and statistics, there is hope. Human beings are extremely adaptable and capable of learning new systems of response. Victims of maltreatment need an alternative to self-blame and self-denigration; they need to have their social skills and self-concepts rebuilt. Finally, they need help sorting through their often intense and confusing emotions. One clinician calls this process "repair work with victims," as he describes a client (a thirty-six-year-old woman) who was abused by her stepmother: "She still cries as the memory comes, unwelcome, to her mind, and one finds a mixture of guilt, sadness, terrible loneliness, and a sense of having been, in her words, 'degraded' by how she was treated." The tragic effects of maltreatment compel us to face it as a social issue, if not for altruistic motives, for reasons of self-preservation. Through the problems it presents us, abuse and neglect drain our society. They drain our criminal justice system, our social welfare system, and our schools. Human suffering costs us all. We all lose the productivity of the incapacitated victim, and we all are potentially vulnerable to the aggressive one.

CHAPTER TEN

In Conclusion
Family Life Development
and Child Protection

James Garbarino
John Eckenrode

———

The maltreatment of children and youth is a problem that reaches beyond victims and perpetrators in its scope. It touches the lives of all professionals and private citizens who are concerned with the quality of life in U.S. families.

• Warren Long is a social worker in a small Midwestern city. As part of the county's Child Protective Services Unit he manages cases of child maltreatment. He feels deeply frustrated about his job. The reports keep coming in, and he keeps investigating them. Despite long hours and a strong commitment to his work, Warren keeps wondering how he can influence the parents he works with. Some parents will not let him into their houses, let alone their lives. Others are so disorganized it is hard to make out the shape of their lives at all. He wants to help, but Warren sometimes feels like it is a losing battle. What strategies should he use?

• Lucy Todd is the mother of three young children. Her husband works for the phone company, and they are saving for a new house. All in all, her life seems to be in pretty good shape. However, there is one thing that bothers her these days, and that is her friend Betty. Betty also has three children, and her husband works for the phone company, too. Maybe that is why they became friends in the first place. Lucy likes Betty, but she is disturbed by the way Betty hits her kids. Sometimes the oldest one has bruises, and there was that time last month when the youngest one had a black eye. Betty said the little girl fell. Lucy was not really convinced, but how do you go about asking your friend if she beats her kids?

• Robert Lane works for the federal government in Washington, D.C. His job is to develop plans for his agency's family assistance program to deal with child abuse and neglect. The available money seems large on paper, $60 million. But when it is spread across the country and filtered through the bureaucracy, it may disappear. How can he propose a plan to use the money so that it will reach the families in greatest need? What route should he take, and how can he justify his decision?

• Elsie Makins lives in rural New York State. She was born less than twenty miles from where she lives today. Last Sunday after church she almost stopped to talk to the minister about her problem, but then did not. That is just it. Is it her problem, or should she mind her own business? The problem is her husband's sister, Maggie, who lives down the road about six miles. There really is not room for the four kids even if they kept the place clean, which they do not. The kids look like they never get a bath, and they are always sick or getting hurt falling over the trash. To top it off, Maggie left the kids with the seven-year-old in charge while she went out barhopping. Elsie's husband says his family always does things their own way, but she wonders how those kids will grow up healthy considering the way they live. Who can she talk to about her problem?

• William Larson is a family practice physician in northern Florida. He is a bit worried about Flora Jones and her baby. He delivered the baby, so he feels some responsibility for it. Flora had a difficult pregnancy, and the birth required a cesarean section. The baby was small—five pounds and two ounces. Mother and baby left the hospital together, but only after nearly two weeks. Larson has not seen either since, and it has been nearly six weeks. With nothing but his uneasiness to go on, where can he turn?

• Ellen Rogers is a graduate student in child and family development at a major West Coast university. After six months of intensive reading, it is time for her to write a proposal for her doctoral dissertation research. She knows she wants to study child maltreatment but has not been able to get any more specific than that. She had hoped her reading would clarify things, but instead it has filled her head with a whirl of hypotheses, data, and theories. She needs someplace to hang what she has learned so she can see what comes next. How does she ask the right question to get her research project off on the right foot?

• Steven and Betty Smithson live in Wichita, Kansas. Their three children have grown up, and their furniture business is running itself these days, so they can devote themselves to the community service projects they feel give them a sense of real accomplishment. They attended a public lecture on child abuse and now they want to do something to help. But what?

THE MAZE OF MALTREATMENT

The social worker, the friend, the policymaker, the relative, the physician, the researcher, and the concerned citizen are all grappling with the problem of child abuse and neglect. Each has special needs and interests. Each perspective is different. What do they have in common? They all are stymied by the social and psychological complexities that surround maltreatment. How do you help when you cannot even gain access to the family? How do you help when to offer may break up a friendship? How do you help when you do not know where to put your resources? How do you help when you are told it is none of your business? How do you help when you do not have hard evidence? How do you help when you do not know what questions to ask? How do we get from here to there? How do we pull together all we know to provide a map to use in our efforts to help and to understand?

The burgeoning of policies, programs, and research dealing with child maltreatment over the past two decades has provided some clues, but we still do not have a comprehensive language for describing child abuse and neglect that cuts across professional lines. Many of us are searching for such a common language. We need an understanding of abusive families that is both ecological and developmental. In this book we have tried to provide some of the vocabulary and principles for such a language. In this chapter we sketch some of our conclusions on solving the problem of maltreatment.

In this concluding chapter we seek an overall ecological integration (from microsytems to macrosystems). We couch our conclusions in terms of suggestions (even exhortations) for change, because we believe understanding comes from actually working with the phenomena in question, as implied in both Dearborn's Dictum ("If you want to understand something, try to change it") and Lewin's Law ("There is nothing so practical as a good theory"). Thus to understand abusive families is to try to change them for the better. (Surely no one would suggest we try to change them for the worse, though the skeptic would say that many of the intervention strategies used thus far have done precisely that.)

Our task, then, is to bring together an agenda for social reform that does justice to the evidence, to the moral principles involved, and to families needing assistance. We do not offer the usual shopping list of social changes needed to better approximate the millennium. We believe the evidence argues persuasively that no quick fix or band-aid intervention program will do. There are some fundamental cultural, socioeconomic, and political forces at work here. But this recognition is consistent with a very pragmatic program of social reform accomplished on the local level, in the communities and neighborhood ecological niches where families play out the dramas of their lives. Perhaps our best course is to be cautious and pragmatic visionaries.

EVIDENCE OF PROGRESS

Developing a social conscience is no small accomplishment. It is a major step in the normal development of an individual; it is also an important step for a whole civilization. As the often grisly history of childhood makes abundantly clear, social conscience is a relatively recent invention with respect to the treatment of children in many cultures, including our own. Without a concept of the child's right to nurturance and integrity (freedom from violation), there is no way even to define abuse and neglect as a problem, let alone solve it. In that sense, then, this discussion is at once both a challenge and a hopeful conclusion. It presumes that there is a social conscience to be appealed to and that the basic right of children and youth to integrity, as we use the term, is recognized and accepted by our civilization.

While both of these presumptions are not completely accurate, it would be wrong totally to deny their validity. We work from them, both because we need to believe in them and because the available evidence documents their existence, albeit in less-than-perfect form. This fact is a necessary resource in meeting the problem of maltreatment. Our other efforts are designed to build upon and expand the integrity of children as guaranteed by individual and collective social conscience. Having argued that there is a basis for meeting the problem of maltreatment, we must immediately refine the issue.

The first step in this process is to be cautious in our claims and our rhetoric. One way of doing this is to refrain from indulging in the now all-too-familiar crisis motif in which social problems are typically cast and then cast off. Are we facing a child abuse and neglect crisis? Does the problem demand an immediate and massive national intervention campaign? More than two decades of this kind of rhetoric have led us to believe that an issue is serious only when it is proclaimed a crisis, particularly in conjunction with a congressional hearing, and is solved only when a government agency is directed to respond by politicians prodded into action by a spirited public demonstration of interest and support for intervention. Hunger, health care, child pornography, declining test scores, poverty, pollution, the budget deficit, and many other genuinely serious issues have gone this crisis intervention route.

While it may be useful and even essential for real progress, this sequence is not in itself the solution. The crux of the matter lies in the activities of what in economic terms is called the private sector. This economic analogy is worth pursuing. Direct government efforts to deal with the problem of unemployment are marginal when compared with the impact of private enterprises: jobs numbering in the tens of thousands versus the millions. Thus government is generally recognized as the employer of last resort, at best. Moreover, its performance as an employer is not always a sterling example of efficiency or productivity. Likewise, government efforts to intervene dramatically in the problem of maltreatment are necessarily limited, both in scope and effectiveness. But they are crucial. Governmental action can set the standard for care, support model programs, and offer leadership to communities, private agencies, and individual citizens.

Certainly, we do not want to pay the price of totalitarianism to deal with the problem of the maltreatment of children and youth. Overall, however, we think our problem is one of too little rather than too much collective action on behalf of children. To protect the integrity of children and avoid totalitarianism we must rely upon a mix of formal and informal family support systems, collaborative networks of good citizens, private service agencies, relatives, neighbors, and friends to support families. In such a scheme, and only in that case, can public agencies effectively perform their function as parent of last resort, without violating the essential principles of a democratic society.

The problem of child maltreatment is so insidiously woven into the fabric of daily life that no single dramatic intervention is likely to succeed. The necessary conditions for maltreatment—an antichild ideology and isolation from potent, prosocial support systems—inextricably link the prevention of maltreatment of children and youth with the development of a more socially integrated and humane society. Having become civilized enough to recognize abuse and neglect as a violation of a child's right to integrity, we must now build the mechanisms to guarantee that right. It is thus a chronic rather than an acute problem. It is not and never will be enough simply and dramatically to remove children from abusive homes, for example. But there is an important role for child advocates to play in giving voice to the human rights of children. The UN Convention on the Rights of the Child provides a global foundation for doing so and can become an effective tool for child protection (Bedard & Garbarino, 1996).

The real test comes in the weeks, months, and years that follow any such declaration. Are the family's fundamental problems addressed? Does action happen to back up the words spoken? Does enlightened policy get translated into effective practice? Many of our most fundamental values, institutional arrangements, and patterns of daily behavior are implicated in the problem and in any genuine solution. Successful coping with the problem does not require some dramatic action by an agency or group of agencies to solve the crisis once and for all. It does not depend on dramatic upheaval. Rather, it calls for a determined effort to readjust many of the day-to-day patterns of our life as a society. This is a task that can only be accomplished in small pieces. It is a matter of individuals and communities amplifying some patterns and suppressing others. It means building up community systems of support for families: values, informal relationships, and institutional structures. It means prevention.

RESOURCES FOR PROTECTING CHILDREN AND YOUTH

Where can we find the resources necessary to meet the problem of maltreatment? To answer this question we must compile an agenda for individuals and communities. The solution, like the problem, lies in ourselves, both individually and collectively. We can begin with efforts to reduce violence in the family.

Quelling Family Violence

Violence is so much a part of our way of life that we hardly notice anything but the most extreme examples. While the connection between violence and child abuse may seem obvious to some, it is not clear in the minds of many; one person's discipline is another's abuse. Moreover, once physical force is legitimized and established as a pattern in one arena, it tends to permeate throughout a social system. Rather than defusing hostility and tension, the expression of violence tends to increase the likelihood of future violence. The little old woman who lived in a shoe is a prime example of just how dangerous it is to maintain physical force as a legitimate weapon against children. She did not know what to do so she spanked them. Some parents become involved in abuse because they do not know what else to do.

But why is violence a natural response when we are frustrated in matters of child control? We believe the answer lies in one of our central hypotheses: maltreatment is fundamentally a cultural problem. By defining the world in such a way that violence seems natural as a tool in family relations, we have set up a situation in which the possibility of abuse is always there, lurking in the background, ready to happen if a parent-child encounter pushes the right button.

There are two things we can do to counter our collective proclivity toward violence. First, we can join in creating an ethic of domestic nonviolence. Spare the child. We can try to live by the principle that people are not for hitting, and children are people, too. Such an ethical commitment is not enough in its own right, of course. But just as progress in civil rights for racial minorities was aided by public declarations, so public expressions of an ethic of nonviolence may contribute to a climate of private nonviolence. This is the spirit of Sweden's much-maligned law against spanking. Certainly we cannot fully legislate morality, but we can legislate a climate that nurtures morality. Although the incest taboo does not preclude sexual encounters between prohibited family members, it does serve as a counterweight to inappropriate expressions of sexuality.

The likelihood of sexual misuse does appear to be controlled in direct proportion to the closeness of the family tie and thus the cultural forcefulness of the taboo. It works better for natural fathers than for stepfathers, for example. In a sense, we are looking for something in the other areas of family violence to serve the function of the incest taboo. Presently, one is more likely rather than less likely to be assaulted the closer the relationship.

Second, we can learn to control children without the use of violence. Everyone knows that children need limits to grow up successfully. But how does one provide discipline without physical punishment? How does one manage without spanking? There are alternatives.

From the field of applied behavioral analysis have come many non-violent techniques for dealing with problem behaviors in children. Some are presented in the form of effective-parenting programs offered by churches, schools, and other groups concerned with parent education. Promoting these nonviolent disciplinary techniques is one of the most important, practical ways to prevent abuse. Using them will result in living proof that nonviolent child rearing is possible, and the techniques will teach others by example. What is more, they will provide a stimulus for changing values and attitudes to conform to new behavioral realities. Finally, these techniques fit well with programs designed to improve the overall quantity and quality of parent-child interaction. They can thus provide a strategy for creating a pattern of more adequate care in families where neglect is present.

Establishing High Standards of Care

If the little old woman who lived in the shoe is involved in child abuse, she is also involved in neglect. Therefore, defusing domestic violence is not enough. For one thing, it does not speak directly to the problem of neglect. Like abuse, neglect is fundamentally a social problem. The key to countering neglect is the standards we set and maintain for minimal child care. If we are to make progress in meeting this aspect of the maltreatment situation, we need to set these standards as high as is scientifically and practically possible. Thus we must make some collective decisions about the legitimate basic needs of children and stick to those decisions. While this may sound simple in the abstract, it is difficult to accomplish practically. The politics of child care are as labyrinthine as almost any (with the exception of energy, perhaps). This, coupled with the low status of children's issues in politics, makes for an uphill fight. In light of these circumstances, the efforts of child-advocacy organizations, such as the Children's Defense Fund, are noble indeed.

What are the minimal standards for the care of children and youth? They fall into three areas.

1. First, we must insist that every child and adolescent has access to basic preventive health care, education, immunization, clothing appropriate to the weather, dental care, adequate nutrition, and so on. A side benefit of these efforts can be greater integration of the family in potent, prosocial support systems. As things stand now, many children and youth lack these elementary aspects of adequate care.

2.   Second, we must insist that every child is provided with adult supervision appropriate to his or her age and level of development. Young children should not be left unattended by an adult or by an adolescent. Teenagers should not be thrown out and left to their own devices; nor should they be denied the freedom to explore the broader world outside the home. As we pointed out in Chapter One, where we defined maltreatment, the issue of appropriateness takes on special meaning during adolescence. Preadolescent children should receive the supervision of an adult. The several million latchkey children who return from elementary school to an empty house run the risk of being neglected. The remedy for this situation also has the effect of increasing the family's integration with prosocial support systems.

3.   Third, we must insist that every child be involved in an enduring relationship with a responsible, caring adult. This is particularly a problem for institutions that offer substitutes for parental care, such as foster care, schools, and day care.

There is growing concern that some institutional treatment is systematically abusive and that some foster care is neglectful. Without a guarantee of permanent placement in a stable and supportive environment, removing children from their homes is itself abusive in many circumstances. If all we can offer is institutionalized neglect, we might better leave all but those children in acute life-threatening circumstances alone. "Above all else, do not harm" is a good motto here as elsewhere. We must insist upon an environment that is responsive to the child. In infancy this means reacting positively with the social stimuli of smiling and vocalization. Later, it means taking an interest in the child's activities, thus avoiding emotional neglect. Where there is anything to work with at all, a creative program of skills development can probably serve to enforce these standards and improve the child's life.

It is easy to say that every child must have these things. How are we to translate such moral injunctions into day-to-day policy and practice? We must form a cooperative effort among professionals, public servants, and, most importantly, concerned citizens. There must be community discussion followed by authoritative action to promulgate these standards. Parent education is as important here as it is in defusing family violence. When we look beyond childhood to adolescence, the issue of appropriately high standards of care includes a requirement that teenagers be given information with which to evaluate their lives and their families for any deviant or socially risky patterns of behavior they may have learned at home, particularly when it comes to norms for family life. We must recognize the existence and prevalence of adolescent abuse and help teenagers deal with the problem in a climate of support. We have yet to face the reality that by insisting on adolescents being dependent upon and answerable to their parents, we lock some teenagers into abusive environments. We must expect disruptive, self-destructive, and even bizarre behavior from youth who are caught in a web of inappropriate and destructive parental behavior.

We need to validate adolescents as victims as a starting point in establishing higher standards of care. As things stand now, abused adolescents have few places to turn, especially if the abuse they suffer leaves no blatant physical wounds. There are, however, signs of help on the horizon. Several communities have organized programs to help abused teenagers by recognizing them as persons in need of assistance. Schools and courts can play an important role in establishing the validity of the adolescent as potential victim. Probably the most urgent need is for the people within each of these systems to become more aware of adolescent abuse and become informed of its central role in the lives of many youth in trouble.

Many victims themselves are not even aware that the treatment they have received is unjustified, and they rarely volunteer details in conversation. We found in our informal discussions with teenagers that, in classrooms containing mainly academically and socially troubled youth, the most common answer to the question, About how many out of each one hundred kids are abused or neglected? was, Between eighty and ninety, while for general high school classrooms the answers clustered between two and ten.

Standards of care need to be communicated to both youth and parents. We need to recognize the fact that one aspect of caring for adolescents is respecting their emerging independent rights. This realization implies some significant changes in the way our laws define and treat adolescents.

The changes just listed would help all teenagers, but for mistreated youth they could mean a legitimate way out of an abusive situation. The cards must be stacked differently between parents and their adolescents. The balance of power in court must be more even, for not all parents can or will provide what is best for their offspring, particularly in adolescence. As things stand now, outside of severely injuring or sexually abusing their teenagers, parents may do almost as they please. Laws have been written to protect youth from neglect and emotional assault, but they generally are interpreted in a framework of nearly supreme parental authority (despite the impotence some parents feel and express). In the future we must be sympathetic with parents who cannot handle the challenge of being responsible for the care of an adolescent in the United States. Parents are often correct in thinking they have too little control and too much responsibility when it comes to their teenagers. Families need help as families, but we must also recognize (if only as a practical necessity) the independent needs and rights of adolescents, particularly those in abusive situations.

Demonstrating the Community's Interest

Psychologist Urie Bronfenbrenner has used the following question to highlight his analysis of U.S. children: Who cares for America's families? This is the question we must continually ask of our communities and ourselves. Do we care? How can a community demonstrate its interest in all its children? Several things stand out. First, a community can provide adequate financial support for the professional agencies providing child care, parent education, and child protective services. While professional services cannot be the answer by themselves, they are an essential part, particularly when they work collaboratively with informal support systems (such as neighborhood social networks) and self-help groups (such as Parents Anonymous) to bring about higher standards of child care and children's rights.

When it comes to the special needs of adolescents, the logical place to begin is with those who are already responding to other human needs, namely, the mental health and social service establishment. Barring some fundamental change in the delivery of human services, this is the mechanism that will provide help to abused youth if such help is to be forthcoming. These agencies are mandated to serve troubled people. Their operations are established. They need only to direct their attention to abused youth and modify programs, policies, and procedures to accommodate them. Although dealing with and preventing adolescent abuse will require changes in many other sectors and in our attitudes, we may as well start where we can accomplish the most in the least amount of time, with the least effort and expense possible. Workers are already trained and settled. Less lead time is necessary than would be the case in creating new agencies. While this is not always the best course of action, in the case of services for adolescents we think it more effective to tinker than to manufacture.

When we speak of services for adolescents, people often conjure up images of yet another group of clients that will burden an already overloaded system. The burden is real, but in part the task is one of shifting resources away from efforts to cope with abused adolescents as "trouble" and toward efforts to help them as "troubled." We advocate two routes for change: (1) tailoring existing agencies to meet adolescent needs; and (2) broadening the capacity of the services that are already offered to make room for all who need help. The first would require little or no extra funding. The second would require an expansion or shifting of resources. The struggle for adequate funding of youth services is a long-standing effort that needs to continue, for even in financial terms the cost of helping pales when compared with the cost of ignoring, particularly if a flexible strategy utilizing volunteers and self-help groups is adopted.

A good first step in adapting the existing social-service structure to the special needs of adolescents is for professionals to become aware that many of the troubled youth with whom they deal are victims of abuse and as such have special needs. With that in mind, established agencies could modify their services to meet the needs of these youth. Crisis hot lines can be expanded to offer twenty-four-hour service, so that a voice is available when needed. Residential units can begin to offer part-time help, allowing teenagers to make regular visits during predictable trouble times, such as weekends. This would allow youth to remain a part of their communities and help them avoid the dangers of institutionalization. There is a crying need for more short-term respite shelters, in which youth can receive no-questions-asked protective care away from home when domestic problems (particularly chronic ones) reach occasional, acute crisis proportions. Another way for the community to demonstrate its concern is for mental health and other agencies to ask their younger clients about abuse at home as part of regular counseling and preventive programs.

Building Institutional Cooperation

One reason our nation's social service system fails to meet the needs of mistreated youth is because of the way it developed, a little at a time, along a rehabilitative medical model. Each agency was established in response to a specific problem and was organized around meeting a specific need. As a result, our system is based on categorical programs that deal exclusively with alcohol or drug abuse or that only aid in family planning, vocational guidance programs, and so on. Professionals within the system need to be able to label the problem before they can assign the person to services and services to the person. Although they may want to help the whole person, individual helpers in these agencies must swim against a strong bureaucratic tide.

Caseworkers know that most of the problems that a given family may present to a variety of different agencies often stem from the same source of dysfunction. A single problem can have many symptoms as well as multiple consequences. A single-parent family headed by an unemployed alcoholic, for example, can (and often does) wind up on numerous case loads. If our agencies were designed to deal with any need a family may have, that family would be served both more comprehensively and with less stigmatization. Some alternative agencies for youth have taken this generic approach, offering medical, legal, and mental health services to any teenager who needs them, regardless of the nature of the problem that brought him or her through the door.

Supporting such programs is one way a community can show that it cares for its youth. A community can make it clear to all families that it abhors domestic violence and insists upon adequate child care. This means electing public officials whose views on these matters clearly support a nonviolent, caring environment for children. It means insisting that the schools be positive models of both nonviolent discipline and active care so that they do not exemplify abuse or neglect.

As we noted earlier, this positive modeling is not to be taken for granted. It means employing judges, county attorneys, and police who implement this goal in their day-to-day handling of child-maltreatment cases. It means providing active support for communitywide child- and family-advocacy efforts, such as an official family week or child abuse awareness week, which include explicit statements by community leaders (particularly from business and government) in support of nonviolent family relations and high standards of child care. Civic groups must take the lead in shaping community consciousness, using "spare the child" as a slogan for community awareness. In addition, the community can demonstrate a special concern for adolescent victims. Instead of requiring caseworkers to make choices between children and adolescents, we advocate that communities underwrite the appointment of one or more staff members as specialists in adolescent abuse.

These people would receive all reports involving teenagers and deal with them exclusively. Protective service agencies usually can authorize some services (such as day care for young children), but they generally provide little treatment on their own. Their role is closer to brokerage, advocacy, or referral, both on behalf of the individuals with specific agencies and on behalf of adolescent victims in general with the total community. This role is just what is needed in many adolescent-abuse cases.

Protective services cannot handle the multiple problems of abusive families. The success of protective services depends upon the success of referrals to human service agencies. This highlights the need for informed and trusting relationships among agencies. Right now, most communities offer sporadic, short-term services to abusive and neglectful families. These services are sometimes independent of other community service programs, in part because referrals often fail: clients refuse service; agencies refuse to serve because criteria are not met; liaisons are inadequate. Many families in trouble need lots of help, from psychotherapy to budget management to family planning. Being crisis-oriented, child protection services generally are not designed to meet such divergent long-term needs. Other agencies must help.

Unfortunately, the current structure of most social service systems encourages competition instead of cooperation. Professionals often are forced to compete for funding and clientele. If all service agencies functioned as a unit (the generic approach) devoted to helping any problem, people might receive more cohesive and comprehensive service. This would require organizational changes, for unless all a community's helping agencies are one in function, they will have a hard time interacting as if they were one in spirit. The community council approach, in which the community's power structure is drawn into a regular relationship with the network of social service agencies around the issue of maltreatment, is one way to forge this alliance.

Such a community council can establish and support norms and structures of cooperation and can provide the muscle needed to make cooperation happen where it otherwise might succumb to interagency rivalries. Working with needy families entails making judgments in many areas: medical, legal, psychological. No individual or agency acting alone can make these far-ranging decisions effectively. Without community support systems providing feedback and nurturance to the protective service agency and others involved, it is unlikely that either the best interests of the youth or the community will be served.

All of this points to asking several people, each with expertise in a different area, to decide collectively which services a given family should receive. The multidisciplinary team concept is a strong one for child-abuse cases and has special relevance to cases involving abused teenagers.

Unfortunately, the concept is too often given only lip service in actual practice. Multidisciplinary teams can assess the situation and make recommendations for both long-term rehabilitation and short-term crisis management. The major participants on such teams are protective service workers, but other professionals such as nurses, pediatricians, foster-care staff, lawyers, law enforcement officials, and psychologists may participate part-time. The team generally is not involved with direct service; it decides which course of action is best and ideally performs the all-important function of following up on cases. Central to these deliberations is the role that out-of-home placement will play in the case. Unless the foster-care implications are realistically considered, case management will be a figment of the team's imagination.

One of the primary responsibilities of the social service community is to make sure that no one is institutionalized needlessly. Mistreated youth are at high risk for institutionalization, primarily because of the psychological damage they have sustained, their frequent bouts of unmanageability, and parental inclination to reject them. They are more likely to behave in some deviant way and they are also less likely to "play the game" well when dealing with a bureaucracy. Service professionals must make sure that institutionalization is only a last resort. Community leaders must work to increase the number and quality of alternative placements so that the last resort is not the first by default.

During the past twenty years, agencies have sprung up to help adolescents with all sorts of problems. They have taken the form of runaway houses, crisis centers, drug rehabilitation programs, family planning clinics, hot lines, and referral agencies. Their presence has no doubt improved the lot of troubled youth, but three main problems block their effectiveness: (1) there are not enough of them, and they are practically nonexistent outside metropolitan areas; (2) most are on shaky fiscal grounds; and (3) many do not have smooth working relationships with the regular social service agencies in their communities. One of the most important functions that an alternative agency can have is that of advocacy. On a collective basis, this means lobbying for the legitimate rights of young people. Individually, it means watching after the interests of the adolescents who have sought help at the agency's door. Both processes can set the alternative agencies in conflict with the established ones. Both processes can work if the agency has good connections with sympathetic professionals and community leaders.

One needs a roster of sympathetic individuals within other community agencies to provide access to speedy and competent help. Individuals within agencies account for much of the success or failure of a particular referral. Workers also need to act as intermediaries between the different institutions that may be dealing with a given teenager. Running interference for a client is a necessary service and is the common denominator of youth-advocacy services. The roster of sympathetic professionals is an essential part of such advocacy efforts if they are to be more than sound and fury. Such a roster should include people who work in both the settings where adolescents normally spend time (schools and youth groups) and in the settings for troubled youth.

It is imperative that child protective service units and other agencies function cooperatively. A caring community can take the lead in forging such cooperative relationships. The inadequacy of community support is one reason why the average social service caseworker does not last long in the field, particularly in protective services. Burnout, the much-discussed problem that stimulates such a high turnover rate, is caused by the burden of large case loads and other stresses that overwhelm workers and make them feel incapable of doing a good job.

Professionals who are in the process of burning out tend to exhibit common symptoms: they tend to minimize involvement with the client through physical distancing, fail to maintain eye contact, shorten interviews, label the client in a derogatory manner, begin to treat their clients as mere cases, and go by the book in every detail; yet they often work excessive overtime. Of all areas of social casework, child protection services must be one of the most arduous. In addition to the normal feelings of responsibility that providing human services brings, workers must literally make life-and-death decisions. They must decide who gets removed from the home, who gets which type of care, and who gets helped at all.

These professionals are given the task of salvaging human beings from very painful circumstances. No training can ever fully protect them from the emotional drain that trying to help so many desperate people will cause. This sort of stress has some predictable effects, including denial and inhibition of anger, anxiety about physical harm, need for emotional gratification from clients, feelings of incompetence, anxiety about the effects of a decision, denial and projection of responsibility, feelings of total responsibility for the assigned families, difficulty separating personal from professional responsibility, the need to be in control, and even feelings of victimization. These workers will probably doubt their own professional and personal fitness at times. They need support. We need to recognize that it is not humanly possible for people to function well under such crushing responsibility for extended periods of time without a great deal of compensatory feedback and encouragement.

We must provide these workers with some sort of occasional diversion to prevent them from systematically burning themselves out. They need breaks: time to attend in-service training or to catch up on their paperwork, for example. Another tool is the professional support group. In these groups, those who deal with abuse professionally share these experiences, frustrations, and solutions. A support group can be as helpful for those who must experience abuse vicariously several times a day as it is for actual victims and perpetrators. Important as such support groups are, however, a supportive community is of equal or greater importance. As mentioned earlier, one reason why abused youth do not receive better help is that our system of helping them is so fragmented. A teenage prostitute who has run away from sexual abuse at home and who also has a drug dependency problem could be processed through the courts, a residential institution, a chemical dependency treatment program, and foster care without anyone ever realizing that she was abused. Until a community makes a concerted effort to coordinate the way it deals with adolescent abuse, people will continue to wind up buried in the files.

The problem of family violence touches nearly every social service agency. The people who must help people cope with these problems need to function within a coherent framework for, regardless of its dedication, no one agency can ever hope to help abused youth alone. Someone needs to call the local service professionals together. It makes very little difference who does it. Alternative agencies, child protective services, the juvenile court, mental health agencies, volunteer groups, and schools are all capable of calling these professionals together. Organizations such as the National Committee to Prevent Child Abuse and APSAC could play a role through affiliated local organizations. Different agencies have taken the lead in different communities. The important thing is that someone does it.

The first step this coalition should take is to find out what is going on in the community. We do not really have a national social service system. It is instead a patchwork of more than three thousand county systems. That entails a local survey of the available resources. This initial survey should be fairly swift. It is, after all, only a means to an end, and an in-depth scrutiny could block the whole process because of the time involved. Once such a survey is done, the organizing force can call a communitywide conference to discuss child and adolescent abuse and the local response to it. This group could then map out a strategy for dealing with victims of abuse.

The idea is to create a system that makes sure that no matter where children and youth enter it, they will be guided to the help they need. Once basic decisions are made, this group can offer training to the local service community designed to raise their consciousness of child and adolescent abuse and to help them deal with it. It can also begin to involve other local groups. For example, it might offer an intensive workshop on empathy for child protective service workers or on outlining the symptoms and dynamics of abuse for mental health counselors. It might sponsor a training session for foster parents on building interpersonal skills and raising the self-esteem of victims in their care. It might gather administrators, commissioners, legislators, and law enforcement officials to discuss their adversary roles with regard to abuse, weighing protection against rehabilitation.

Those individuals who process abuse cases through the courts could be asked for their opinions on specific problems, such as the precise ingredients that a doctor's statement in court should include. One essential task for this group is public education. Letting people know that they do not need to be mistreated does no good if there is no place for them to go for help.

Communities that have started public awareness campaigns report a predictable increase in reporting. The machinery to respond must be in place before the public is informed. A foundation of public sympathy and concern, not a knee-jerk response, is the goal. The needs exist, and they will overwhelm any system that is not ready to deal with the cases. For this reason, public education programs should emphasize the importance of self-help groups and volunteers as adjuncts to professional service programs.

Strengthening Families

One way to help prevent child maltreatment is to support families in times of crisis, such as when unemployment or illness produces acute stress. A second way is to provide special services to families at high risk for maltreatment because of the values or prior experience of the parents or some special developmental difficulty of the child. A third way is to strengthen the family as a social entity. This last area is at the heart of the matter and can be accomplished in several ways. It is easy to see how strengthening families is an essential part of our efforts to solve the problem of maltreatment. If we increase the psychological and social resources of parents, we increase the likelihood that they can and will provide adequate care for their children.

But we cannot ignore the fact that our analysis clearly points to a need to go beyond conventional notions of strengthening families by equipping them to stand on their own and be self-sufficient. Indeed, it is precisely this go-it-alone mentality that we have repeatedly criticized. We believe one of the most important ways to strengthen families is by building bridges between their members and the outside world. Positive dependency (interdependency, really) is our goal, in addition to individual coping skills.

Our ecological perspective tells us that families are dependent upon other social systems, like it or not. These connections must work for rather than against families. This idea undergirds our ideas about opening up and building social bridges as a way of strengthening families. Use the health care system as a support system for families. The birth of a child is an event that offers a special opportunity to promote social connection. Even isolated and alienated families can be ready for increasing their social relationships when a child is born. We can capitalize on this receptivity. We could provide a "health visitor" to every family when a child is born, as has been recommended by the U.S. Advisory Board on Child Abuse (Melton & Barry, 1994). This person would begin visiting even before the baby is born and continue well afterward. The data are not yet in as to whether paraprofessionals can perform this role as well as trained professionals such as nurses, but the key is to provide an enduring relationship with the same caring person.

Such arrangements could be made with other institutions also, such as schools. In fact, our goal should be a seamless social fabric in which the family is smoothly handed over from institution to institution as the child and family move through the life course. The physician or midwife bridges to the health visitor, who bridges to the Head Start or preschool teacher or day-care center worker, who bridges eventually to the elementary school teacher. Such an approach builds strength into the family-community relationship and stands on firm ground as a part of the ecology of the child's life.

This health-visitor approach is part of a broader concept, however. Many observers have commented that our nation's approach to medicine tends to focus on curing diseases rather than promoting health. The former is much less useful in dealing with child abuse and neglect than is the latter. If we think of the health care system as a family support system, we quickly recognize that it goes hand-in-hand with preventive medicine, for example, well-baby visits, immunization, dietary counseling, and lifestyle management. In both cases, the family develops a relationship with health care providers. For our purposes, however, that relationship is best when it combines connections to specific individuals over a long period (to develop feelings of attachment) with contact with a variety of individuals (to add a note of objectivity). Let us be clear that we are not talking about some intrusive "Big Brother" approach but rather a natural extension of our traditional family practice, ministering to the family's needs—perhaps more like a "Big Sister" approach. This begins with the birth of a child.

As we have learned more and more about childbirth and early infancy, it has become apparent that the more actively involved and in control of the situation the parents are, the greater is their feeling of attachment to the infant. The stronger these feelings, the less likely it is that the family will have trouble caring for the baby. Thus family-centered childbirth (such as the Lamaze method), father involvement in delivery, breast-feeding, and parent-infant contact in the first minutes of life all can be used to promote a stronger family bond. Here, as in all our efforts, the goal is to increase the family's social and psychological resources. By viewing birth as a social event and capitalizing on its implicit power, we can take advantage of the opportunity it presents us to recognize and encourage the role of natural helping networks and natural neighbors. Where do most people get most of the help they need and receive on a day-to-day basis? Most of us rely mainly on friends, relatives, and neighbors. Just as our economy depends on the free enterprise system, so our social services are mainly provided by exchanges of assistance that are not professionally run. Once we recognize this, we have taken an important step.

Several questions leap out at us: What are the existing networks in which the family is already involved or could potentially become involved? Are there individuals who are particularly adept at or interested in helping others in their neighborhood? Can they provide the missing link between the professional responsible for child protection and the families in a given area? If we invest the time and energy to gain the trust of an area's natural helping networks, we can use that relationship to enhance prevention, case identification, and treatment. All our efforts are a coherent campaign aimed at increasing the professional's access to the community's social resources and the community's access to the professional's expertise.

Everybody needs a friend, and every friend sometimes needs help to be both a good friend and a good citizen. Alice Collins and Diane Pancoast (1976) called this strategy the consultation model. In it, the professional works with key citizens and neighbors on behalf of children and their families. Wherever possible, use trained volunteers and self-help groups. Self-help groups, such as Parents Anonymous, are effective and cost relatively little to operate. This cost effectiveness promises to be of increasing importance in coming years. But volunteers, no matter how well trained and how highly motivated, and self-help groups, no matter how emotionally involved and caring, are not going to solve all problems. No one specific strategy will. They can, however, handle many situations, thus freeing the professional for the situations that are too volatile or too unattractive for lay intervention. Moreover, professional resources can be concentrated in a way that is rarely possible now.

Programs such as Homebuilders can be used more widely. In the Homebuilders Program a team of counseling specialists can rally around a family in trouble when all conventional approaches have failed and family breakup is imminent. The therapeutic team spends all its time with the family—for up to six weeks if necessary—trying to rescue parents and children from dysfunction.

By the time the children of abusive families reach adolescence, their parents may have exposed them to more than a decade's worth of inadequate care. Neither the teenagers nor the parents are likely to feel good about their relationships, nor will they be particularly disposed to discuss the matter, a source of failure, with outsiders. In contrast, while parents who have never abused their child before may not have had an idyllic family life, they have refrained from abuse for at least ten years. This means that they have managed as parents (at least in comparison with those who began abuse during childhood) until they fail to meet the challenge of coping with a teenager. They may be more inclined to discuss parenthood because they have some positive feelings about parenthood and they may therefore be more willing to change their behavior in order to regain their original state of equilibrium. The task here may be much more one of rehabilitation.

One very important aspect of the problem is the need to work with parents while a teenager is out of the home (for example, because of running away) to smooth the youth's reentry into the family. If a well-designed group home or therapeutic foster care is available, it may well be the best course of action for long-term victims. The relative wisdom of removal is in part a developmental matter; it may be more appropriate for teenagers than for children, more for chronic than for acute problems. There are many specific services that local agencies could provide to abused youth and their families, some to one group more than another. Mental health agencies could offer peer self-help groups for abuse victims. They could also offer support groups for abusive parents. They could counsel the parents of a runaway while the youth is absent in order to smooth the eventual reentry. They could offer training in development for families that would include information about the adolescent stage in the life cycle. They could also alert concerned parents to the consequences of physical punishment, promote nonviolent forms of conflict resolution, and deal with the knotty problems of adolescent sexuality, particularly where stepparents are concerned. Agencies dealing with the foster-care system should treat the placement of an adolescent for what it is: a deal. Teenagers are completely capable of leaving any setting they do not like.

With adolescents, a foster-care relationship is a mutual arrangement in that the youth's consent must be received if it is to be successful. Caseworkers also should consider the possible wrenching effect of placing a teenager in an unfamiliar community. Greater attention to an adolescent's own social network might pay off in terms of more durable and effective placements. Concerned relatives may offer an untapped resource to workers making placements, but legislative and policy revisions may be necessary to make use of them. One particularly promising concept for successful placement of teenagers is therapeutic foster care. Therapeutic foster homes differ from traditional foster homes in that the foster parents are specifically recruited to work with the seriously disturbed children; they are paid a stipend above and beyond the money paid to regular foster parents; they receive special training; and they have additional professional and social supports built in. In most cases only one child is placed per home, and rarely would there be more than two children per home.

A professional counselor or caseworker is assigned to from eight to twelve youngsters, generally, with the expectation of conducting at least one treatment session per week for each youngster. In addition, the foster parents receive the benefits of a face-to-face contact with the professional staff member weekly. This is a marked contrast with regular foster care, where the foster parents may go several weeks or even months in between visits from caseworkers. A specific attempt is often made in therapeutic foster homes to build amongst the various families a cohesive network that provides emotional and social support for its members. This is almost akin to creating an "extended family" for each household, since the foster parents are encouraged to assist each other in ways that extended family members have traditionally done.

CHANGING VALUES

But all the important changes that agencies and institutions combined can make are probably insufficient. Our ecological perspective points out that there are sources of risk in our macrosystem, in the blueprints we use to define and organize our lives. We need to make the difficult and slow progress on these basic cultural issues. There are two major areas that deserve attention here: (1) our criteria for determining personal worth and (2) our standards of acceptable behavior during family conflict. Our materialistic ethic undermines the sense of self-worth in people of moderate means and contributes to family conflict. People who feel they are not good enough, based upon their lack of accumulated wealth, will not feel especially good about their activities. This applies to parenthood. For the economically secure, ascription to this materialistic ethic is lamentable. It may cause needless problems, since a strong sense of self-worth is the key element in sensitive, responsive parental behavior.

Obviously, a shift in values would solve the problem for the middle class. But for the poor this is not enough, and poverty remains the central problem facing child-abusing families. In our materialistic society, economic inadequacy is widespread and is related to social impoverishment. It is no wonder people who are reminded every day that they are worth less than most other people because they earn less do not always feel or act like competent parents. In this way, child abuse really is a class phenomenon. Certainly, adolescent victims who have a history of abuse come from this context. Every time abusing parents hit their children, they reinforce their own conviction that they are inadequate parents. Rejection of our materialistic ethic and redistribution of the wealth of this country are goals that many have and will continue to work for.

The role that resource redistribution would play in defusing the problem of abuse is just one more reason for advocating it. In terms of direct impact upon abuse, however, the ground rules we set for family conflict are more important than the economic issues. We do not get upset about family members hitting or slapping each other the way we would if strangers were to be similarly assaultive: the first is normal; the second, criminal. If someone will not listen to reason, we generally permit a family member to use violence. We must take violence within families as seriously as we do violence between strangers. To do that we need to provide families with nonviolent mechanisms for resolving conflicts.

The family-teaching model offers one example in this area. People need to learn to fight fairly and to air their grievances in a controlled, nonviolent way. The model requires greater reliance on the rational presentation of grievances without value judgments, on bargaining toward compromise, and on effective action that carries out the dictates of the resolution. Parents need practical suggestions to do this, particularly when the natural forces at work in the family facing adolescence work in the opposite direction.

STUDYING THE HUMAN ECOLOGY OF CHILD MALTREATMENT

No discussion of child abuse and neglect is complete without a request for more thoughtful research on the topic. The methodological problems involved are staggering (National Research Council, 1993). Finding an adequate sample to study, devising appropriate measures to use, and designing valid comparisons between groups and treatments is enough to drive the investigator either into despair or into some less-than-adequate compromise between expediency and validity. The very difficulty of the challenge makes it more important that communities support further research. The evidence drawn from the research that's been done so far is helpful despite its limitations and inability to provide comprehensive answers.

Still, we need to know more, and our discussion thus far contains many hypotheses for studies of how to prevent child maltreatment by working on the human ecology of the family from the microsystem to the macrosystem. This need for improved information is particularly pressing when it comes to adolescents.

BRINGING THE DEVELOPMENTAL PERSPECTIVE TO FRUITION

Our agenda can harness our practical social conscience in pursuit of an idealized world in which community and family work together on behalf of the development of children and youth. Some of the issues have greater relevance for children than for teenagers (and vice versa), though most are important across the board. We believe basic economic issues are most important in protecting young children, while "rights" issues are particularly important for adolescents who need the community's support in negotiating ground rules with parents. The special issues for adolescents come from the poor credibility of the adolescent as victim and the necessity of "empowering" adolescents (to use Edward Albee's term) in their own defense.

In the matter of prevention, there are two central issues: (1) providing more effective community responses to child maltreatment to cut off the flow of "child-abuse cases grown up" and (2) increasing the social skills of both parents and youth to aid them in navigating the tricky currents and crosscurrents of early adolescence.

The mistreatment of youth is a social problem. Manis (1974) proposed three criteria for assessing the seriousness of social problems: (1) *primacy,* or how much the problem acts as a cause of other problems and is the result of multiple factors; (2) *magnitude,* or the extent or frequency in the population; and (3) *severity,* or the degree or level of harmfulness. In these terms, maltreatment is a serious problem primarily because of its primacy and severity. It stimulates many other problems (including running away, delinquency, future child abuse, and psychological deficiencies), and it evolves from a complex set of social and psychological forces at work in the family. It is a severe problem because it appears that many of its victims experience highly impaired functioning that may well continue into adulthood. The least serious aspect of the problem is its magnitude. Most families do not mistreat their offspring.

However, the primacy and severity of the problem, even in the relatively small percentages of the population involved, make maltreatment a very serious problem. As we see it, we need to change many things on many levels to cope with this problem. We need to make some organizational changes in our social service systems. We need more information about abuse and maltreatment. We need to mobilize the resources of our schools. We need legislated change in the status of youth in general and in relation to their families in particular. More fundamentally, we need to change the way we think about families, violence, power, and youth. As always, we must examine these patterns in the social contexts in which they occur. Teachers, counselors, probation officers, and police need to be constantly alert to the possibility that the youth with whom they are dealing may be abused or neglected. This parallels the need for these gatekeepers to consider the role of learning disabilities in the behavior of troubled youth. It is especially important that key people in the schools and law enforcement agencies know the local social service system and its people. No effort to change the way a community deals with adolescent abuse can afford to ignore these two institutions—schools and the criminal justice system—and the people who run them. There is no substitute for personal connections.

Bring Schools into the Prevention Movement

Schools have made great gains in some aspects of helping abuse victims, primarily in compliance with mandatory reporting laws. Nearly all large school districts and most small ones now provide referrals and some counseling services for abuse victims. Most school districts now have a formal policy on abuse. And many of our large school districts have even conducted their own campaigns to educate the public about abuse. But the school has yet to perform its most effective role in the area of prevention. Schools cannot be ignored in any community campaign that hopes to improve the lot of abused children. Through the schools we can reach nearly all youth without any fear of labeling. Preventive efforts can take many forms.

Concerned schools can attune educators in elementary and junior high schools to issues of parent-child conflict, so they can better address those issues informally with students. Teachers can also become more sensitive to the special needs of abused youth, even providing them with special in-class attention. Parent-teacher organizations could sponsor classes for parents in nonviolent conflict resolution, sexuality, and the dynamics of reconstituted families involving stepparents and take an official stand against physical punishment at school. Schools can offer classes in life management and human development; some already do. These classes can begin to prepare youth for the decisions they will need to make as parents. By showing teenagers exactly what babies are capable of doing, the classes also could help eliminate the unrealistic expectations held by many abusing parents. A course in adolescent development could give students insight into themselves. If they gain a thorough understanding of adolescence, such a course might even help when their own children reach that age, though the long-term effectiveness of parent education is undocumented. Schools might also help teenagers in foster care or in group homes to become integrated into classroom life. Such help is crucial for youth returning to schools from institutions.

There is another way that the schools can help teenagers: by recognizing the fact that traditional education is frustrating to those who do not succeed at it. People do not like to encounter their defeats on a daily basis; yet those who do not perform well academically are expected to attend regularly and behave themselves properly while in school. Instead of planning some alternate form of education for these students, schools often expel them. Schools also can become active in promoting youth self-help groups and general awareness of adolescent abuse so that the powerful processes of the adolescent peer group are working on behalfoof victims.

Reform the Juvenile Justice System

More than schools, the criminal justice system deals directly with the abuse of children and adolescents. Since many abused youth come to the courts because of theiroown offensive acts, attorneys and judges need to be alert to abuse symptoms. The correlations we drew earlier between abuse and serious hard-core delinquency (particularly if it involves violence) are so strong that it is not unrealistic to recommend an attitude of assuming the youth has been mistreated until proven otherwise. The assumption of "innocent by virtue of abuse" is a good starting point with criminally violent youth, because it simultaneously tells the court that intervention is required and that rehabilitation of the offender's social skills is a precondition for future good behavior. The acknowledgment and introduction of a juvenile's family history in the courtroom can change the disposition of his or her case dramatically.

The juvenile justice system itself is slow. Adolescents who encounter the court solely as a result of abuse should be given priority on the docket because of the potential for developmental damage. Cases that involve both adult criminal charges for the parents and child-dependency hearings for the adolescent should be coordinated to avoid undue delay. Because the system is so complicated, teenagers need someone to help them navigate it. Courts could provide volunteers to watch over a given case and appear in court with the youth to make sure his or her interests are protected. The volunteers are called guardian ad litem, and they usually need some legal or paralegal training. Such services are becoming more common.

The burden of proof must be lightened in abuse cases. Since teenage bodies are less likely to show physical damage, the grounds for providing services to adolescents need to be broader. Someone—perhaps the multidisciplinary team we described earlier—must be empowered to decide whether or not the family can be helped. Once that decision is made, the wheels should move quickly.

One little-used response to dysfunctional families with adolescents is *emancipation,* the process that allows minors to live independently of their parents, giving them the rights they would need to do so. Many states have emancipation procedures, but almost all require parental consent. When the home is inhospitable, and the youth is capable of living alone, emancipation is a nonrestrictive solution. Providing the small amount of support that an older teenager would need to maintain a household takes much less time and energy than does placing her or him in the care of an adult or an institution. It also increases the likelihood that the adolescent will not be mistreated by the person who is supposed to be providing care. For many youth, especially those who have suffered severe, prolonged abuse, independent living may present an insurmountable challenge because of their damaged social skills and psyches. But there are adolescents who could manage quite well independently. Obviously, parental permission is often an obstacle that prevents such an arrangement, and laws might be changed so that a neutral third party can play a larger role. This was the thrustof Swedish legislative initiatives dealing with procedures to permit children to be divorced from their parents.

When circumstances permit, independent living is a legitimate solution that should be an option. We need every option to meet the wide range of needs manifest among mistreated youth. In the same vein, we need to recognize that runaway youth are functionally emancipated. As things stand now, a lack of rights and resources leaves runaways with no means of legitimate support. We must recognize that regardless of the reason for leaving home, these youth already are living independently, and we may need to allow them to do so within the law. Underage runaways should be able to attend school, enter into contracts, rent housing, consent to the provision of medical care, and work nights.

We need to allow youth to get help without parents' permission. Granting these rights would not condone or encourage running away; it would merely allow those who have left home to survive. It would recognize the fact that many runaways had no other choice but to leave their parents. It would begin to lift the burden of the situation from the teenager. Counseling parents of runaways while the youth is out of the home could help to determine the underlying causes of the behavior and smooth the runaway's reentry into the family when such an arrangement is possible. The jailing of children is a repugnant practice that has been terminated on the federal level and in many states. Youth advocates now are pressing states to comply with the federal directive to deinstitutionalize status offenders, a group that includes many victims of abuse.

We need also to protect youth from abuse when they are institutionalized both outside the penal system and within it. Studies are underway to investigate the nature, causes, and effects of abuse and neglect within residential institutions. Other projects have sought to develop procedures for handling complaints of abuse within institutions. This may include encouraging reports of abuse, establishing ways of dealing with reports, and taking corrective action. Through its Developmental Disabilities Program, the federal government helped states establish advocates for youth in residential institutions. Institutional abuse, like parental abuse, flourishes in secrecy and isolation. We need to more consistently open institutions if we are to strengthen them in fulfilling their missions.

Mobilize the Community

If our understanding of abusive families is to be of benefit, it must become the foundation for action. The ecological perspective developed in this book implies that action cannot be limited to intervention strategies designed to change directly the family or the environment at only one level. As frequently stated, the maltreatment of children and youth is a social indicator describing the quality of life in a community or a society. The problems of maltreatment, then, cannot be adequately addressed by only one segment of a community, be it helping professionals, abusive parents, or researchers. Based on this knowledge, we define our ultimate goal as the primary prevention of child maltreatment, and we foresee it being accomplished by the mobilization of the total community.

One model for such total community organization relies on concepts from the fields of evaluation research and marketing. Michael Patton (1978) developed an approach toward evaluation that involves the users of the evaluation throughout the process of research. Applied to community organization as the primary preventive of child maltreatment, Patton's concept involves the total community in such a way that people are committed to and invested in the process of making society more supportive of effective childrearing.

From the field of marketing we draw on Philip Kotler's (1975) principles for nonprofit organizations. These principles provide a systematic conceptual framework for selling and implementing a program of primary prevention in a given community. The initial step in the process of community mobilization for primary prevention is the identification and organization of relevant decision makers and information users. We suggest that the community attempt to identify people from among social service professionals, city and county government officials, business and labor representatives, leaders in education and health care, and family members (including adolescents) from diverse neighborhoods.

An educational group process with these people could be implemented to focus evaluation questions. To begin, the group would study, among other things, insights into the developmental process as it relates to maltreatment and the ecological perspective proposed in this book. The second stage of the process would break the larger group into smaller task groups that would view the geographic area of the community as a market and segment it into neighborhoods that would be defined around variables such as age, lifestyle, socioeconomic status, and employment characteristics. It would also define formal and informal social networks around variables such as kinds of services and demographic characteristics.

The task groups would then choose the targets for action. At this point ownership of decisions by community members is crucial. These decision makers and information users must identify the systems and the neighborhoods needing change and those already functioning in a preventive mode. Financial and policy support can be planned and given to those systems in the community identified as already providing child care and homemaker, home health, parent support, and recreation services. Of course, the community needs to identify and empower a leader who coordinates the works of the task groups, monitors the functioning of the subsidized services, hires other part- or full-time workers to carry out the plans of the group, and coordinates public relations efforts.

As unmet needs are identified and commitment to programs for change are developed, they are presented to the total community in a systematic way through the use of a marketing model. The philosophy of primary prevention and our ecological perspective demand that these programs be planned to be supportive of all families rather than just those identified as high risk. Possible agenda items include identifying natural helping networks and providing consultation services to them; initiating a program of family-centered childbirth; developing exosystem supports, particularly between family and school; planning a campaign to change the image of teenagers as troublemakers; or developing youth self-help and support groups. Informal social systems such as neighborhood or support groups can be targeted and described according to demographic and other characteristics. Decisions related to the promotion variable revolve around use of mass media, face-to-face, and small group contacts to advertise the product. While mass media are important for public education, face-to-face contacts are essential for consultation in natural helping networks. Finally, both psychological and financial costs must be studied, especially in such a sensitive area as family support for the protection of children and youth.

HOPE FOR THE FUTURE

If people can be convinced that the wrong treatment they have received is really behind them and that they are not substandard individuals because they were abused, they tend to recover from the effects of abuse. We must get that message across to abuse victims and to the helping community, so that the community will attempt to give the victims realistic grounds for believing that help is available. We are in the hope business, if we are anything at all. Our interviews with mistreated youth convince us that it does happen:

QUESTION: Do you think other kids who have had the same kind of trouble that you've had—is there any hope for them?

ANSWER: There is if they're strong. You gotta be very strong to handle something like that. You gotta be able to let the past be the past, not the present. Which I have. I have faced up to the fact that things like this do happen. And I'm not the only one. And I know it. The other kids that won't say nothing or won't do nothing about it are the ones who are hurting the most.

Q: Who helped you?

A: If it wasn't for the school counselor and the teacher and my girlfriend's mother, I wouldn't have made it through high school and got my diploma. I would have just ended it all.

Q: What was most helpful to you during this time?

A: I'd have to say my social worker. She was the greatest help. I don't know. It wasn't really my social worker, just the attention I got from her. She treated me like a human being. Not just like a little gnat that you walk over like my parents did.

Q: Was that really a big change?

A: Oh yeah. It really was. It changed my whole outlook on life. I thought I was just not good. She changed my whole outlook. I felt like a human being. I felt like I had something to live for.

These young people are making it because they found community through its formal or informal support systems. Everyone needs this caring community, but the victims of maltreatment are critically dependent on it.

Q: Does it feel pretty risky?

A: Yeah—it's like walking on thin ice. You gotta remember that the past is the past, too. And you can't walk around with these parents that are beating you up all your life. You can grieve over it, but grieve and then walk, you know. Go away from it. Yeah, just don't get stuck there.

—⁓—

Our hope is that by approaching maltreatment ecologically and developmentally we can all get unstuck in dealing with this problem.

~~~ References

Aber, J. L., Allen, J. P., Carlson, V., & Cicchetti, D. (1989). The effects of maltreatment on development during early childhood: Recent studies and their theoretical, clinical and policy implications. In D. Cicchetti & V. Carlson (Eds.), *Child maltreatment* (pp. 579–619). New York: Cambridge University Press.

Adams-Tucker, C. (1982). Proximate effects of sexual abuse in childhood: A report on 28 children. *American Journal of Psychiatry, 139,* 135–152.

Albee, G. (1979, June). *Politics, power, prevention and social change.* Paper presented at the Vermont Conference on the Primary Prevention of Psychopathology, Burlington, VT.

Alexander, J. F. (1973). Defensive and supportive communications in normal and deviant families. *Journal of Consulting and Clinical Psychology, 40,* 223–231.

Alexander, P. C. (1990). Interventions with incestuous families. In S. W. Henggeler & E. M. Borduin (Eds.), *Family therapy and beyond: A multisystematic approach to treating the behavior problems in children and adolescents.* Pacific Grove, CA: Brooks/Cole.

Alfaro, J. (1976, January 1). Report of the New York State Assembly Select Committee on Child Abuse. *Child Protection Report, 2.*

Alfaro, J. D. (1981). Report on the relationship between child abuse and neglect and later socially deviant behavior. In R. J. Hunner & Y. E. Walker (Eds.), *Exploring the relationship between child abuse and delinquency* (pp. 175–219). Monclair, NJ: Allanheld, Osman.

Allen-Hagen, B., & Sickmund, M. (1993). *Juveniles and violence: juvenile offending and victimization.* Washington, DC: Office of Juvenile Justice and Delinquency Prevention.

Alley, J., Cundiff, B., & Terry, J. (1976, January 26). Child abuse in Georgia, 1975–1977. *Morbidity and mortality report* (pp. 33–35). Atlanta: Centers for Disease Control.

American Humane Association. (1977). *Annual report of the national clearinghouse on child abuse and neglect.* Denver, CO: Author.

American Humane Association. (1988). *Highlights of official child neglect and abuse reporting—1986.* Denver, CO: Author.

American Professional Society on the Abuse of Children (APSAC). (1995). *Practice guidelines: Psychosocial evaluation of suspected psychological maltreatment in children and adolescents.* Chicago: Author.

Aries, P. (1962). *Centuries of childhood: A social history of family life.* New York: Random House.

Aronfreed, J., & Paskal, V. (1969). Altruism, empathy and the conditioning of positive affect. In L. Berkowitz (Ed.), *Advances in experimental social psychology.* Orlando: Academic Press.

Astley, R. (1953). Multiple metaphyseal fractures in small children: Metaphyseal fragility of bone. *British Journal of Radiology, 26,* 577.

Attanucci, J. (1995). Timely characterization of mother-daughter and family-school relations: narrative understandings of adolescence. *Journal of Narrative and Life History, 3,* 99–116.

Atten, D., & Milner, J. (1987). Child abuse potential and work satisfaction in day-care employees. *Child Abuse & Neglect, 11,* 117–123.

Bandura, A. (1977). *Social learning theory.* Englewood Cliffs, NJ: Prentice Hall.

Bandura, A., & Walters, R. (1959). *Adolescent aggression.* New York: Ronald Press.

Barnett, D., Manley, J. T., & Cicchetti, D. (1991). Continuing toward and operational definition of psychological maltreatment. *Development and Psychopathology, 3,* 19–29.

Baumrind, D. (1971). Current patterns of parental authority. *Developmental Psychology Monograph, 4,* 1–103.

Baumrind, D. (1979). A dialectical materialist's perspective on knowing social reality. *New Directions in Child Development, 2,* 61–82.

Bavolek, S., Kline, D., McLaughlin, J., & Publicover, P. (1979). *The development of the adolescent parenting inventory (API): Identification of high-risk adolescents prior to parenthood.* Paper prepared at the Utah State University, Department of Special Education, Provo, UT.

Becker, J. V. (1994). Offenders: Characteristics and treatment. In R. E. Behrman (Ed.), *The future of children, 4*(2), 176–197. Los Altos, CA: The David and Lucille Packard Foundation.

Bedard, C., & Garbarino, J. (1996). *The UN convention on the rights of the child as a tool in child protection.* Ithaca, NY: Cornell University, Family Life Development Center.

Bee, H. L. (1967). Parent-child interaction and distractibility in 9-year-old children. *Merrill-Palmer Quarterly, 13,* 175–190.

Bell, C. (1991). Traumatic stress and children in danger. *Journal of Health Care for the Poor and Underserved, 2,* 175–188.

Bender, L., & Curran, F. (1940). Children and adolescents who kill. *Criminal Psychologist, 1,* 297–322.

Berdie, J., Berdie, M., Wexler, S., & Fisher, B. (1983). *An empirical study of families involved in adolescent maltreatment: Final report* (Grant No. 90-CA-837/01). Washington, DC: National Center on Child Abuse and Neglect, Department of Health and Human Services.

Berenson, A. B., San Miguel, V. V., & Wilkinson, G. S. (1992). Violence and its relationship to substance use in adolescent pregnancy. *Journal of Adolescent Health, 13*(6), 470–474.

Berkowitz, L. (1957). Effects of perceived dependency relationships upon conformity to group expectations. *Journal of Abnormal and Social Psychology, 55,* 350–354.

Berliner, L., & Conte, J. R. (1990). The process of victimization: The victim's perspective. *Child Abuse and Neglect, 114,* 29–40.

Berliner, L., & Elliott, D. M. (1996). Sexual abuse of children. In J. Briere, L. Berliner, J. A. Bulkley, C. Jenny, & T. Reid (Eds.), *The APSAC handbook on child maltreatment* (pp. 51–71). Thousand Oaks, CA: Sage.

Beutler, L. E., Williams, R. E., & Zetzer, H. A. (1994). Efficacy of treatment for victims of child sexual abuse. In R. E. Behrman (Ed.), *The future of children, 4*(2), 156–175. Los Altos, CA: The David and Lucille Packard Foundation.

Binet, A., & Simon, T. (1916). *The development of intelligence in children.* (E. S. Kite, Trans.). Baltimore, MD: Williams and Wilkins.

Blatt, E. (1990). Staff supervision and the prevention of institutional abuse and neglect. *Journal of Child and Youth Care, 4,* 73–80.

Blatt, E., & Brown, S. (1985, April). *Reporting practices of workers in New York State psychiatric facilities.* Paper presented at the New York State Conference on Child Abuse and Neglect, Albany, NY.

Blos, P. (1979). *Adolescent passage.* New York: International University Press.

Blum, R., & Runyan, C. (1980). Adolescent abuse: The dimensions of the problem. *Journal of Adolescent Health Care, 1,* 121–126.

Bourne, R., & Newberger, E. (Eds.). (1979). *Critical perspectives on child abuse.* Lexington, MA: Lexington Books.

Brannan, C., Jones, R., & Murch, J. (1992). *Castle Hill report: Practice guide.* Shrewsbury, England: Shropshire County Council.

Brazelton, B. (1977, October). *How the normal newborn shapes his environment.* Address presented at a seminar on Treatment of the Abused and Neglected Child, Denver, CO.

Briere, J. N., & Elliott, D. M. (1994). Immediate and long-term impacts of child sexual abuse. In R. E. Behrman (Ed.), *The future of children, 4*(2), 54–69. Los Altos, CA: The David and Lucille Packard Foundation.

Bronfenbrenner, U. (1970). *Two worlds of childhood.* New York: Russell Sage Foundation.

Bronfenbrenner, U. (1975). The origins of alienation. In U. Bronfenbrenner & M. Mahoney (Eds.), *Influences on human development.* Hinsdale, IL: Dryden Press.

Bronfenbrenner, U. (1979). *The ecology of human development.* Cambridge, MA: Harvard University Press.

Bronfenbrenner, U., & Mahoney, M. (1975). The structure and verification of hypothesis. In U. Bronfenbrenner & M. Mahoney (Eds.), *Influences on human development* (pp. 3–37). Hinsdale, IL: Dryden Press.

Bronfenbrenner, U., McClelland, P., Wethington, E., Moen, P., & Ceci, S. (1996). *The state of Americans.* New York: Free Press.

Browne, A., & Finkelhor, D. (1986). Impact of sexual abuse: A review of the research. *Psychological Bulletin, 99,* 66–77.

Budlong, M., Holden, M., & Mooney, A. (1993). *Therapeutic crisis intervention: A train the trainer curriculum* (3rd ed.). Ithaca, NY: Family Life Development Center.

Burgess, R., & Conger, R. (1978). Family interaction patterns in abusive, neglectful and normal families. *Child Development, 49,* 163–173.

Burgess, A., Janus, M., McCormack, A., & Wood, J. (1986). *Canadian runaways: Youth in turmoil and running for their lives.* Paper presented at the Symposium on Street Youth, Toronto, Ontario, Canada.

Bybee, D., & Mowbrary, C. T. (1993). Community response to child sexual abuse in day-care settings. *Families in Society, 74*(5), 268–281.

Caffey, J. (1946). Multiple fractures in long bones of infants suffering from chronic subdural hematoma. *American Journal of Roentgenology, 56,* 163–173.

Campbell, A. (1976). Subjective measures of well-being. *American Psychologist, 31,* 117–124.

Caspi, A., & Bem, D. (1990). Personality continuity and change across the life course. In L. Pervin (Ed.), *Handbook of personality theory and research* (pp. 549–575). New York: Guilford Press.

Chamberland, C., Bouchard, C., & Bevadry, J. (1986). Abusive and negligent behavior toward children: Canadian and American realities. *Canadian Journal of Behavioural Sciences, 18,* 391–412.

Cicchetti, D. (1989). How research on child maltreatment has informed the study of child development: Perspective from developmental psychopathology. In D. Cicchetti & V. Carlson (Eds.), *Child maltreatment* (pp. 377–431). New York: Cambridge University Press.

Cicchetti, D., Toth, S., & Bush, M. (1988). Developmental psychopathology and incompetence in childhood: Suggestions for intervention. In B. Lahey & A. Kazdin (Eds.), *Advances in clinical child psychology* (pp. 1–73). New York: Plenum.

Cochran, M., & Brassard, J. (1979). Social networks and child development. *Child Development, 50,* 601–616.

Collins, A., & Pancoast, D. (1976). *Natural helping networks.* Washington, DC: National Association of Social Workers.

Conte, J. R., & Schuerman, J. R. (1987). Factors associated with an increased impact on child sexual abuse. *Child Abuse and Neglect, 11,* 201–211.

Coopersmith, S. (1967). *The antecedents of self-esteem.* San Francisco: H. W. Freeman.

Corder, B. (1976). Adolescent parricide: A comparison with other adolescent murder. *American Journal of Psychiatry, 133,* 957.

Coser, R. (1975). The complexity of roles as a seedbed of individual autonomy. In L. C. Coser (Ed.), *The idea of social structure: Papers in honor of Robert K. Merton* (pp. 256–263). New York: Harcourt.

Coulton, J., Korbin, J., Su, M., & Chow, J. (1995). Community level factors and child maltreatment rates. *Child Development, 66,* 1262–1276.

Crane, J. (1991). The epidemic theory of ghettos and neighborhood effects on dropping out and teenage childbearing. *American Journal of Sociology, 96*(5), 1226–1259.

Crittenden, P. M. (1985). Social networks, quality of child rearing, and child development. *Child Development, 56,* 1299–1313.

Crittenden, P. M., Claussen, A. H., & Sugarman, D. B. (1994). Physical and psychological maltreatment in middle childhood and adolescence. *Development and Psychopathology, 6,* 145–164.

Crockenberg, S. B. (1981). Infant irritability, mother responsiveness, and social support influences on the security of infant-mother attachment. *Child Development, 52,* 857–865.

Crockenberg, S., & McCluskey, K. (1986). Change in maternal behavior during the baby's first year of life. *Child Development, 57,* 746–753.

Curtis, G. C. (1963). Violence breeds violence. Perhaps? *American Journal of Psychiatry, 120,* 386–387.

Daly, D. L., & Dowd, T. P. (1992). Characteristics of effective, harm-free environments for children in out-of-home care. *Child Welfare, 71*(6), 487–496.

Deccio, G., Horner, W., & Wilson, D. (1994). High-risk neighborhoods and high-risk families: Replication research related to the human ecology of child maltreatment. *Journal of Social Service Research, 18*(3–4), 123–137.

Devereux, E. C. (1970). The role of peer group experience in moral development. In J. P. Hill (Ed.), *Minnesota Symposia on Child Psychology, 4,* 94–140. Minneapolis: University of Minnesota Press.

Dickens, C. (1839). *Oliver Twist.* Philadelphia: Lea and Blanchard.

Dodge, K. A., Pettit, G. S., Bates, J. E., & Valente, E. (1995). Social information-processing patterns partially mediate the effect of early physical abuse on later conduct problems. *Journal of Abnormal Psychology, 104,* 632–643.

Dodge-Reyome, N. (1990). Executive directors' perceptions of the prevention of child abuse and maltreatment in residential facilities. *Journal of Child and Youth Care, 4,* 45–60.

Donabedian, A. (1980). *The definition of quality and approaches to its assessment.* Ann Arbor: Health Administration Press.

Doris, J., Mazur, R., & Thomas, M. (1995). Training in child protective services: A commentary on the amicus brief of Bruck and Ceci (1993/1995). *Psychology, Public Policy and Law, 1,* 479–493.

Downing, D. (1978). A selective study of child mortality. *Child Abuse and Neglect, 2,* 101–108.

Dubanoski, R., Inaba, M., & Gerkewicz, K. (1983). Corporal punishment in the schools: Myths, problems and alternatives. *Child Abuse and Neglect, 7*(3), 271–278.

Duncan, J. (1977). The immediate management of suicidal attempts in children and adolescents: Psychological aspects. *Journal of Family Practice, 4,* 77–80.

Durkin, R. (1982). No one will thank you: First thoughts on reporting institutional abuse. *Child and Youth Services, 4*(1–2), 109–113.

Eckenrode, J., & Wethington, E. (1990). The process and outcome of mobilizing social support. In S. Duck & R. C. Silver (Eds.), *Personal relationships and social support* (pp. 83–103). Thousand Oaks, CA: Sage.

Edens, F. M., & Smit, G. N. (1992). Effectiveness of a skills training program for residential child care workers. *Children and Youth Services Review, 14,* 541–552.

Egeland, B., Jacobvitz, D., & Sroufe, L. A. (1988). Breaking the cycle of abuse: Relationship predictors. *Child Development, 59,* 1080–1088.

Egeland, B., Pianta, R., & O'Brien, M. A. (1993). Maternal intrusiveness in infancy and child maladaptation in early school years. *Development and Psychopathology, 5,* 359–370.

Egeland, B., Sroufe, L. A., & Erickson, M. (1983). The developmental consequence of different patterns of maltreatment. *Child Abuse and Neglect, 7,* 459–469.

Ehrenshaft, D. (1992). Pre-school child sexual abuse: The aftermath of the Presidio case. *American Journal of Orthopsychiatry, 62*(2), 234–244.

Elder, G. (1974). *Children of the Great Depression.* Chicago: University of Chicago Press.

Elder, G., Nguyen, T., & Caspi, A. (1985). Linking family hardship to children's lives. *Child Development, 56,* 361–375.

Elliott, D. S., Huizinga, D., & Menard, S. (1989). *Multiple problem youth: Delinquency, substance use, and mental health problems.* New York: Springer-Verlag.

Elmer, E. (1979). Child abuse and family stress. *Journal of Social Issues, 35,* 60–71.

Erikson, E. (1963). *Childhood and society* (2nd ed). New York: Norton.

Ewigman B., Kivlahan C., & Land, G. (1993). The Missouri child fatality study: Underreporting of maltreatment fatalities among children younger than five years of age, 1983 through 1986. *Pediatrics, 91,* 330–337.

Ewing, C. P. (1990). *When children kill: The dynamics of juvenile homicide.* Lexington, MA: Lexington Books.

Faller, K. C. (1989). The myth of the "collusive mother": Variability in the functioning of mothers of victims of intrafamilial abuse. *Journal of Interpersonal Violence, 3,* 190–196.

Farber, E., & Joseph, J. (1985). The maltreated adolescent: Patterns of physical abuse. *Child Abuse and Neglect, 9,* 201–206.

Farber, E., Kinast, C., McCoard, W., & Falkner, D. (1984). Violence in families of adolescent runaways. *Child Abuse and Neglect, 8,* 295–299.

Fawcett, S., Bernstein, G., Czyzewski, M., & Greene, B. (1988). Behavior analysis and public policy. *Behavior Analysis, 11,* 11–25.

Fellin, P., & Litwak, E. (1968). The neighborhood in urban American society. *Social Work, 13,* 72–80.

Feshbach, N. (1973). The effects of violence in childhood. *Journal of Clinical Child Psychology, 28,* 28–31.

Finkelhor, D. (1979). What's wrong with sex between adults and children? Ethics and the problem of sexual abuse. *American Journal of Orthopsychiatry, 49,* 692–697.

Finkelhor, D. (1994). Current information on the scope and nature of child sexual abuse. In R. E. Behrman (Ed.), *The future of children, 4*(2), 31–53. Los Altos, CA: The David and Lucille Packard Foundation.

Finkelhor, D. (1995). The victimization of children: A developmental perspective. *American Journal of Orthopsychiatry, 65*(2), 177–193.

Finkelhor, D., & Baron, L. (1986). High-risk children. In D. Finkelhor (Ed.), *A sourcebook on child sexual abuse* (pp. 60–88). Thousand Oaks, CA: Sage.

Finkelhor, D., Hotaling, G., Lewis, I. A., & Smith, C. (1990). Sexual abuse in a national study of adult men and women: Prevalence, characteristics, and risk factors. *Child Abuse and Neglect, 14,* 19–28.

Finkelhor, D., Hotaling, G., & Sedlak, A. (1990). *National incidence study of missing, abducted, runaway, and throwaway children.* A final report to the Office of Juvenile Justice and Delinquency Prevention, Washington, DC.

Fischer, R. (1976). Consciousness as role and knowledge. In L. Allman & D. Jaffe (Eds.), *Readings in abnormal psychology: Contemporary perspectives.* New York: Harper and Row.

Fisher, B., Berdie, J. Cook, J., Radford-Barker, J., & Day, J. (1979). *Adolescent abuse and neglect: Intervention strategies and treatment approaches.* San Francisco: Urban and Rural Systems Associates.

Fitchen, J. (1981). *Poverty in rural America: A case study.* Boulder, CO: Westview Press.

Fontana, V. J. (1968). Further reflections on maltreatment of children. *New York State Journal of Medicine, 68,* 2214–2215.

Fox, K. A. (1974). *Social indicators and social theory.* New York: John Wiley and Sons.

Francis, C. (1978). Adolescent suicidal attempts: Experienced rejection and personal constructs. *Dissertation Abstracts International, 38*(9-B), 4453.

Freud, A., & Dann, S. (1951). An experiment in group upbringing. *The Psychoanalytic Study of the Child, 6,* 127–168.

Freudenberger, H. (1977). Burn-out: Occupational hazard of the child care worker. *Child Care Quarterly, 6,* 90–99.

Friedman, R. (1978, February). *Adolescents as people: No kidding around.* Paper presented at the conference of A Community Response to the Adolescent in Conflict, Jacksonville, FL.

Friedrich, W. N. (1991). *Casebook of sexual abuse treatment.* New York: Norton.

Garbarino, J. (1976). A preliminary study of some ecological correlates of child abuse: The impact of socioeconomic stress on mothers. *Child Development, 47,* 178–185.

Garbarino, J. (1977). The human ecology of child maltreatment: A conceptual model for research. *Journal of Marriage and the Family, 39,* 721–736.

Garbarino, J. (1981). An ecological perspective on child maltreatment. In L. Pelton (Ed.), *The social context of child abuse and neglect.* New York: Human Sciences Press.

Garbarino, J. (1982). *Children and families in the social environment.* Hawthorne, New York: Aldine de Gruyter.

Garbarino, J. (1987). Family support and the prevention of child maltreatment. In S. Kagan, R. Powell, B. Weissbourd, & E. Zigler (Eds.), *America's family support programs.* New Haven, CT: Yale University Press.

Garbarino, J. (1995). *Raising children in a socially toxic environment.* San Francisco: Jossey-Bass.

Garbarino, J., & Associates. (1992). *Children and families in the social environment* (2d ed.). Hawthorne, NY: Aldine de Gruyter.

Garbarino, J., & Bronfenbrenner, U. (1976, May). *Research on parent-child relations and social policy: Who needs whom?* Paper presented at the Symposium on Parent-Child Relations: Theoretical, Methodological and Practical Implications, University of Trier, West Germany.

Garbarino, J., & Carson, B. (1979a). *Mistreated youth in one community.* Paper. Boys Town, NE: Center for the Study of Youth Development.

Garbarino, J., & Carson, B. (1979b). *Mistreated youth versus abused children.* Boys Town, NE: Center for the Study of Youth Development.

Garbarino, J., & Crouter, A. (1978a). Defining the community context of parent-child relations: The correlates of child maltreatment. *Child Development, 49,* 604–616.

Garbarino, J., & Crouter, A. (1978b). A note on assessing the construct validity of child maltreatment report data. *American Journal of Public Health, 68,* 898–899.

Garbarino, J., Dubrow, N., Kostelny, K., & Pardo, C. (1992). *Children in danger: Coping with the consequences of community violence.* San Francisco: Jossey-Bass.

Garbarino, J., & Gilliam, G. (1980). *Understanding abusive families.* Lexington, MA: Lexington Books.

Garbarino, J., Guttman, E., & Seeley, J. (1986). *The psychologically battered child: Strategies for identification, assessment, and intervention.* San Francisco: Jossey-Bass.

Garbarino, J., & Kostelny, K. (1992). Child maltreatment as a community problem. *International Journal of Child Abuse and Neglect, 16*(4), 455–464.

Garbarino, J, Schellenbach, C., Sebes, J., & Associates. (1986). *Troubled youth, troubled families.* Hawthorne, NY: Aldine de Gruyter.

Garbarino, J., & Sherman, D. (1980). High-risk neighborhoods and high-risk families: The human ecology of child maltreatment. *Child Development, 5*(1), 188–198.

Garbarino, J., Stocking, S. H., & Associates. (1980). *Protecting children from abuse and neglect.* San Francisco: Jossey-Bass.

Garbarino, J., Wilson, J., & Garbarino, A. (1986). The adolescent runaway. In J. Garbarino, C. Schellenbach, & J. Sebes. (Eds.), *Troubled youth, troubled families* (pp. 41–56). Hawthorne, NY: Aldine de Gruyter.

Gardner, J. J., & Cabral, D. A. (1990). Sexually abused adolescents: A distinct group among sexually abused children presenting to a children's hospital. *Journal of Pediatric Child Health, 26,* 22–24.

Garmezy, N. (1977). Observations on research with children at risk for child and adult psychopathology. In M. F. McMillan & S. Henao (Eds.), *Child psychiatry treatment and research.* New York: Brunner/Mazel.

Gelles, R. (1978). Violence toward children in the United States. *American Journal of Orthopsychiatry, 48,* 580–592.

Gelles, R. J., & Cornell, C. P. (1990). *Intimate violence in families* (2nd ed.). Thousand Oaks, CA: Sage.

Germain, C. (1978). Space: An ecological variable in social work practice. *Social Casework, 59,* 522.

Gil, D. (1975). Unraveling child abuse. *American Journal of Orthopsychiatry, 45,* 346–356.

Gil, D. G. (1970). *Violence against children: Physical child abuse in the United States.* Cambridge, MA: Harvard University Press.

Gil, E. (1991). *The healing power of play.* New York: Guilford.

Gilligan, C. (1982). *In a different voice.* Cambridge, MA: Harvard University Press.

Gilligan, J. (1992). *Violence: Our deadly epidemic and its causes.* New York: Putnam.

Gilligan, J. (1996). *Violence: Our deadly epidemic and its cure.* New York: Putnam.

Gilmartin, B. (1978). The case against spanking. *Human Behavior, 7*(2), 18–23.

Giovannoni, J. (1991). Social policy considerations in defining psychological maltreatment. *Development and Psychopathology, 3,* 51–59.

Giovannoni J., & Becerra, R. (1979). *Defining child abuse.* New York: Free Press.

Gladwell, M. (1996, June 3). The tipping point. *The New Yorker*, 32–38.

Goldstein, A. P., & Glick, B. (1987). *Aggression replacement training*. Champaign, IL: Research Press.

Goleman, D. (1995). *Emotional intelligence*. New York: Bantam Books.

Goodall, J. (1990). *Through a window*. Boston: Houghton Mifflin.

Gordon, L. (1988). *Heroes of their own lives: the politics and history of family violence: Boston 1880–1960*. New York: Viking-Penguin.

Gray, C. (1978). *Empathy and stress as mediators in child abuse: Theory, research and practical implications*. Unpublished doctoral dissertation, University of Maryland.

Grotberg, E. (1976). *200 years of children* (DHEW Publication No. (OHD) 77–30103). Washington, DC: U.S. Department of Health, Education and Welfare, Office of Human Development, Office of Child Development.

Gutierres, S., & Reich, J. (1981). A developmental perspective on runaway behavior: Its relationship to child abuse. *Child Abuse and Neglect, 60*, 89–94.

Haggerty, R. J., Sherrod, L. R., Garmezy, N., & Rutter, M. (Eds.). (1994). *Stress, risk, and resilience in children and adolescents*. New York: Cambridge University Press.

Haldopoulos, M. A., & Copeland, M. (1991). Case studies of child care volunteers found to be at risk for abuse. *Early Child Development and Care, 68*, 149–158.

Hall, V. D. (1954). *A primer of Freudian psychology*. New York: World Publishing.

Halpern, R. (1995). *Rebuilding the inner city: A history of neighborhood initiatives to address poverty in the United States*. New York: Columbia University Press.

Harris, H., & Howard, K. (1979). Phenomenological correlates of perceived quality of parenting: A questionnaire study of high school students. *Journal of Youth and Adolescence 8*(2), 171–180.

Hart, S. N., Brassard, M., & Carlson, H. C. (1996). Psychological maltreatment. In J. Briere, L. Berliner, J. Bulkley, C. Jenny, & R. Reid (Eds.), *The APSAC handbook on child maltreatment* (pp. 72–89). Thousand Oaks, CA: Sage.

Haugaard, J., & Garbarino, J. (1997). *Catastrophic maltreatment*. Ithaca, NY: Cornell University, Family Life Development Center.

Hawes, J. (1828). Lecture addressed to the young men of Hartford and New Haven. Hartford, CT: O. D. Cooke. Cited in President's Science Advisory Committee (1974). *Youth: Transition to adulthood*. Chicago: University of Chicago Press.

Hawley, A. (1950). *Human ecology: The theory of community structure.* Somerset, NJ: Ronald Press.

Hechler, D. (1988). *The battle and the backlash: The child sexual abuse war.* San Francisco: New Lexington Press.

Herrenkohl, R. (1977, April). *Research: Too much, too little?* Proceedings of the Second Annual Conference on Child Abuse and Neglect. Vol. 1: Issues on Innovation and Implementation, Houston, TX.

Hershberger, S. (1996). *Violence within the family: Social psychological perspectives.* Boulder, CO: Westview Press.

Hill, J. (1980). The early adolescent and the family. In M. Johnson (Ed.), *Seventy-ninth yearbook of the National Society for the Study of Education.* Chicago: University of Chicago Press.

Hirschi, T. (1969). *Causes of delinquency.* Berkeley: University of California Press.

Hoffman, M. L., & Saltzstein, H. D. (1967). Parent discipline and the child's moral development. *Journal of Personality and Social Psychology, 5,* 45–57.

Homans, G. (1975). *The human group.* London: Routledge and Kegan Paul.

Houten, T., & Golembiewski, M. (1976). *A study of runaway youth and their families.* Washington, DC: Youth Alternatives Project.

Howard, J. (1978). *Families.* New York: Simon & Schuster.

Hunter, J., Goodwin, D. W., & Wilson, R. J. (1992). Attributions of blame in child sexual abuse victims: An analysis of age and gender influences. *Journal of Child Sexual Abuse, 1,* 75–90.

James M., & Krisberg, B. (1994). *Images and reality: juvenile crime, youth violence, and public policy.* San Francisco: National Council on Crime and Delinquency.

Janus, M., McCormack, A., Burgess, A., & Hartman, C. (1987). *Adolescent runaways: Causes and consequences.* Lexington, MA: Lexington Books.

Jeffrey, M. (1976). Practical ways to change parent-child interaction in families of children at risk. In R. Helfer & H. C. Kempe (Eds.), *Child abuse and neglect.* Cambridge, MA: Ballinger.

Johnson, R. N. (1972). *Aggression in man and animals.* Philadelphia: W. B. Saunders.

Jordan, T. (1987). *Victorian childhood: Themes and variations.* Albany: State University of New York Press.

Jurich, A. (1979). Parenting adolescents. *Family Perspective, 3,* 137–149.

Justice, B., & Justice, R. (1976). *The abusing family.* New York: Human Sciences Press.

Kandel, D., & Lesser, G. (1972). *Youth in two worlds.* San Francisco: Jossey-Bass.

Katz, I. (1967). The socialization of academic motivation in minority group children. In D. Levine (Ed.), *Nebraska symposium on motivation, 1967* (pp. 133–191). Lincoln: University of Nebraska Press.

Kaufman, J., & Zigler, E. (1989). Do abused children become abusive adults? *American Journal of Orthopsychiatry, 57,* 186–192.

Keller, M. (1975). Development of role-taking ability. *Human Development, 19,* 120–132.

Keller, R. A., Cicchinelli, L. F., & Gardner, D. M. (1989). Characteristics of child sexual abuse treatment programs. *Child Abuse and Neglect, 13,* 361–368.

Kelly, J., & Drabman, R. (1977). Generalizing response, suppression of self-injurious behavior through an overcorrection punishment procedure: Case study. *Behavior Therapy, 3,* 468–472.

Kempe, C. H. (1973). A practical approach to the protection of the abused child and rehabilitation of the abusing parent. *Pediatrics, 51,* 804–812.

Kempe, C. H., & Helfer, R. E. (1975). *Helping the battered child and his family.* New York: Lippincott.

Kempe, C. H., Silverman, F. N., Steele, B. F., Droegemueller, W., & Silver, H. K. (1962). The battered child syndrome. *Journal of the American Medical Association, 181,* 17–24.

Kendall-Tackett, K. A. (1994a). Postpartum depression and the mother-infant relationship. *APSAC Advisor, 7,* 11–38.

Kendall-Tackett, K. A. (1994b). Postpartum rituals and the prevention of postpartum depression: A cross-cultural perspective. *Newsletter of the Boston Institute for the Development of Infants and Parents, 13,* 3–6.

Kendall-Tackett, K. A., Williams, L. M., & Finkelhor, D. (1993). Impact of sexual abuse on children: A review and synthesis of recent empirical studies. *Psychological Bulletin, 113,* 164–180.

Kent, J. (1976). A follow-up study of abused children. *Journal of Pediatric Psychology, 1,* 25–31.

Kessen, W. (Ed.). (1975). *Childhood in China.* New Haven, CT: Yale University Press.

King, C. H. (1975). The Ego and integration of violence in homicidal youth. *American Journal of Orthopsychiatry, 45,* 134–135.

Kogan, L., Smith, J., & Jenkins, S. (1977). Ecological validity of indicator data as predictors of survey findings. *Journal of Social Service Research, 1,* 117–132.

Kohn, M. (1977). *Class and conformity: A study of values* (2nd ed.). Chicago: University of Chicago Press.

Konopka, G. (1966). *The adolescent girl in conflict.* Englewood Cliffs, NJ: Prentice-Hall.

Korbin, J. (1987). Child sexual abuse: Implications from the cross-cultural record. In N. Scheper-Hughes (Ed.), *Child survival: Anthropological perspective on the treatment and maltreatment of children* (pp. 247–267). Dordrecht, Holland: Reidel.

Korbin, J. E. (1991). Cross-cultural perspectives and research directions for the 21st Century. *Child Abuse and Neglect, 15,* 67–77.

Kotler, P. (1975). *Marketing for nonprofit organizations.* Englewood Cliffs, NJ: Prentice-Hall.

Kratcoski, P. (1985). Youth violence directed toward significant others. *Journal of Adolescence, 8*(2), 145–157.

Kreider, D. G., & Motto, J. (1974). Parent-child role reversal and suicidal states in adolescence. *Adolescence, 9*(35), 365–370.

Kromkowski, J. (1976). *Neighborhood deterioration and juvenile crime.* South Bend, IN: South Bend Urban Observatory.

Lazoritz, S. (1990). Whatever happened to Mary Ellen? *Child Abuse and Neglect, 14,* 143–149.

Leichter, H. J., & Mitchell, W. E. (1967). *Kinship and casework.* New York: Russell Sage Foundation.

Lempers, J. D., Clark-Lempers, D., & Simons, R. L. (1989). Economic hardship, parenting, and distress in adolescence. *Child Development, 60,* 25–39.

Lenoski, E. F. (1974). *Translating injury data into preventive and health care services—Physical child abuse.* Los Angeles: University of Southern California School of Medicine.

Lerman, P. (1994). Child protection and out-of-home care: System reforms and regulating placements. In G. B. Melton & F. D. Barry (Eds.), *Protecting children from abuse and neglect* (pp. 353–437). New York: Guilford Press.

Levine, M. L., & Levine, A. (1970). *A social history of helping services: Clinic, court, school and community.* New York: Appleton-Century-Crofts.

Levy, A., & Kahan, B. (1991). *The pindown experience and the protection of children: The report of the Staffordshire child care inquiry 1990 (No. 903363496).* Scotland: Staffordshire County Council.

Lewis, D. O. (1992). From abuse to violence: Psycho-physiological consequences of maltreatment. *Journal of the American Academy of Child Adolescent Psychiatry, 31,* 383–391.

Lewis, D. O., Mallouh, C., & Webb, V. (1989). Child abuse, delinquency, and violent criminality. In D. Cicchetti & V. Carlson (Eds.), *Child maltreatment: Theory and research on the causes and consequences of child abuse and neglect.* Cambridge: Cambridge University Press.

Lewis, D. O., Moy, E., Jackson, D. D., Aaronson, R., Restifo, N., Serra, S., & Simos, A. (1985). Biopsychosocial characteristics of children who later murder: A prospective study. *American Journal of Psychiatry, 142*(10), 1161–1167.

Lewis, D. O., Pincus, J. H., Feldman, M., Jackson, L., & Bard, B. (1986). Psychiatric, neurological and psychoeducational characteristics of fifteen death row inmates in the United States. *American Journal of Psychiatry, 143*(7), 838–845.

Lewis, D. O., Shanok, S. S., Pincus, J. H., & Glaser, G. H. (1979). Violent juvenile delinquents: Psychiatric, neurological, psychological, and abuse factors. *Journal of the American Academy of Child Psychiatry, 18,* 307–319.

Libbey, P., & Bybee, R. (1979). The physical abuse of adolescents. *Journal of Social Issues, 35,* 101–126.

Loeber, R., & Dishion, T. (1983). Early predictors of male delinquency: A review. *Psychological Bulletin, 94,* 68–99.

Loeber, R., & Strouthammer-Loeber, M. (1986). Family factors as correlates and predictors of juvenile conduct problems and delinquency. In N. Tonry & N. Morris (Eds.), *Crime and justice: An annual review of research* (Vol. 7, pp. 29–150). Chicago: University of Chicago Press.

Lofquist, W. (1983). *Discovering the meaning of prevention: A practical approach to positive change.* Tucson, AZ: AYD Publications.

Lourie, I. (1977). The phenomenon of the abused adolescent: A clinical study. *Victimology, 2*(2), 268–276.

Madonna, P. G., Van Scoyk, S., & Jones, D. P. H. (1991). Family interactions within incest and nonincest families. *American Journal of Psychiatry, 148,* 46–49.

Magnuson, E. (1983). Child abuse: The ultimate betrayal. *Time.*

Manis, J. (1974). Assessing the seriousness of social problems. *Social Problems, 22,* 1–15.

Mannarino, A. P. , Cohen, J. A., & Berman, S. R. (1994). The Children's Attributions and Perceptions Scale: A new measure of sexual abuse–related factors. *Journal of Clinical Child Psychology, 23,* 204–211.

Margolin, L. (1990). Child abuse by babysitters: An ecological-interactional interpretation. *Journal of Family Violence, 5*(2), 95–105.

Margolin, L. (1991). Child sexual abuse by non-related caregivers. *Child Abuse and Neglect, 15*(3), 213–221.

Martin, H. (1976). *The abused child: A multidisciplinary approach to developmental issue at treatment.* Cambridge, MA: Ballinger.

Maslow, A. (1954). *Motivation and personality.* New York: Harper and Row.

Masten, A. S., Morison, P., Pelligrini, D., & Tellegen, A. (1990). Competence under stress: Risk and protective factors. In J. Rolf, A. S. Masten, D. Cicchetti, K. H. Nuechterlein, & S. Weintraub (Eds.), *Risk and protective factors in the development of psychopathology* (pp. 236–256). Cambridge: Cambridge University Press.

Mattingly, M. (1977). Sources of stress and burn-out in professional child care work. *Child Care Quarterly, 6,* 127–137.

Maxwell, M. G., & Widom, C. S. (1996). The cycle of violence revisited 6 years later. *Archives of Pediatric and Adolescent Medicine, 150,* 390–395.

McClain, P., Sacks, J., Froehlke, R., & Ewigman, B. (1993). Estimates of fatal child abuse and neglect, United States, 1979 through 1988. *Pediatrics, 91,* 338–343.

McClelland, D. (1973). Testing for competence rather than intelligence. *American Psychologist, 28,* 1–14.

McClelland, J. (1986). Job satisfaction of child care workers: A review. *Child Care Quarterly, 15,* 82–89.

McIntire, S., Angle, C., & Schlicht, M. (1977). Suicide and self-poisoning in pediatrics. *Advances in Pediatrics, 24,* 291–309.

McGee, R. A., & Wolfe, D. A. (1991). Psychological maltreatment: Toward an operational definition. *Development and Psychopathology, 3,* 3–18.

McGrath, T. (1985–1986). Overcoming institutionalized child abuse: Creating a positive therapeutic climate. *Journal of Child Care, 2,* 59–65.

McLeer, S. V., Deblinger, E. B., Atkins, M. S., Foa, E. B., & Ralphe, D. L. (1988). Post-traumatic stress disorder in sexually abused children. *Journal of the American Academy of Child and Adolescent Psychiatry, 27,* 650–654.

Megargee, E. I. (1971). The role of inhibition in the assessment and understanding of violence. In J. L. Singer (Ed.), *Control of aggression in violence* (pp. 125–147). New York: Academic Press.

Melton, G., & Barry, F. (Eds.). (1994). *Protecting children from abuse and neglect: Foundations for a new national strategy.* New York: Guilford Press.

Mercer, M. (1982). Closing the barn door: The prevention of institutional abuse through standards. *Child and Youth Services, 4,* 127–132.

Milgram, S. (1974). *Obedience to authority.* New York: Harper and Row.

Miller, A. (1984). *Thou shalt not be aware: Society's betrayal of the child.* New York: Farrar, Straus & Giroux.

Miller, G. (1987). State-sponsored child abuse. *Child and Adolescent Social Work, 4,* 10–11.

Miller, P. A., & Eisenberg, N. (1988). The relation of empathy to aggressive and externalizing/antisocial behavior. *Psychological Bulletin, 103,* 324–344.

Mirringhoff, M. (1996). America's social health: Trends and comments. *The Social Report.* New York: Fordham University.

Moffitt, T. E. (1993). Adolescence-limited and life-course persistent antisocial behavior: A developmental taxonomy. *Psychological Review, 100,* 674–701.

Moran, P., & Eckenrode, J. (1992). Protective personality characteristics among adolescent victims of maltreatment. *Child Abuse and Neglect, 16,* 743–754.

Mundy, P., Robertson, M., Roberts, J., & Greenblatt, M. (1990). The prevalence of psychotic symptoms in homeless adolescents. *Journal of the American Academy of Child and Adolescent Psychiatry, 29*(5), 724–731.

Nadler, R. (1979). Child abuse in gorilla mothers. *Caring, 5,* 1–3.

National Center on Child Abuse and Neglect (NCCAN). (1978). *Child sexual abuse: Incest, assault, and sexual exploitation.* (Publication No. 79–30166). Washington, DC: Department of Health, Education and Welfare.

National Center on Child Abuse and Neglect (NCCAN). (1993). *A report on the maltreatment of children with disabilities.* Washington, DC: Department of Health and Human Services.

National Center on Child Abuse and Neglect (NCCAN). (1995). *Child maltreatment 1993: Reports from the states to the National Conference on Child Abuse and Neglect.* Washington, DC: U.S. Department of Health and Human Services.

National Child Abuse Coalition. (1993a, July/August). President signs family support bill. *Memorandum,* 1–2.

National Child Abuse Coalition. (1993b, August/September). Title XX funding increases, addresses child maltreatment. *Memorandum,* 2–3.

National Child Abuse Coalition. (1994, April/May). Home visiting services funded. *Memorandum,* 3.

National Committee to Prevent Child Abuse. (1996). *Current trends in child abuse reporting and fatalities: The results of the 1995 annual fifty state survey.* (Working Paper No. 808). Chicago: Author.

National Network of Runaway and Youth Services. (1988, January). *Preliminary findings from the National Network's survey of runaway and homeless youth.* Testimony before the U.S. House of Representatives Subcommittee on Human Resources.

National Research Council. (1993). *Understanding and preventing violence.* Washington, DC: National Academy Press.

Nelson, B. (1984). *Making an issue of child abuse.* Chicago: University of Chicago Press.

Newberger, C. M., & White, K. M. (1989). Cognitive foundations for parental care. In D. Cicchetti & V. Carlson (Eds.), *Child maltreatment: Theory and research on the causes and consequences of child abuse and neglect* (pp. 302–316). New York: Cambridge University Press.

New York State Commission on Quality of Care (1992). *Child abuse and neglect in the New York State Office of Mental Health and Office of Mental Retardation and Developmental Disabilities Residential Programs.* Albany, NY: Author.

Newell, H. W. (1934). Psychodynamics of maternal rejection. *American Journal of Orthopsychiatry, 4,* 387–403.

Nilson, P. (1981). Psychological profiles of runaway children and adolescents. In C. F. Wells & I. R. Stuart (Eds.), *Self-destructive behavior in children and adolescents* (pp. 84–98). New York: Van Nostrand Reinhold.

Nunno, M., & Motz, J. (1988). The development of an effective response to the abuse of children in out-of-home care. *Child Abuse and Neglect, 12,* 521–528.

Nye, F. I. (1959). Family relationships. In W. McCord & J. McCord (Eds.), *Origins of crime.* New York: Columbia University Press.

Oates, R. K., Forest, D., & Peacock, A. (1985). Self-esteem of abused children. *Child Abuse and Neglect, 9,* 159–163.

Offer D., & Offer, J. (1974). Normal adolescent males: The high school and college years. *Journal of the American College Health Association, 22,* 209–215.

O'Keefe, M. (1995). Predictors of child abuse in martially violent families. *Journal of Interpersonal Violence, 10,* 3–25.

Olafson, E., Corwin, D., & Summit, R. (1993). Modern history of child sexual abuse awareness: Cycles of discovery and suppression. *Child Abuse and Neglect, 17,* 7–24.

Olsen, L., & Holmes, W. (1986). Youth at risk: Adolescents and maltreatment. *Children and Youth Services Review, 8,* 13–35.

Osofsky, J., Wewers, S., Hann, D., & Fick, A. (1993). Chronic community violence: What is happening to our children? *Psychiatry, 56,* 36–45.

Osterrieth, P. A. (1969). Adolescence: Some psychological aspects. In G. Caplan & S. Leborici (Eds.), *Adolescence: Psychosocial perspectives.* (pp. 11–21). New York: Basic Books.

Parke, R., & Collmer, C. W. (1975). Child abuse: An interdisciplinary analysis. In E. M. Hetherington (Ed.), *Review of child development research* (Vol. 5). Chicago: University of Chicago Press.

Patterson, G. R. (1982). *Coercive family process.* Eugene, OR: Castalia.

Patterson, G. R. (1986). Performance models for antisocial boys. *American Psychologist, 41*(4), 432–444.

Patterson, G. R., & Reid, J. B. (1970). Reciprocity and coercion: Two facets of social systems. In C. Neuringer & J. Michael (Eds.), *Behavior modification in clinical psychology* (pp. 133–177). New York: Appleton-Century Crofts.

Patton, M. (1978). *Utilization-focused evaluation.* Thousand Oaks, CA: Sage.

Paulson, M., & Stone, D. (1974). Suicidal behavior of latency-age children. *Journal of Clinical Child Psychology, 3*(2), 50–53.

Paykel, E. S. (1976, September). Life stress, depression and attempted suicide. *Journal of Human Stress,* 3–12.

Pelcovitz, D., Kaplan, S., Samit, C., Krieger, R., & Cornelius, P. (1984). Adolescent abuse: Family structure and implications for treatment. *Journal of Child Psychiatry, 23,* 85–90.

Pelton, L. (1978). The myth of classlessness in child abuse cases. *American Journal of Orthopsychiatry, 48,* 569–579.

Pelton, L. (1981). *The social context of child abuse and neglect.* New York: Human Sciences Press.

Pelton, L. (1994). The role of material factors in child abuse and neglect. In G. Melton & F. Barry (Eds.), *Protecting children from abuse and neglect* (pp. 131–181). New York: Guilford Press.

Piaget, J. (1952). *The origins of intelligence in children* (M. Cook, Trans.). New York: International Universities Press.

Pianta, R. C., Egeland, B., & Hyatt, A. (1986). Maternal relationship history as an indicator of developmental risk. *American Journal of Orthopsychiatry, 56,* 385–398.

Polansky, N., Chalmers, M., Buttenweiser, E., & Williams, D. (1979). The isolation of the neglectful family. *American Journal of Orthopsychiatry, 49,* 149–152.

Polansky, N., Chalmers, M., Buttenweiser, E., & Williams, D. (1981). *Damaged parents: An anatomy of child neglect.* Chicago: University of Chicago Press.

Polit, D. G., White, C. M., & Morton, T. D. (1990). Child sexual abuse and premarital intercourse among high-risk adolescents. *Journal of Adolescent Health Care, 11*(3), 231–234.

Powers, J., & Eckenrode, J. (1988). The maltreatment of adolescents. *Child Abuse and Neglect, 12*(2), 189–199.

Powers, J., Eckenrode, J., & Jaklitsch, B. (1990). Maltreatment among runaway and homeless youth. *Child Abuse and Neglect, 14*, 87–98.

Powers, J., & Jaklitsch, B. (1989). *Understanding survivors of abuse: Stories of homeless and runaway adolescents.* Lexington, MA: Lexington Books.

Powers, J., Mooney, A., & Nunno, M. (1990). Institutional abuse: A review of the literature. *Journal of Child and Youth Care, 4*, 81–95.

Putnam, R. (1993). What makes democracy work? *National Civic Review, 82*, 101–107.

Quinton, D., Rutter, M., & Liddle, C. (1984). Institutional rearing, parenting difficulties and marital support. *Psychological Medicine, 14*, 107–124.

Radke, M. J. (1946). *The relation of parental authority to children's behavior and attitudes.* Minneapolis: University of Minnesota Press.

Rao, K., DiClemente, R. J., & Ponton, L. E. (1992). Child sexual abuse of Asians compared with other populations. *Journal of the American Academy of Child and Adolescent Psychiatry, 31*, 880–886.

Reidy, T. J. (1977). The aggressive characteristics of abused and neglected children. *Journal of Clinical Psychology, 33*, 1140–1145.

Riesman, D. (1950). *The lonely crowd.* New Haven, CT: Yale University Press.

Rindfleisch, N., & Baros-Van Hull, J. (1982). Direct careworkers' attitudes toward the use of physical force with children. *Child and Youth Services, 4*, 115–125.

Rindfleisch, N., & Foulk, R. C. (1992). Factors that influence the occurrence and the seriousness of adverse incidents in residential facilities. *Journal of Social Service Research, 16*(3–4), 65–87.

Rindfleisch, N., & Nunno, M. (1992). Progress and issues in the implementation of the 1984 out-of-home care protection amendment. *Child Abuse and Neglect, 16*, 693–708.

Robertson, M. (1989). *Homeless youth: Patterns of alcohol use.* A report to the National Institute of Alcohol Abuse and Alcoholism. Berkeley, CA: Alcohol Research Group.

Rodning, C., Beckwith, L., & Howard, J. (1989). Characteristics of attachment organization and play organization in prenatally drug-exposed toddlers. *Development and Psychopathology, 1*, 277–289.

Rohner, R. (1975). *They love me, they love me not.* New Haven, CT: Human Relations Area Files Press.

Rohner, R., & Nielsen, C. (1978). *Parental acceptance and rejection: A review of research and theory.* New Haven, CT: Human Relations Area Files Press.

Rosenbaum, J., Fishman, N., Brett, A., & Meaden, P. (1993). Can the Kerner Commission's housing strategy improve employment, education and social integration for low-income blacks? *North Carolina Law Review, 71,* 1519–1556.

Rosenthal, J., Motz, J., Edmonson, D., & Groze, V. (1991). A descriptive study of abuse and neglect in out-of-home placement. *Child Abuse and Neglect, 15,* 249–260.

Rotenberg, M. (1977). Alienating individualism and reciprocal individualism: A cross-cultural conceptualization. *Journal of Humanistic Psychology, 17,* 3–17.

Russell, D. (1984). The prevalence and seriousness of incestuous abuse: Stepfathers vs. biological fathers. *Child Abuse and Neglect, 8,* 15–22.

Rutter, M. (1989). Pathways from childhood to adult life. *Journal of Child Psychology and Psychiatry, 4,* 91–115.

Rutter, M., & Quinton, D. (1984). Parental psychiatric disorder: Effects on children. *Psychological Medicine, 14,* 853–880.

Sameroff, A. J., & Feil, L. A. (1985). Parental concepts of development. In I. Sigel (Ed.), *Parental belief systems: The psychological consequences for children.* Hillsdale, NJ: Erlbaum.

Sattin, D., & Miller, J. (1971). The ecology of child abuse within a military community. *American Journal of Orthopsychiatry, 53,* 127–143.

Satir, V. (1972). *Peoplemaking.* Palo Alto, CA: Science and Behavior Books.

Saunders, B. E., Villeponteaux, L. A., Lipovsky, J. A., & Kilpatrick, D. G. (1992). Child sexual assault as a risk factor for mental disorder among women: A community survey. *Journal of Interpersonal Violence, 7,* 189–204.

Schmitt, B. (1987). Seven deadly sins of childhood: Advising parents about difficult developmental stages. *Child Abuse and Neglect, 2,* 421–432.

Schorr, L. B. (1988). *Within our reach: Breaking the cycle of disadvantage.* New York: Doubleday.

Schwartz, I. M. (1991). Out-of-home placement of children: Selected issues and prospects for the future. *Behavioral Sciences and the Law, 9,* 189–199.

Sedlak, A. J., & Broadhurst, D. D. (1996). *The third national incidence study of child abuse and neglect (NIS-3): Final report.* Washington, DC:

U.S. Department of Health and Human Services, National Center on Child Abuse and Neglect.

Seely, H., & Craig, J. (1993, July 25). Beaten by the system. *Syracuse Herald American,* 1–13.

Sendi, I., & Blomgren, P. (1975). A comparative study of predictive criteria in the predisposition of homicidal adolescents. *American Journal of Psychiatry, 132,* 423–425.

Seng, M. J. (1989). Child sexual abuse and adolescent prostitution: A comparative analysis. *Adolescence, 24*(95), 665–675.

Sgroi, S. M. (1982). *Handbook of clinical intervention in child sexual abuse.* Lexington, MA: Lexington Books.

Shaffer, D., & Caton, C. (1984). *Runaway and homeless youth in New York City: A report to the Ittleson Foundation.* New York: Division of Child Psychiatry, New York State Psychiatric Institute and Columbia University of Physicians and Surgeons.

Shaver, P. R., Goodman, G. S., Rosenberg, M. S. & Orcutt, H. (1991). The search for a definition of psychological maltreatment. *Development and Psychopathology, 3,* 79–86.

Silverman, F. (1953). Roentgen manifestations of unrecognized skeletal trauma in infants. *American Journal of Roentgenology, 69,* 413.

Slater, P. E. (1970). *The pursuit of loneliness: American culture at the breaking point.* Boston: Beacon Press.

Smith, C. J. (1976). Residential neighborhoods as humane environments. *Environment and Planning, 8,* 311–326.

Smith, M. B. (1968). School and home: Focus on achievement. In A. H. Passow (Ed.), *Developing programs for the educationally disadvantaged.* New York: Teachers College Press.

Snow, K. (1994). "Aggression: Just part of the job?" The psychological impact of aggression on child and youth workers. *Journal of Child and Youth Care, 9*(4), 11–30.

Snyder, H., & Sickmund, M. (1995). *Juvenile offenders and victims: A national report.* Washington, DC: Office of Juvenile Justice and Delinquency Prevention.

Solarz, A. (1988). Homelessness: Implications for children and youth. *Social Policy Report, 3,* 1–16. Society for Research in Child Development, Washington, DC.

Spencer, J. W., & Knudsen, D. D. (1992). Out-of-home maltreatment: An analysis of risk in various settings for children. *Children and Youth Services Review, 14,* 485–492.

Sroufe, A., & Rutter, M. (1984). The domain of developmental psychopathology. *Child Development, 55,* 17–29.

Stacey, W., & Shupe, A. (1983). *The family secret.* Boston: Beacon Press.

Stack, C. B. (1974). *All our kin: Strategies for survival in a Black community.* New York: Harper and Row.

Steele, B. (1970). Violence in our society. *The Pharos of Alpha Omega Alpha, 33,* 42–48.

Steinberg, L. (1977, August). Research in the ecology of adolescent development: *A longitudinal study of the impact of physical maturation on changes in the family system in early adolescence.* Paper presented at the Conference on Research Perspectives in the Ecology of Human Development, Cornell University, Ithaca, NY.

Steirlin, H. (1974). *Separating parents and adolescents.* New York: Quadrangle.

Stern, G., & Kruckman, L. (1983). Multi-disciplinary perspectives on postpartum depression: An anthropological critique. *Social Science and Medicine, 17,* 1027–1041.

Straus, M. (1980). Stress and child abuse. In C. H. Kempe & R. E. Helfer (Eds.), *The battered child* (3rd ed., pp. 86–103). Chicago: University of Chicago Press.

Straus, M. (1988). Abused adolescents. In M. B. Straus (Ed.), *Abuse and victimization across the life span.* Baltimore: Johns Hopkins University Press.

Straus, M. (1994). *Beating the devil out of them: Corporal punishment in American families.* New York: Free Press.

Straus, M., & Gelles, R. (1987). Measuring intrafamily conflict and violence: The conflict tactics (CT) scales. *Journal of Marriage and the Family, 41,* 75–88.

Straus, M., Gelles, R., & Steinmetz, S. (1980). *Behind closed doors.* New York: Doubleday.

Streit, J. (1974). A test and procedure to identify secondary school children who have a high probability of drug abuse. *Dissertation Abstracts International, 34,* 10–13.

Sugarman, M. (1977). Paranatal influences on maternal-infant attachment. *American Journal of Orthopsychiatry, 47,* 407–421.

Summit, R., & Kryso, J. (1978). Sexual abuse of children: A clinical spectrum. *American Journal of Orthopsychiatry, 48,* 237–251.

Sundrum, C. (1984). Obstacles to reducing patient abuse in public institutions. *Hospital and Community Psychiatry, 35,* 238–243.

Symonds, P. (1938). A study of parental acceptance and rejection. *American Journal of Orthopsychiatry, 8,* 679–688.

Teicher, J. (1973). Why adolescents kill themselves. In J. Segal (Ed.), *The mental health of the child.* New York: Arno Press.

Thomas, G. (1980). Dimensions of the problem of child abuse and neglect in residential placement that distinguish it from child abuse and neglect in the family context. In *Testimony before the US House of Representatives*. Athens GA: Regional Institute of Social Welfare Research.

Thomas, G. (1990). Institutional child abuse: The making and prevention of an un-problem. *Journal of Child and Youth Care, 4*, 1–22.

Thomas, W., & Thomas, D. (1928). *The child in America*. New York: Knopf.

Thompson, R. (1994). Social support and the prevention of child maltreatment. In G. Melton & F. Barry (Eds.), *Protecting children from abuse and neglect* (pp. 40–130). New York: Guilford Press.

Thompson, R. A. (1995). *Preventing child maltreatment through social support*. Thousand Oaks, CA: Sage.

Tietjen, A. (1980). Integrating formal and informal support systems: The Swedish experience. In J. Garbarino & H. Stocking (Eds.), *Protecting children from abuse and neglect* (pp. 15–36). San Francisco: Jossey-Bass.

Tolan, P., & Guerra, N. (1993). *What works in reducing adolescent violence: An empirical review of the field*. Chicago: University of Chicago Press.

Toolan, J. M. (1975). Suicide in children and adolescents. *American Journal of Psychotherapy, 29*, 339–344.

Tronick, E., Als, H., Adarnson, L., Wise, S., & Brazelton, B. (1978). The infant's response to entrapment between contradictory messages in face-to-face interaction. *Child Psychiatry, 17*, 1–13.

Tucker, L. (1976). A comparison of the value preferences of emotionally disturbed adolescents and their parents with normal adolescents and their parents. *Adolescence, 11*, 549–567.

Twain, M. (1885). *Adventures of Huckleberry Finn (Tom Sawyer's companion)*. New York: Charles L. Webster.

U.S. Advisory Board on Child Abuse and Neglect. (1990). *Child abuse and neglect: Critical first steps in response to a national emergency* (Stock No. 017–092–00104–5). Washington, DC: U.S. Government Printing Office.

U.S. Advisory Board on Child Abuse and Neglect. (1991). *Creating caring communities: Blueprint for an effective federal policy on child abuse and neglect*. Washington, DC: U.S. Department of Health and Human Services, Administration for Children and Families.

U.S. Advisory Board on Child Abuse and Neglect. (1994). *A nation's shame: Fatal child abuse and neglect in the United States*. Washington, DC: U.S. Department of Health and Human Services, Administration for Children and Families.

U.S. Advisory Board on Child Abuse and Neglect. (1995). *A nation's shame: Fatal child abuse and neglect in the United States*. Washington, DC: U.S. Department of Health and Human Services.

U.S. Department of Health and Human Services, National Center on Child Abuse and Neglect. (1996). *Child maltreatment 1994: Reports from the states to the National Center on Child Abuse and Neglect.* Washington DC: U.S. Government Printing Office.

U.S. Department of Health and Human Services, Office of Human Development Services Administration for Children, Youth and Families. (1984). *Runaway youth centers: FY 1984 report to Congress.* Washington, DC: Author.

U.S. Department of Justice. (1992). *Crime in the United States, 1992.* Washington, DC: Author.

U.S. Federal Bureau of Investigation. (1978). *Crime in the United States, 1977.* Washington, DC: U.S. Department of Justice.

U.S. Federal Bureau of Investigation. (1995). *1994 uniform crime reports, supplemental homicide reports.* Washington, DC: U.S. Department of Justice.

U.S. Government Accounting Office. (1992). *Child abuse: Prevention programs need greater emphasis* (GAO/HRD-92–99). Washington, DC: Author.

Vissing, T., Straus, M., Gelles, R., & Harrop, J. (1991). Verbal aggression by parents and psychosocial problems of children. *Child Abuse and Neglect, 15,* 223–238.

Walker, E., Downey, G., & Bergman, A. (1989). The effects of parental psychopathology and maltreatment on child behavior: A test of the diathesis-stress model. *Child Development, 60,* 15–24.

Wallace, R. (1989). Homelessness, contagious destruction of housing, and municipal service cuts in New York City: Demographics of a housing deficit. *Environment and Planning, 1,* 1585–1603.

Wallace, R. (1990). Urban desertification, public health and public order: "planned shrinkage," violent death, substance abuse and AIDS in the Bronx. *Social Science and Medicine, 31,* 801–813.

Walters, D. (1975). *Physical and sexual abuse of children: Causes and treatment.* Bloomington: Indiana University Press.

Walters, R., & Parke, R. (1964). Social motivation, dependency, and susceptibility to social influence. In L. Berkowitz (Ed.), *Advances in experimental social psychology* (pp. 232–276). New York: Academic Press.

Wandersman, A., Florin, P., Friedmann, R., & Meir, R. (1987). Who participates, who does not, and why? An analysis of voluntary neighborhood organizations in the United States and Israel. *Sociological Forum, 2,* 534–555.

Warren, D. (1980). Support systems in different types of neighborhoods. In J. Garbarino & H. Stocking (Eds.), *Protecting children from abuse and neglect* (pp. 61–93). San Francisco: Jossey-Bass.

Weatherly, D. (1963). Self-perceived rate of physical maturation and personality in late adolescence. *Child Development, 35,* 1197–1210.

Webb, W. (1952). *The great frontier.* Austin: University of Texas Press.

Weissman, M., & Paykel, E. (1973). Moving and depression in women. In R. S. Weiss (Ed.), *Loneliness* (pp. 154–164). Cambridge, MA: MIT Press.

Weissman, M., & Paykel, E. (1974). *The depressed woman.* Chicago: University of Chicago Press.

Welsch, R. S. (1976). Severe parental punishment and delinquency: A developmental theory. *Journal of Clinical Child Psychology, 5,* 17–21.

Wexler, R. (1990). *Wounded innocents: The real victims of the war against child abuse.* Amherst, NY: Prometheus.

White, R. (1959). Motivation reconsidered: The concept of competence. *Psychological Review, 66,* 297–333.

White, R., & Watt, N. (1973). *The abnormal personality.* New York: Ronald Press.

Widom, C. S. (1989). The cycle of violence. *Science, 244,* 160–166.

Widom, C. S. (1991). Childhood victimization: Risk factor for delinquency. In M. E. Colten & S. Gore (Eds.), *Adolescent stress: Causes and consequences* (pp. 201–221). Hawthorne, NY: Aldine de Gruyter.

Wiehe, V. (1990). *Sibling abuse: Hidden physical, emotional and sexual trauma.* San Francisco: New Lexington Press.

Williams, L. (1994). Recall of childhood trauma: A prospective study of women's memories of child sexual abuse. *Journal of Consulting and Clinical Psychology, 62,* 1167–1176.

Williamson, J. M., Borduin, C. M., & Howe, B. A. (1991). The ecology of adolescent maltreatment: A multilevel examination of adolescent physical abuse, sexual abuse and neglect. *Journal of Consulting and Clinical Psychology, 59*(3), 449–457.

Wilson, W. J. (1987). *The truly disadvantaged: The inner city, the underclass and public policy.* Chicago: University of Chicago Press.

Wolberg, L. (1944). The character structure of the rejected child. *Nervous Child, 3,* 74–88.

Wolfe, D. A. (1985). Child-abusive parents: An empirical review and analysis. *Psychological Bulletin, 97,* 462–482.

Wolfe, D. A. (1987). *Child abuse: Implications for child development and psychopathology.* Thousand Oaks, CA: Sage.

Wollack, I., & Magura, S. (1996). Parental substance abuse as a predictor of child maltreatment re-reports. *Child Abuse and Neglect, 20,* 1183–1193.

Women report past abuse. (1991, May 4). *The Boston Globe.*

Woodson, R. (1996). Welfare reform: a message from the receiving end, *National Forum: The Phi Kappa Phi Journal, 76,* 15–19.

Woolley, P., & Evans, W. (1955). Significance of skeletal lesions in infants resembling those of traumatic origin. *Journal of the American Medical Association, 158,* 539–543.

Wyatt, G. E., & Powell, G. J. (Eds.). (1988). *Lasting effects of child sexual abuse.* Thousand Oaks, CA: Sage.

Wynne, E. (1975, March). *Privacy and socialization to adulthood.* Paper presented at the annual meeting of the American Educational Research Association, Washington, DC.

Yahares, H. (1978). *Why young people become antisocial.* Washington: U.S. Government Printing Office.

Yates, G., MacKenzie, R., Pennbridge, J., & Cohen, E. (1988). A risk profile comparison of runaway and non-runaway youth. *American Journal of Public Health, 78,* 820–821.

Yoshikawa, H. (1994). Prevention as cumulative protection: Effects of early family support and education on chronic delinquency and its risks. *Psychological Bulletin, 115,* 28–54.

Young, R., Godfrey, W., Mathews, B., & Adams, G. (1983). Runaways: A review of negative consequences. *Family Relations, 32,* 275–281.

Zierler, S., Feingold, L., Laufer, D., Velentgas, P., Kantrowitz-Gordon, I., & Mayer, X. (1991). Adult survivors of childhood sexual abuse and subsequent risk of HIV infection. *American Journal of Public Health, 81*(5), 572–575.

Zuckerman, B. (1994). Effects on children and parents. In D. Besharov (Ed.), *When drug addicts have children* (pp. 49–63). Washington, DC: Child Welfare League of America.

Zuravin, S., & Taylor, R. (1987). The ecology of child maltreatment: Identifying and characterizing high-risk neighborhoods. *Child Welfare, 66,* 497–506.

~~ About the Authors

JAMES GARBARINO is director of the Family Life Development Center and professor of Human Development and Family Studies at Cornell University in Ithaca, New York. Prior to coming to Cornell he
served as president of the Erikson Institute for Advanced Study in
Child Development in Chicago, Illinois. Garbarino is author or editor of sixteen books, including *Children and Families in the Social
Environment* (1992), *Children in Danger: Coping with the Consequences
of Community Violence* (1992), *No Place to Be a Child: Growing Up in
a War Zone* (1991), *Raising Children in a Socially Toxic Environment*
(1995), *What Children Can Tell Us* (1989), *The Psychologically Battered
Child* (1986), and, for children, *Let's Talk About Living in a World with
Violence* (1993).

Garbarino has been a consultant to television, magazine, and newspaper reports on children and families and in 1981 received the Silver
Award at the International Film and Television Festival of New York
for coauthoring *Don't Get Stuck There: A Film on Adolescent Abuse.* In
1985, he collaborated with John Merrow to produce "Assault on the
Psyche," a videotaped program dealing with psychological abuse. He
has served as a scientific expert witness in criminal and civil cases
involving issues of violence and children.

The National Conference on Child Abuse and Neglect honored Dr.
Garbarino in 1985 with its first C. Henry Kempe Award, in recogni-
tion of his efforts on behalf of abused and neglected children. In 1975,
Dr. Garbarino was named a Spencer Fellow by the National Academy
of Education and, in 1981, named a National Fellow by the Kellogg
Foundation. In 1979 and again in 1981 he received the Mitchell Prize
from the Woodlands Conference on Sustainable Societies. In 1987, he
was elected president of the American Psychological Association's
Division on Child, Youth and Family Services, In 1988, he received the
American Humane Association's Vincent De Francis Award for
nationally significant contributions to child protection. In 1989, he

255

received the American Psychological Association's Award for Distinguished Professional Contributions to Public Service. In 1992, he received the Society for Psychological Study of Social Issues prize for research on child abuse. In 1993, he received the Brandt F. Steele Award from the Kempe National Center on Child Abuse and Neglect. In 1994 the American Psychological Association's Division on Child, Youth and Family Services presented him with its Nicholas Hobbs Award. Also in 1994, he received the Dale Richmond Award from the American Academy of Pediatrics Section on Behavioral and Developmental Pediatrics. In 1995, he was awarded an honorary Doctor of Humane Letters by St. Lawrence University.

JOHN ECKENRODE is professor of human development and family studies and associate director of the Family Life Development Center in the College of Human Ecology at Cornell University. He earned his B.S. degree (1972) in psychology at the University of Notre Dame, and both his M.S. (1975) and Ph.D. (1979) degrees in psychology at Tufts University. Before joining the faculty at Cornell University, he was a research associate in behavioral sciences at the Harvard School of Public Health for four years.

Eckenrode's main research activities have focused on stress and coping processes, child abuse and neglect, and the evaluation of early intervention programs for at-risk mothers and children. He has authored numerous research articles and book chapters and in 1995 received the Robert Chin Memorial Award from the Society for the Psychological Study of Social Issues for the best research paper in child abuse and neglect for that year. Eckenrode has edited two previous books, with Susan Gore, *The Social Context of Coping* (1991) and *Stress Between Work and Family* (1990).

FRANK BARRY is a senior extension associate at the Family Life Development Center at Cornell University in Ithaca, New York, and a member of the Community Development Society in Milwaukee, Wisconsin. He received his M.S. degree (1970) in agricultural economics at Cornell after receiving his B.A. degree (1959) in social sciences from Earlham College. He served four years on the U.S. Advisory Board on Child Abuse and Neglect, established in 1989 to advise the federal government on child abuse policy. He coauthored the board's 1993 major policy recommendations, culminating a four-year effort. He also coauthored *Protecting Children from Child Abuse and Neglect* (1994, with Gary Melton); recent writings have focused on the effect of community environment on child abuse and other social problems.

In 1996 Barry received the Florence Halpern prize for Extension Outreach at Cornell, and the Pioneer Award from the National Committee to Prevent Child Abuse, New York Chapter.

KERRY BOLGER, a developmental psychologist, is a research associate at the Family Life Development Center, Cornell University. She received her B.S. degree (1985) in behavioral sciences from the University of Chicago and her Ph.D. degree (1996) in psychology from the University of Virginia. Bolger's research currently focuses on children's social and emotional development in the context of family and peer relationships. For her previous research project on children growing up in high-risk environments, she received the 1997 Dissertation Award from the American Professional Society on the Abuse of Children.

PATRICK COLLINS is the Project Director of the National Data Archive on Child Abuse and Neglect. Since 1987, Collins has managed research projects in the areas of child abuse, elder abuse, and sexual victimization. He received his B.S. degree with Honors (1986) in human development and family studies from Cornell. Before coming to the Family Life Development Center he worked as a systems analyst for the Cornell Institute for Social and Economic Research and as a research analyst for ABT Associates.

MARTHA HOLDEN is a senior extension associate with the Family Life Development Center and the director of the Residential Child Care Project. As project director, she provides a train-the-trainer program in therapeutic crisis intervention to residential child care supervisory staff, a program in the investigation of institutional maltreatment, and a program in institutional assessment throughout the United States, Canada, and the United Kingdom. Holden received her M.S. degree (1975) in mental health counseling from Wright State University. She was lead editor and writer in the 1991 update and redevelopment of the center's therapeutic crisis intervention curriculum in use from 1982. In addition to her extensive experience in training and curriculum development, Holden served as an administrator of a residential child-care facility overseeing the day-to-day operation of a residential treatment facility for children, including its education resources, from 1979 to 1988. Since 1982, she has been studying ways to prevent the occurrence of institutional abuse of children through training, reporting, investigating, and influencing organizational culture.

BRIAN LEIDY is a senior research associate with the Family Life Development Center in the College of Human Ecology at Cornell University. Since coming to the center he has worked primarily as the evaluation manager for military projects, developing evaluation protocols for child maltreatment and domestic violence prevention programs provided by the Family Advocacy Program in the United States Army and Marine Corps. His current work includes the evaluation of home visiting programs for new parents in the Army and a youth violence prevention program in the Marines. Other work for the military includes a review of out-of-home child maltreatment and the co-occurrence of child abuse and domestic violence in military families. He also contributed to an evaluation of the child safety curriculum developed by the National Center for Missing and Exploited Children. Prior to this, Leidy worked as a senior extension associate in the Human Service Studies Department in the College of Human Ecology at Cornell University providing professional training for adult protective service workers and adult care facility administrators.

Leidy received his Ph.D. degree (1991) from Cornell University in human service studies with concentrations in administration and program evaluation. He received his M.S. degree (1985) in public administration from Marywood College and his B.A. degree (1972) in psychology from Mansfield State University. He is a member of Pi Alpha Alpha—the National Honor Society for Public Affairs and Administration—and the American Evaluation Association.

MICHAEL NUNNO is a senior extension associate with the Family Life Development Center. He is currently the coprincipal investigator of the New York State Child Protective Services Training Institute, one of the largest child protective services training programs in the United States. It is responsible for training over two thousand child protective services personnel annually in New York State in a series of core and advanced courses. The institute's curriculum has been highlighted at national and international conferences. He is also principal investigator for the Residential Child Care Project, which trains residential child-care staff in the identification and prevention of child maltreatment in residential child-care facilities. This project's three training programs and curricula were originally developed under a grant from the National Center on Child Abuse and Neglect and have been delivered on a fee-for-service basis since 1982 throughout the United States, Canada, Puerto Rico, and the United Kingdom.

Nunno has considerable experience working with community and state agencies and private nonprofit organizations throughout the United States and the United Kingdom in the development of monitoring and prevention programs in the area of institutional abuse of children. He has published in the *New Child Protective Services Team Handbook* (1988) and in *Child Abuse and Neglect: An International Journal, Children and Society,* and *Protecting Children.* In addition, Nunno was editor of the *Journal of Child and Youth Care*'s dedicated issue on institutional maltreatment. He received his D.S.W. degree (1996) in social welfare at the Graduate Center of the City University of New York.

JANE LEVINE POWERS has been a senior research associate at Cornell University's Family Life Development Center since 1985, working on a variety of projects concerned with child abuse and neglect and problems related to high-risk youth and families. A specialist in adolescent development, she has directed several research projects at the center, including Statewide Teamwork for Abused Runaways (STAR), a federal research and demonstration project concerned with improving services to maltreated runaway and homeless youth in New York State. Most recently, she was director of a major project examining the long-term effects of an early intervention nurse home visitation program on high-risk mothers and their adolescent children. She is author of *Understanding Survivors of Abuse: Stories of Homeless and Runaway Adolescents* (1989) and of numerous articles. She received her Ph.D. degree (1985) from Cornell University in developmental psychology.

MARNEY THOMAS is senior extension associate with the Family Life Development Center at the College of Human Ecology, Cornell University and is currently the coprincipal investigator and director for the center's military Child and Spouse Abuse Prevention projects. These projects conduct researchoon home visiting and family violence prevention in the military and provide technical assistance and training for United States Army and Marine Corps Family Advocacy Programs worldwide. From 1988 to 1992 she managed the New York State Child Protective Services Training Institute and has taught courses in child abuse and neglect, risk assessment, forensic interviewing, measurement and testing, and child development.

She is currently studying the relationship between positive drug testing in newborns and subsequent maltreatment. Her most recent article was published in *Psychology, Public Policy and the Law.* Thomas received her B.S. degree (1964) from Carnegie Institute of Technology, her M.S. degree (1968) from Cornell University, and her Ph.D. degree (1973) in developmental psychology from Cornell University.

⟋⟋⟋ Name Index

⟶ Subject Index

A

Adolescent abuse: antisocial behavior and, 184–190; autonomy and independence issues in, 161–162; versus child maltreatment, 154–159; characteristics of, 157–159; concept of inappropriateness and, 9–10, 146–147, 154; corporal punishment as, 13–14, 160–161; damaging consequences of, 155–156, 174–178, 181–185, 187–192; developmental perspective in, 146–148; family stability and, 162, 163–164, 167, 168; gender differences in, 157–158; incidence rates, 156–157; long-term versus recent initiation of, 147–148, 159–160, 162–164, 167–170; as motivation for delinquency, 168; neglect as, 17; parental sex roles in, 162–163; patterns of, 159–162; prevention of, 204–205; psychological, 14–15, 174–178; roots of, 147–148; self-destructive and suicidal behavior and, 181–183, 191; self-reporting of, 167–168; social isolation and, 178–181; societal costs of, 193; societal view of adolescence and, 148, 155; socioeconomic factors in, 157, 163–164, 167, 168–169

Adolescent delinquency and violence: domestic violence and, 187–190; gender and, 187; history of abuse and, 184–186; homicide and, 187–190

Adolescent development: in authoritarian and overcontrolling homes,

154, 180–181; change and autonomy issues in, 148–149, 152–153, 170; damage processes in, 170–181; peer influences in, 151–152; physical, social, and psychological aspects of, 149–154; processes of identification/imitation in, 171–172; sexual experience in, 149–150

American Humane Association (AHA), 27

Antisocial behavior: chronic pattern in, 186; parent-child relations and, 184–186; sex-typed pattern in, 186–187

Anxiety, 176–177

C

Causation factors: environmental and psychological, 45–46, 54; familial cycle of abuse as, 91–92, 121–122; in family sexual abuse, 123–124; high-risk neighborhoods as, 46, 57–60, 65–73, 75; substance abuse as, 46, 94–95. *See also* Parent-child relations

Child abuse definitions, 5–8, 9

Child Abuse Prevention and Treatment Act (CAPTA), 27, 41–42, 48, 49

Child development. *See* Human development

Child maltreatment: catastrophic, 10–11, 18; chronic, 160, 162–164; definitions of, 43–45; evolution of public response to, 33–37; poverty and, 44–46, 51, 57, 62–63, 163–165;